GREAT
COMMANDERS
OF THE
EARLY MODERN
WORLD

GREAT COMMANDERS OF THE EARLY MODERN WORLD

Edited by

Andrew Roberts

Quercus

Dedicated to Alex Coulson and Alec Foster-Brown

First published in Great Britain in 2009 by Quercus

This paperback edition published in 2011 by

Quercus
55 Baker Street
7th Floor, South Block
London
W1U 8EW

CONTENTS

INTRODUCTION TO THE HISTORY OF EARLY MODERN MILITARY COMMAND

This third volume of the *Great Commanders* covers the time from the opening of the Age of Gunpowder in the late sixteenth century to the end of the American Civil War in 1865. I believe it can be seen as a discrete period in military history, the moment when campaigns and battlefields underwent two great revolutions. Although gunpowder had of course been invented by the Chinese many centuries earlier, it only really made its presence fully felt in global terms once it was used in the muskets and cannons of the armies that warred over the continental plains of western Europe.

The first revolution it effected was massively to reduce the importance of the castle and the defended city in grand strategy. With the capacity to bombard and destroy city walls using gunpowder and shot, as demonstrated so effectively by Oliver Cromwell during the English Civil

Wars, the impregnable urban stronghold quickly lost its central place in the unfolding of a campaign. Indeed from hitherto being literal 'strongholds', the possession of cities that required feeding could turn into an incubus rather than an asset. The art of warfare moved to the open battlefield, whereas once it had been cooped up in a series of sieges.

The second revolution was of course to be seen on the battlefield itself. Where once topography only mattered insofar as no commander wanted his men to have to fight uphill with the sun in their eyes, once muskets and cannon using gunpowder were able to sweep lethal fire over battlefields from significant distances, the folds in the landscape suddenly afforded protection from otherwise devastating arcs of fire. Commanders who knew how to use topography to their tactical as well as strategic advantage during this period – Marlborough, Napoleon and Wellington are the classic exemplars – could win campaigns against less skilled opponents.

Gunpowder thus changed the world as comprehensively as any of the more positive inventions such as the printing press or the Internet. Gunpowder's major ingredient, saltpetre (literally: stone salt), is a chemical compound (potassium nitrate) that was manufactured in a truly disgusting way. Heaps of manure and/or guano, wood ash, rotting straw and copious amounts of urine (the sourer the better) were all left to bubble away for a year or so.

The ammonia thus generated causes the chemical reactions that produce this remarkably efficient oxidizer and give it its explosive qualities. The best saltpetre was produced in India, which was why British gunpowder during the Napoleonic Wars was considered of a far higher quality than French. (It was also believed to have some medicinal properties, and veterans would swear by sprinkling gunpowder in their soup, as it was meant to be good for high blood pressure. Napoleon's senior military surgeon, the admiral Baron Larrey, added it to the broth he gave the wounded that was cooked up in cavalry cuirasses after the battle of Aspern-Essling in 1809.)

'Greatness is not universal,' thundered the military historian and theorist Major-General J. F. C. Fuller to Captain Basil Liddell Hart after reading his 1926 biography of Scipio Africanus, provocatively entitled *Greater Than Napoleon*. 'To say that Homer is greater than Shakespeare, or Shakespeare than Goethe, is absurd. Each may have been the great of his epoch. You may rightly say that Scipio was greater than Hannibal, but you cannot logically say that he was greater than Alexander or Napoleon or Frederick.' Of course there are omissions and seemingly arbitrary choices in this volume; there have to be. Why Nathanael Greene and not George Washington? Was not Ney a greater marshal than Davout? I have chosen solely on the grounds that I believe the great commanders in these volumes fulfil better than anyone else the ultimate criterion for successful military leadership, the one that the great Prussian military theorist Carl von Clausewitz returned to again and again in his seminal work *On War*: genius.

For when we consider the question of whether great commanders are born great, achieve greatness or have greatness thrust upon them, the answer seems to be both all and none of the above. Although the more viscous social structures of early times militated towards regal and noble commanders until the end of the Age of Gunpowder, death and the fear of death was always democratic enough to ensure that soldiers of merit rose faster in war than in periods of peace, just as revolutions fling up the kind of leaders that would never emerge in tranquil times. Talent will always out, even in the most hidebound societies: Clive was a debt-ridden clerk, Napoleon a Corsican outsider, and so on.

Nor is there any definable connection between fighting well and fighting in a good cause. If there are a large number of generals in these pages who fought for barbarism and enslavement rather than civilization and liberty, that is because the righteousness of the ultimate goal seems to be pretty immaterial when it comes to military genius. 'It is a piece of idle sentimentality,' wrote John Stuart Mill, 'that truth, merely as truth, has any inherent power denied to error, of prevailing against the dungeon and the stake.' The same goes for the twenty-four-pounder cannon or the Martini-Henry rifle.

André Malraux once said that the purpose of war was to do the utmost to ensure that fragments of metal penetrated human flesh. It is a severe but essentially fair summation of the art of the great commander, at least once the period of pre-battle manoeuvre is over. On rare occasions manoeuvre alone is enough, and these are paid tribute to in this book.

Andrew Roberts, May 2011
www.andrew-roberts.net

CONTRIBUTORS

JOHN CHILDS

Educated at the University of Hull and King's College, London, John Childs is Professor of Military History and Director of the Centre for Military History in the University of Leeds. As well as publishing a pioneering investigation of the military use of land and co-authoring a *Dictionary of Military History*, he has written a number of books on European armies and warfare during the seventeenth and eighteenth centuries, principally a trilogy on the social and political history of the British army from 1660 to 1702, a study of the Nine Years War, and, most recently, *Warfare in the Seventeenth Century* (2001) and *The Williamite Wars in Ireland, 1688–1691* (2007). He is currently writing a history of the War of the Spanish Succession. A former trustee of the Royal Armouries, John Childs chairs the Royal Armouries Development Trust and the Battlefields Panel of English Heritage.

STEPHEN BRUMWELL

Dr Stephen Brumwell is a freelance writer and independent historian based in Amsterdam. Leaving school to work as a newspaper reporter, he subsequently attended the University of Leeds as a mature student. After gaining a First in History, Brumwell was awarded British Academy funding to research eighteenth-century North America. His doctoral dissertation was published by Cambridge University Press as *Redcoats: The British Soldier and War in the Americas, 1755–63* (2002). Drawing upon his research interests Brumwell has since published *White Devil: A True Story of War, Savagery and Vengeance in Colonial America* (2004); and *Paths of Glory: The Life and Death of General James Wolfe* (2006). All of Brumwell's books have been widely acclaimed for engaging general readers and specialists alike – what Canada's *Globe & Mail* characterized as a combination of 'first-rate, innovative scholarship, and page-turning readability'. He is currently writing a biography of George Washington for Quercus.

ANTONIA FRASER

Since 1969, Antonia Fraser has written many acclaimed historical works which have been international bestsellers, including *Mary Queen of Scots* (1969, James Tait Black Memorial Prize); *Cromwell: Our Chief of Men* (1973); *The Six Wives of Henry* VIII (1992) and *The Gunpowder Plot: Terror and Faith in 1605* (1996, St Louis Literary Award; CWA Non-Fiction Gold Dagger); and *Marie Antoinette* (2001). Antonia Fraser was made CBE in 1999, and awarded the Norton Medlicott Medal by the Historical Association in 2000. She is married to the playwright Harold Pinter and lives in London.

CHARLES SPENCER

Charles Spencer was educated at Eton and at Magdalen College, Oxford, where he read Modern History. He was a reporter for seven years with the News Division of the American television network NBC. His books include *Althorp: The Story of an English House* (1998); *The Spencer Family* (1999); *Blenheim: Battle for Europe* (2004), which was shortlisted for History Book of the Year at the 2005 National Book Awards; and *Prince Rupert: The Last Cavalier* (2007). He is a book reviewer for the *Independent on Sunday*, and has written for the *Spectator*, the *Guardian* and many other newspapers and magazines in the UK and the USA. Charles Spencer has been the owner of Althorp, Northamptonshire, since 1992, and founded the Althorp Literary Festival. He is the father of six children.

GILES MACDONOGH

Giles MacDonogh went to school in London, and university in Oxford and Paris, where he first read and later undertook research into modern history. He is the author of twelve books, six of them on the history of Germany. He has written biographies of Frederick the Great (1999), the Kaiser and the resistance leader Adam von Trott. He has also published histories of Prussia and Berlin and *After the Reich* (2007) which looks at Germany and Austria at the end of the Second World War. His most recent book is *1938: Hitler's Gamble* (2009). MacDonogh has written for the main British newspapers such as *The Times*, *Financial Times* and the *Guardian*. He has lectured at universities in France, Germany, Italy and Bulgaria. He also works as a translator from French and German and produced *The Hitler Book* for John Murray (2005) and *A Garden of Eden in Hell* for MacMillan (2007).

ROBERT HARVEY

Robert Harvey has been a columnist for the *Daily Telegraph*, assistant editor of *The Economist* and an MP. He is the author of many books, including a highly popular biography of Lord Cochrane. He is a former member of the House of Commons Foreign Affairs Committee, and foreign affairs leader writer for the *Daily Telegraph*. His books include *Portugal: Birth of a Democracy* (1978); *The Undefeated: The Rise, Fall and Rise of Modern Japan* (1994); *Liberators* (2000); and *Cochrane* (2000). Robert Harvey lives in Powys, Wales.

PHILIP DWYER

Philip Dwyer is Senior Lecturer in Modern European History at the University of Newcastle, Australia. His primary research interest is eighteenth-century Europe with particular emphasis on the Napoleonic Empire. His most recent publications include: *Napoleon and Europe*, ed. (2001); *The French Revolution and Napoleon. A Sourcebook*, with Peter McPhee (2002); *Talleyrand (Profiles in Power)* (2002); *Napoleon and His Empire: Europe, 1804–1814*, ed. with Alan Forrest (2007); and *Napoleon, 1769–1799: The Path to Power* (2007). He is currently writing the sequel.

ANDREW ROBERTS

Andrew Roberts took a first in modern history from Gonville & Caius College, Cambridge, from where he is an honorary senior scholar and PhD. His biography of Winston Churchill's foreign secretary Lord Halifax, entitled *The Holy Fox*, was published by Weidenfeld & Nicolson in 1991, followed by *Eminent Churchillians* (Weidenfeld & Nicolson, 1994); *Salisbury: Victorian Titan*, which won the Wolfson Prize and the James Stern Silver Pen Award (Weidenfeld & Nicolson, 1999); *Napoleon and Wellington* (Weidenfeld & Nicolson, 2002); *Hitler and Churchill: Secrets of Leadership* (Weidenfeld & Nicolson, 2003) and *Waterloo: Napoleon's Last Gamble* (HarperCollins, 2005).

He has also edited a collection of twelve counterfactual

essays by historians entitled *What Might Have Been* (Weidenfeld & Nicolson, 2004) as well as *The Correspondence of Benjamin Disraeli and Mrs Sarah Brydges Willyams* (2006). His *A History of the English-Speaking Peoples Since 1900* (Weidenfeld & Nicolson, 2006) won the US Intercollegiate Studies Institute Book Award for 2007. Dr Roberts is a Fellow of the Royal Society of Literature, an honorary Doctor of Humane Letters, and reviews history books for more than a dozen newspapers and periodicals. His *Masters and Commanders: How Churchill, Roosevelt, Alanbrooke and Marshall Won the War in the West, 1941–45* (Allen Lane 2009) won the International Churchill Society Award, and his *The Storm of War: A New History of the Second World War* (Allen Lane, 2010) won the British Army Military Book of the Year Award. His website can be found at www.andrew-roberts.net.

ANDREW UFFINDELL

Andrew Uffindell has written extensively on the Napoleonic period. His books include *Napoleon's Immortals* (2007), a major reassessment of the Imperial Guard; *Waterloo Commanders* (2007); *Great Generals of the Napoleonic Wars* (2007); *The Eagle's Last Triumph: Napoleon's Victory at Ligny* (1994); and (as a co-author) *On the Fields of Glory: The Battlefields of the 1815 Campaign* (1986). He has edited a collection of essays by the late Jac Weller, *On Wellington* (1998); and also wrote *The National Army Museum Book of*

Wellington's Armies (2003), part of a series that collectively won the Royal United Services Institute's Duke of Westminster Medal for Military Literature (2004). His published articles include studies of the Franco-Austrian War of 1859 and friendly fire at Waterloo.

ALAN PALMER

Alan Palmer was Head of History at Highgate School, London, for eighteen years before retiring early to concentrate on historical writing and research. The author of more than three dozen narratives, biographies and reference books, he was elected a Fellow of the Royal Society of Literature in 1980. Subjects of his biographies include Tsar Alexander I, Marshal Bernadotte, Metternich, Bismarck, Kaiser William II, Emperor Francis Joseph, Frederick the Great, King George IV and Kemal Atatürk. His other books include *Napoleon in Russia* (1967); *Russia in War and Peace* (1973); *The Decline and Fall of the Ottoman Empire* (1993) and *Northern Shores, A History of the Baltic Sea and its Peoples* (2005). His most recent book was *The Salient, Ypres 1914–1918* (2007).

MALCOLM DEAS

Malcolm Deas has been a Fellow of St Antony's College, Oxford, since 1966, where he was one of the founders and subsequently the Director of the University's Latin American Centre. He has written extensively on the history and politics of Colombia and its neighbouring republics. For five years after the Falklands War he wrote leader columns on Latin American affairs for *The Times*, and he has contributed articles and reviews to the *TLS*, *The Spectator* and the *London Review of Books*. He has also worked as an adviser to the Colombian government.

SAUL DAVID

Saul David is Visiting Professor of Military History at the University of Hull, and Professorial Research Fellow at the Humanities Research Centre of the University of Buckingham. His many books include *The Indian Mutiny: 1857* (2002); shortlisted for the Westminster Medal for Military Literature, *Zulu: the Heroism and Tragedy of the Zulu War of 1879* (2004, a Waterstone's Military History Book of the Year) and, most recently, *Victoria's Wars: The Rise of Empire* (2006). He has presented history programmes for most of the major TV channels, appeared as an expert on the BBC2 virtual battle series *Time Commanders*, and was the historical consultant for the BBC *Timewatch* documentary *Zulu: The True Story*.

LUCY RIALL

Lucy Riall is Professor of History at Birkbeck College, University of London, and the editor of *European History Quarterly*. She was educated at the London School of Economics and

Cambridge University. She has held previous appointments at Cambridge and the University of Essex, and been a visiting professor at the Ecole Normale Supérieure, Paris, and the Freie Universität, Berlin. Her publications include *Risorgimento: The History of Italy from Napoleon to Nation-state* (2008); *Garibaldi: Invention of a Hero* (2007); *Sicily and the Unification of Italy: Liberal Policy and Local Power, 1859–1866* (1998); and the edited volume (with David Laven), *Napoleon's Legacy: Problems of Government in Restoration Europe* (2000).

JOHN A. BARNES

A native New Yorker, John Barnes took a bachelor's degree in journalism from New York University in 1982 before embarking on a seventeen-year career as a reporter and editorial writer for columnists Rowland Evans and Robert Novak, the *Detroit News* and the *New York Post*. He joined Pfizer Inc. in 1999 as part of its corporate communications unit. He is the author of three books: *Irish-American Landmarks: A Traveler's Guide* (1995); *Ulysses S. Grant on Leadership: Executive Lessons from the Front Lines* (2001); and *John F. Kennedy on Leadership: The Lessons and Legacy of a President* (2005). He lives in Manhattan with his wife Mary and their two children.

RICHARD J. SOMMERS

Richard J. Sommers was born in Hammond, Indiana, and raised in suburban Chicago. He earned his BA from Carleton

College and his Ph.D. from Rice University. His numerous publications on the American Civil War include *Richmond Redeemed: The Siege at Petersburg* (1980), which won the National Historical Society's Bell Wiley Prize as the best Civil War book of 1981–2. Since 1970, he has served as the US Army Military History Institute's Chief Archivist-Historian, Assistant Director for Archives, and Chief of Patron Services. In 2007 he held the General Harold Keith Johnson Chair of Military History at the Institute and the US Army War College. In 2008 he assumed his current position as the Institute's Senior Historian. He has served on the boards of the Society of Civil War Historians, the Jefferson Davis Association, the Richmond Battlefields Association, and the Harrisburg Civil War Round Table. He lives in Carlisle, Pennsylvania.

MAURICE OF NASSAU

1567–1625

JOHN CHILDS

MAURICE OF NASSAU, the most admired soldier in Europe at the turn of the seventeenth century, saved the infant Dutch Republic from reconquest by Spain, leading to the truce that effectively recognized the state's legal right to exist. He also reformed the Dutch armed forces and in doing so established the basis for new tactical and organizational methods that spread widely across western Europe.

Maurice was born in Dillenburg Castle in the Duchy of Nassau, Germany, on 14 November 1567, the second son of William the Silent of Nassau, Prince of Orange, and his second wife Anna of Saxony. He became heir to his father's titles and estates before his first birthday, after his elder half-brother Philip William was abducted to Spain as a hostage in 1568. The same year, his father, stadholder (royal representative or governor) of the mainly Calvinist provinces of Holland, Zeeland and Utrecht, led the Dutch forces in open revolt against Spain, thus initiating a struggle for independence that was to continue for eighty years and to which Maurice was to devote his career.

The states of Holland and Zeeland funded Maurice's education at Heidelberg and then Leiden, where he was tutored by the mathematician and engineer Simon Stevin (1548–1620). After his father's assassination at the hands of a French Catholic in 1584, Holland and Zeeland invited the 16-year-old Maurice to succeed as stadholder – Utrecht, Gelderland and Overijssel following suit in 1587 – and, in 1586, conferred upon him the title Prince of Orange. In 1588, at the age of 21, he was appointed Admiral-General of the United Netherlands and Captain-General of the troops in Brabant and Flanders. His cousin William Louis (1560–1620) was chosen as stadholder of Friesland, Groningen and Drenthe.

Dour, taciturn, careful and slow to make decisions, Maurice was not a sovereign ruler but an appointee of the States General, the central representative institution and effective government of the nascent Dutch Republic, so his authority and independence were prescribed by the civil power. As admiral-general, he was answerable to five provincial admiralty boards, whilst a committee of the States

General, the Council of State (Raad van State), coordinated military affairs and supervised field operations through civilian 'field deputies'. His own natural caution complemented the States General's watchful, methodical strategy, which sought to conduct military operations with minimum risk. However, the States General pursued neither military traditions nor aspirations and was usually content to leave martial business to the stadholders. Maurice lacked political ambitions of his own, so this arrangement worked satisfactorily.

Military reforms

Maurice needed to weld the Dutch army's ineffective and unreliable mixture of mercenaries and city militias into a professional army capable of resisting the Spanish forces. The programme, which he began in 1589, was largely achieved within ten years. Maurice's *more Romano* ('in the Roman style') combined contemporary practice with ideas and models derived from Classical authors, particularly Vitruvius, Caesar, Aelianus, Vegetius Renatus and the Byzantine Emperor Leo VI. He also owed much to the teaching of the philosopher Justus Lipsius, professor of history at Leiden from 1579 to 1590, whose treatises on the Roman army, *De Militia Romana* (1595), and siege warfare, *Poliorceticon* (1596), provided the underlying historical information.

Although pressed by Lipsius to create an army of

citizen-soldiers, Maurice was forced to use mercenaries because the Dutch population only numbered about 1 million people, most of whom were engaged in the agricultural, commercial and maritime activities essential to provide the revenues for the continuation of the war. Thus, the majority of the rank-and-file in Maurice's army were English, Scots, French, German, Swiss and Danish, but quality and loyalty were enhanced through careful selection and the provision of comparatively attractive and extended periods of service. In return, these long-term mercenaries came to accept enhanced standards of discipline and expectations of unit loyalty.

To foster instant obedience and cohesion, at the suggestion of William Louis the men were trained daily at routines partly devised from Aelianus and Leo, with the original Greek words of command translated into Dutch, French, English and German. Drills for handling pikes and reloading muskets were reduced to numerical sequences, chanted in unison. Prompt and uniform execution of the manual of arms developed combat effectiveness and became the obvious manifestation of discipline. Daily exercises allowed more precise evolutions, permitting improved coordination between shot (muskets) and pike, and increased the rate of infantry fire. The problem of delivering a sufficient weight of shot from the inaccurate and unwieldy matchlock muskets was solved in 1594 by the introduction of the counter-march (based on Roman javelin drill), again at the recommendation of William Louis.

Constant training and the more independent combat role allotted to sub-units required more numerous and better-educated junior officers, preferably Dutch. However, the military expertise of foreigners remained indispensable because many native officers continued to owe their appointments to non-military factors: the publication of a table of ranks was delayed until 1618. Maurice began the gradual change in the ethos of the military profession from a foundation of noble birth, honour and chivalry to a publicly recognized authority derived from a commission issued by the state.

The field army was cut to a size that was financially and logistically supportable: before 1600, it rarely amounted to more than 12,000 men (2,000 mounted and 10,000 infantry), accompanied after 1595 by six field guns and a siege train of forty-two cannon. The effectiveness of the artillery was improved by establishing a gun foundry in The Hague in 1589 and, from 1590, limiting production to just three calibres: 12-, 24- and 48-pounders. In tune with the general European tendency to improve articula-tion by making infantry units smaller – Spanish *tercios* (the distinctive pike-and-musket infantry formations that formed the basis of Spanish triumphs on the battlefield in the sixteenth century) had been halved to 1,500 men in

1584 – Maurice trimmed his companies to 130, all ranks, raised the number of musketeers until there was one for every pikeman, and arrayed his men in ten ranks, later reduced to six. In 1592 William Louis organized the companies into 'half regiments', or battalions, of around 800 men, later slimmed to 580, which were arranged on the battlefield in a chequerboard formation reminiscent of the deployment of a Roman legion. Troops of cavalry protected the vulnerable battalion flanks.

In combat, Maurice's reforms achieved two objectives. First, the new battalions were more mobile and better suited to operating in the 'great bog of Europe'. Secondly, they were much handier than the larger tercios both in conducting sieges and defending field works and fixed fortifications. Maurice of Nassau was less concerned about performance in pitched battle, although the new system functioned effectively at Turnhout in 1597 and Nieuport in 1600.

The conduct of sieges
Siege warfare was particularly apposite to the situation: it decreased operational risk though at an increased financial cost which the United Provinces could afford through its burgeoning trade and commerce. Maurice developed the siege techniques established by the Spanish governors Alva and Parma. Target towns and cities would be block-

aded and then enclosed within a double ring of redoubts (contravallation and circumvallation) which protected the besiegers' camp. First trenches then zigzagged saps (mines) were excavated towards the 'front' selected for attack, and the artillery installed in batteries. Lighter cannon destroyed breastworks and countered the garrison's artillery while the heavier guns concentrated on breaching the fortifications. When the defending fire had been substantially subdued, the besiegers sapped up the glacis (sloping earthwork rampart) to capture the counterscarp (the outer slope of the ditch in front of the main wall or scarp). The artillery was then advanced to begin battering the main ramparts, while the attacking infantry built a bridge or causeway over the wet ditch ready to assault the breach; occasionally hydraulic engineers had to be summoned to assist with drainage and diversion of watercourses.

Rather than rely upon gangs of unwilling, conscripted civilian labour, Maurice trained his soldiers to dig their own siege works and field fortifications, a reform that greatly increased the speed and effectiveness of siege operations. Shovels and hand-tools were routinely carried in the siege train.

Two treatises by Stevin, *Legermeting* (*The Marking Out of Army Camps*; 1617) and *Nieuwe maniere van Stercktebouw door spilsluysen* (*New Manner of Fortification by Means of Pivoted Sluice Locks*; 1617), provided the theoretical basis for Dutch fortification techniques. In 1600, he and Maurice established a course in surveying and military engineering at Leiden, in which the lectures were given in Dutch rather than the traditional Latin. Stevin did not confine himself to theory and by 1592 was serving as engineer and quartermaster to the army of the States General, designing entrenched camps and drawing up instructions and standing orders for men engaged in building fortifications and undertaking siege operations. He was often present at sieges, and indicated the mode of attack to be employed.

Stevin's prominence in military engineering supports the view that many of the military reforms developed by the Dutch were actually team efforts in which Maurice himself may not have played the leading role. In recruiting and financing the army, the political and moral support of Johan van Oldenbarneveldt (1547–1619), the Landsadvocaat of Holland, was central, as administration of the field forces rested with the Raad van State, which he dominated; whilst in tactical and operational matters, Maurice was ably supported by his cousins William Louis and John VII, Count of Nassau-Siegen, who devised drill movements and supervised the publication of instruction manuals.

Dutch strategy

Oldenbarneveldt and Maurice appreciated that Dutch strategy had to concentrate upon defending the central provinces of

Holland, Zeeland and Utrecht. This was best achieved by checking Spanish attempts at further reconquest while employing cautious, positional warfare to recapture fortified towns and cities to extend the outlying areas of the state, comprising the four 'land' provinces of Friesland, Groningen, Overijssel and Gelderland, which protected the three key provinces. Usually after very close consultation with Maurice, the States General decided upon targets to be besieged. Mostly he was content with this arrangement; indeed it strengthened his position, although the emphasis of the States General upon protecting the particular interests of the individual provinces and keeping costs to a minimum occasionally clashed with wider strategic priorities.

Maurice sought to avoid open battle: between 1589 and 1609, twenty-nine fortresses were recaptured, three sieges relieved but only two battles fought. Interior lines and the great rivers acted as force multipliers enabling the small Dutch army to move rapidly between the eastern and southern fronts. When obliged to use overland routes, as in an abortive campaign into Brabant in 1602, results were less impressive.

Keeping the Spaniards at bay

Alexander Farnese, Duke of Parma, who arrived in the Netherlands in 1578, successfully reduced the opposition to Spanish rule in the southern Netherlands, but the northern provinces continued to hold out. At the end of 1587, however, the Dutch Republic held only Holland, Zeeland and Utrecht, a few isolated outposts in Overijssel, Gelderland and Friesland, plus Ostend and Bergen-op-Zoom south of the great rivers. Parma was then called away to Dunkirk to provide troops for the Spanish Armada against England and, when ready to resume his offensive in 1589, was redirected into France to support the Catholic League against the Huguenots. These distractions provided Maurice with the opportunity to begin rebuilding the army, safe within the defences of the waterline in *Vesting Holland* ('Fortress Holland', with natural defensible borders formed by the rivers Rhine and Meuse to the south and west and the Ijsselmeer to the east), while the States General concentrated upon building fortifications. Maurice surprised Breda on 26 February 1590, the first major town to be captured since 1580, but when Parma departed for France in July, the States General was unprepared to exploit the occasion and could only authorize an excursion into Brabant which retook some small forts.

Confident that some of Parma's forces would again be deployed in France in 1591, the States General mounted a major campaign to secure the line of the River Ijssel and retake the northeastern towns seized during the 1580s. Commanding 10,000 men and a train of artillery, Maurice captured Zutphen on 30 May following a seven-day siege, and Deventer on 10 June. The next target was Nijmegen but, despite having to send 6,000 men to France and losing another 2,000 to a mutiny over pay, Parma parried Maurice's thrust. His health failing, in August Parma travelled to Spain for medical treatment but was back in Brussels by November, assembling 20,000 men for the French wars to relieve Henry of Navarre's siege of Rouen. Maurice moved his troops rapidly by barge and seized Hulst on 24 September. Then he doubled back to Dordrecht and marched overland to Nijmegen, which fell on 21 October after a siege lasting only six days. These results were achieved by rapid movement, swift siege operations and the offer of generous terms to enemy garrisons. Maurice continued to campaign in the northeast during 1592, taking Steenwijk and Coevorden, but further operations were compromised by the localist attitudes of the four 'land' provinces. Nevertheless, after a long siege during which Maurice and Stevin demonstrated the improved techniques, Gertruidenberg fell in June 1593, and on 23 July in the following year Maurice captured Groningen. Their principal objectives realized, the States General cut back military expenditure, obliging Maurice to suspend major operations; reform of the army continued, however, during the ensuing long pause in campaigning.

With 6,800 men, Maurice surprised a marching column of 5,000 Spanish troops near Turnhout on 24 January 1597, but the resulting Dutch victory had little impact on the overall situation. Later the same year, when Spain was again heavily committed in France, Maurice took Rheinberg and Groenlo, further securing the eastern borders. In 1598, however, peace between France and Spain altered the strategic balance. Reinforced, a Spanish army pushed north through Bommel across the river lines, but again the troops mutinied and all the captured towns and forts were regained by the Dutch in 1599, some purchased from the rebellious garrisons. Oldenbarneveldt ordered Maurice to exploit the opportunity and the inexperience of the new governor of the Spanish Netherlands, Archduke Albrecht of Austria, by advancing down the Flemish coast to link up with the isolated Dutch garrison at Ostend before moving against the Spanish privateer bases at Nieuport and Dunkirk. Maurice was reluctant, favouring a more cautious strategy, but was overruled by Oldenbarneveldt, who was willing to accept the risk. On 2 July 1600, Maurice's 11,400 men defeated a hastily mustered Spanish army of 9,000 in the sand dunes outside Nieuport. However, it was only a tactical victory because the Dutch army was not strong enough to besiege either Nieuport or Dunkirk and had to be evacuated into Zeeland by sea. Archduke Albrecht then attacked Ostend. Leading 5,442 cavalry and around 19,000 infantry, Maurice invaded Brabant, intending to march into Flanders to lift the siege, but the thrust was abandoned because insufficient horse forage was available.

The States General ordered Maurice to stand on the defensive, passing the initiative to the newly arrived Ambrogio Spinola, the best Spanish general to serve during the Eighty Years War (1568–1648). While the siege of Ostend dragged on for three years, the States General began the construction of a line of defensive redoubts along the River Ijssel to improve the defences of the vulnerable eastern front. Even so, when Spinola transferred his attention to the east in 1606, he made progress into Overijssel and Gelderland before heavy rains prevented further advance. Aware of Spain's catastrophic financial condition, Spinola now advocated an end to hostilities and, following a cease-fire in 1607, a twelve-year truce came into effect in 1609, marking the end of the solitary struggle of the Dutch Republic: when fighting resumed in 1621, the conflict was subsumed within the larger Thirty Years War.

Maurice considered the truce to be a betrayal, as only military victory over Spain could guarantee the long-term viability of the Dutch state; his close working relationship with Oldenbarneveldt, the leading advocate of the truce, was irrevocably ruptured. Political differences were expressed in religious terms. Maurice was supported by the orthodox Calvinists of the Reformed Church, the Contra-Remon-strants, many of whom were exiles from the southern provinces that remained in Spanish hands, whilst the Arminians, or Remonstrants, favoured greater religious latitude and toleration and looked to Oldenbarneveldt for leadership. Maurice himself claimed little theological knowledge and once remarked that he did not know whether predestination was blue or green, but he was firmly committed to the Reformed Church and convinced that it formed the bedrock of the Dutch revolt against Spain: to attack the church was to imperil the state and therefore an act of treason. Although enjoying a more sophisticated understanding of the theological issues, Oldenbarneveldt differed sharply from the Contra-Remonstrants over the relationship of church to state. He upheld the state's right to determine church government and favoured keeping the doctrinal door wide open to admit all loyal and obedient subjects. To Oldenbarneveldt, the state was not the States General but the individual provinces, especially Holland. In 1618, on the authority of the States General, Maurice arrested Oldenbarneveldt for treason; he was tried and executed in 1619.

Demoralized, prematurely aged and badly damaged by the judicial murder of Oldenbarneveldt, on the resumption of the war in 1621 Maurice had lost the vigour and zest required to lead his troops to victory. When Spinola besieged Breda in 1624, Maurice was unable to effect a relief. His health collapsed and he asked the States General to commission a deputy commander. His brother, Frederick Henry, was appointed on 12 April, and eleven days later, on 23 April 1625, Maurice died.

Reputation

Maurice's reforms were enthusiastically imitated throughout Europe. In the Electorate of Brandenburg they were known as the *exercitia Mauritiana*. The French writer Louis de Montgomery, Siegneur de Corbouzon, devoted part of his book on tactics (1603) to '*les évolutions et les exercises, qui se font en la milice de Hollande avec les mots dont il faut user ...*' Another French author, Jeremias de Billon, wrote of '*ce grand Capitaine le Prince Maurice de Nassau*', while the English writer John Bingham added an appendix to his book *The Tactiks of Aelian* (1616) entitled 'The Exercises of the English in the Service of the high and mighty lords, the Lords of Estate in the United Provinces of the Low Countries'. The engraver Jakob de Gheyn translated Maurice's infantry drills into a series of pictorial representations, *Wapenhandling van roers, musquetten ended spiessen* (*The Exercise of Armes*; Amsterdam, 1607), quickly followed by English, German, French and Danish editions (see pp. 19–21). Johann von Wallhausen taught only the Mauritian method at the *Kriegs und Ritterschule* in Siegen, 1616–23. Even the Swiss, master exponents of the pike square, switched to Dutch tactics during the 1620s. The 'Nassau Doctrine' was thus given the widest possible circulation across western Europe and directly informed the tactical methods of Gustavus Adolphus of Sweden.

GUSTAVUS ADOLPHUS

1594–1632

STEPHEN BRUMWELL

HAILED AS A DAUNTLESS PROTESTANT CHAMPION, King Gustav II Adolph of Sweden (known elsewhere as Gustavus Adolphus) was a charismatic commander who propelled his kingdom from backwater to Great Power. His influential tactical innovations, which underpinned Sweden's dramatic intervention in the Thirty Years War (1618–48), exploited lessons learned during a decade of conflict in northeastern Europe.

Born in Stockholm in December 1594, Gustavus Adolphus was well prepared for his role as king, learning ancient and modern languages, law and Lutheran theology. But his real passions were history, particularly tales of Sweden's early warrior kings, and the art of war itself.

Gustavus grew up tall and burly, inclining to paunch-iness, but of great strength and endurance. A keen sportsman and accomplished horseman, he was well suited to the rigours of campaign life. His golden-red mane of hair and small, pointed beard helped to inspire his nick-name, 'the Lion of the North'. Proud and moody, he was nonetheless capable of deploying great charm when required. Gustavus shunned luxury and finery: his usual dress was the simple buff coat and broad-brimmed hat of the soldier, a plain ensemble relieved only by a scarlet sash. Yet Gustavus was no bluff swordsman but an astute statesman and a gifted commander. Both skills were honed through hard experience.

Prussian apprenticeship
At his accession in 1611, Gustavus was just 16. He inher-ited wars with Denmark and Muscovy (Russia), although by 1617 peace treaties had been concluded with both powers. Through the latter, Sweden acquired Estonia on the Baltic's southern shore, a development that sparked hostilities with Poland, which considered that territory part of Polish Livonia. Over the coming decade, the protracted Polish war would provide Gustavus with an intensive mili-tary apprenticeship.

In 1621 Gustavus invaded Livonia, swiftly capturing the vital port of Riga. This was his first significant victory.

Over the next four years the Poles were pushed out of most of Livonia, and in 1626 Gustavus turned his attention to Polish East Prussia. The Swedish army won significant battles: at Mewe, on 1 October 1626 a picked corps of infantry and artillery stormed a strong Polish position, and at Dirschau, on 17 August 1627, the Swedish cavalry proved its worth, vanquishing the vaunted Polish hussars; a general action on the following day began well for the Swedes, only to be abandoned after Gustavus was shot through the shoulder.

On a tactical level, these small-scale engagements testified to the growing confidence of Swedish troops, itself a consequence of reforms initiated by Gustavus. In strategic terms, however, the king overreached himself in Prussia. Although key ports were captured, the Swedes stalled in the face of fierce local resistance that hemmed them in within a band of territory along the shore of the Baltic Sea.

Events now turned against Gustavus. In August 1628 his bid to destroy the Polish commander Stanislas Koniecpolski, who was encamped around Mewe with 10,000 men, ended in fiasco. The canny Pole refused to risk a battlefield clash with Gustavus's 15,000 men, instead devastating the countryside and obliging the hungry Swedes to conduct an ignominious retreat to winter quarters.

Worse was to follow in 1629. Sigismund III of Poland was not only Gustavus's cousin but also the brother-in-law of the Holy Roman Emperor Ferdinand II, who loaned him

12,000 of his soldiers under Hans George von Arnim. Gustavus had 23,000 men in Prussia, but garrison commitments left him with a field force of just 14,000 to pitch against the 26,000 Poles and Imperialists led by Koniecpolski and Arnim. Unable to confront his opponents before they could unite, Gustavus suffered a heavy defeat at Honigfelde on 27 June, barely escaping with his life.

At Altmark, in September 1629, Gustavus had no option but to sign a six-year truce with Poland. With his own kingdom exhausted, the relieved Sigismund conceded generous terms to Sweden, which not only retained Livonia and some of her Prussian conquests, but was also granted licences to collect lucrative tolls on shipping using Prussian and Polish ports, thus giving a vital boost to Sweden's war chest.

Military reform

Gustavus's punishing Polish war provided a valuable opportunity to learn from a formidable enemy, to identify weaknesses in his own army, and to overhaul its structure and tactics. The extent to which these reforms contributed to a 'military revolution' – a term which is likewise controversial – has been hotly debated. Yet whether 'revolutionary' or not, by 1630 Gustavus had implemented changes destined to have a profound impact upon the battlefields of western Europe.

The king's military reforms built upon his own long-standing interest in the theory of warfare, both past and present. He was the most dedicated – and influential – disciple of Maurice of Nassau, who had remodelled the Dutch army in the 1590s (see pp. 19–21), placing an emphasis upon shallower and more flexible formations, improved drill and increased firepower.

At the outset, Gustavus inherited a national army, based upon a system of conscription (*utskrivning*) dating from 1544. In 1620 this was regulated, with one infantry conscript provided by every *rota*, or 'file', of ten men. By contrast, the Swedish cavalry were either foreign mercenaries or native-born volunteers. Throughout the 1620s there had been experiments to find the most effective administrative and tactical units. Both merged in the infantry regiment of two squadrons, each at 'battalion' strength of 480 men. By 1630 the infantry was employing the 'Swedish brigade' of 1,500–2,000 men, formed of three or four squadrons, or two regiments, arrayed in wedge or arrow-shaped formation, with one squadron held in reserve. An unusually high proportion of officers and non-commissioned officers ensured discipline and control.

Intensive drill permitted the Swedish infantry to adopt a far thinner formation than usual. At just six ranks deep, this was even shallower than Maurice's recommended ten, and only a fifth of the depth of the unwieldy blocks of infantry employed by most western armies. By 1631, the Swedish musketeers were using the salvo, an innovation attributed to Gustavus himself. Here, the musketeers doubled up their ranks, so that they were only three deep, allowing them to deliver a concentrated, devastating volley, intended, in the words of the Scottish volunteer Sir James Turner, to 'pour as much lead in your enemies' bosom at one time'.

Each infantry squadron enjoyed the close support of two or three light 3-pounder guns. Mobile enough to be manhandled, they augmented the infantry's firepower with blasts of the newly introduced close-range projectile canister. Neither was cold steel neglected. While the proportion of pikemen to musketeers was typically declining elsewhere, Gustavus retained a higher than usual ratio, using the pike as an offensive, rather than a purely defensive, weapon.

In the cavalry, as with the infantry, formation depths were reduced. In contrast to many armies, where cavalry employed the 'caracole', a technique by which successive relays of troopers fired their pistols before peeling off to reload and repeat the process, the Swedes were trained to deliver their fire and then immediately charge home with the sword. The Swedish cavalry's effectiveness was increased by close support from parties of musketeers.

Gustavus's reforms forged a well-organized and highly disciplined army, capable of punching its weight through a fusion of close-range firepower and shock action. As events would demonstrate, this was a formidable combination.

Intervention in Germany

Peace with Poland freed Gustavus to turn towards Germany, where hostilities between the Catholic forces of Emperor Ferdinand and a loose alliance of Protestant princes had escalated since 1618. By 1630 the conflict – which would continue until 1648, thus becoming known as the Thirty Years War – was going badly for the Protestants. Gustavus was the devout leader of a staunchly Lutheran state, but he played down the ideological justification for intervention: despite his future reputation as champion of the beleaguered Protestant cause, this was no anti-Catholic 'crusade'; indeed, vital financial support for Sweden came from Catholic France, which was chiefly concerned with curbing Habsburg power. For Gustavus too, *Realpolitik* was the prime motivator: Ferdinand's military aid to Poland still rankled, but above all there were growing fears that Imperial ambitions threatened Sweden's security.

In 1627, after Christian IV of Denmark had rashly taken a direct hand in the war, Ferdinand retaliated by sending an army to the Baltic. The Imperialists invaded southern Denmark, and their defeat of Christian at Wolgast in September 1628 permitted the diversion of manpower into Prussia that led to Gustavus's stinging defeat at

Honigfelde. It seemed clear that the Habsburgs aimed to extend their influence by creating a naval base on the shores of the 'Scandinavian Lake'. This so-called 'Baltic Design' angered Sweden and Denmark alike. Back in 1627, while still mired in his Prussian campaigns, Gustavus had informed his trusted chancellor Axel Oxenstierna that war with the emperor was already inevitable: the lapping waves of the 'Popish League', which had now inundated much of Denmark, must be stemmed in good time if they were not to swamp Sweden, too.

In June 1630 Gustavus told the *Riksdag*, or parliament, of his decision to intervene personally in Germany. He predicted a gruelling struggle in which all Swedes must be prepared to make sacrifices, not least himself: 'just as the pitcher taken often to the well would finally be broken, so he, who had on so many occasions risked his life for his realm, must surely lose it at last.'

On 27 June Gustavus sailed from Stockholm with 13,000 men, landing at Peenemünde in the Oder estuary on 6 July. A swift conquest of Usedom and Stettin forced the local ruler, the Duke of Pomerania, to grant the invaders a foothold from which to step onwards into Germany. But for the rest of 1630 the Swedes stayed in Pomerania, waiting for the North German princes to rally to them. Major figures such as Electors John George of Saxony and George William of Brandenburg proved wary of defying the emperor, but support came from others with less to lose and more to gain, notably the dispossessed Duke of Mecklenburg, and Margrave Christian William of Brandenburg, the former administrator of the archbishopric of Magdeburg, a strategically important city on the Elbe.

The Swedish bridgehead gradually expanded, and by February 1631, most of Mecklenburg had been occupied. Gustavus continued his methodical advance southwards into Brandenburg, taking Küstrin and Frankfurt-an-der-Oder. But he arrived too late to save his ally, Magdeburg. On 20 May that Protestant bastion was stormed by the Imperialists under John 't Serclaes von Tilly, and sacked with a savagery that sent shock waves of horror across Europe. Prompted by Magdeburg's grim fate, George William of Brandenburg finally sided with Gustavus on 21 June 1631. This was a timely pact. By the Peace of Cherasco, ratified two days earlier, the Imperialist army in northern Italy was freed to fight elsewhere. Encouraged by the prospect of reinforcement, Tilly vacated the smoking ruins of Magdeburg to tackle Gustavus.

With Swedes and Imperialists alike short of supplies, much now hinged on Saxony, the rich and hitherto unravaged territory between them. On 4 September, after the Elector, John George, refused his formal request to enter Saxony, Tilly invaded regardless, storming Merseburg and Leipzig. John George immediately joined forces with

Gustavus, adding 18,000 raw Saxons to his own army of 23,000 veterans, by now a kernel of Swedes outnumbered by foreign mercenaries. Heading down the Elbe, Gustavus encountered Tilly's 31,000 men on 17 September near Breitenfeld, a village amid gently rolling countryside north of Leipzig (see also pp. 58–9).

At Breitenfeld near Leipzig the rival armies offered a striking contrast. The Imperial infantry were arrayed across Tilly's centre in seventeen tercios (mixed infantry formations of pikemen and musketeers), each fifty files wide and thirty ranks deep. Cavalry formed each wing, and all the guns were massed in the middle of the line. The Swedish–Saxon force was in reality composed of two separate armies: the untried Saxons took the left, the experienced Swedes held the centre and right. Each army was flanked by cavalry. Unlike the Saxons, the Swedish infantry fought in its unique six-rank, 500-man battalions; every three of these were grouped into T-shaped brigades – at 1,500 men, equivalent in manpower to Tilly's dense tercios. Unlike their opponents, the Swedish infantry were formed in depth, so providing reserves. Detachments of musketeers were threaded between the Swedish cavalry squadrons. Each Swedish brigade was supported by at least six 3-pounder guns. In addition, Gustavus deployed fifty-one heavy field guns. With just twenty-seven artillery pieces, Tilly was not only heavily outnumbered, but also outgunned. Yet the

Imperialists could deploy a powerful weapon of their own: the aura of invincibility.

The action commenced with the traditional artillery duel. Then Tilly's ponderous tercios lumbered forward, initially making for the centre of the allied line before veering towards the nervous Saxons. By now the cavalry on both flanks were in action. Gottfried Heinrich von Pappenheim led forward the Imperial horse of the left, riding at the head of his dreaded cuirassiers, all clad from crown to knee in sinister blackened armour. Under the personal command of Gustavus, and stiffened by the musketeers posted among them, the Swedish cavalry held its ground. On the Imperialist right, it was a very different story. Here, Egon von Fürstenberg's troopers swiftly broke the Saxon cavalry, allowing Tilly's foot to grind its way through Elector John George's infantry. The Saxon army was eliminated, and another Imperial victory seemed assured.

The Swedish left – 4,000 men under General Gustav Horn – lay dangerously exposed. At this crisis, the flexibility of the Swedish battalion system proved its worth: Horn calmly formed a new front to cover his vulnerable flank, drew upon reserves, and then counter-attacked. He struck Tilly's tercios while they were still winded and disorganized from their clash with the Saxons. Meanwhile, a combination of cavalry charges and infantry firepower had finally rebuffed the persistent Pappenheim. Gustavus's triumphant right wing now wheeled inwards, captured Tilly's guns and turned them upon his own reeling infantry. This clinched the Swedish victory. The wounded Tilly withdrew northwest, the remnants of his army covered by the indefatigable Pappenheim.

Some 7,600 Imperialists were killed, with 9,000 wounded or taken prisoner, and another 4,000 deserters. Swedish casualties totalled 1,500, with Saxon losses at 3,000. Gustavus's triumph, which rested upon the effective integration of infantry, cavalry and artillery, was overwhelming.

The virtual annihilation of Tilly's previously unstoppable army took Europe's rulers by surprise, not least because Gustavus was unknown outside the Baltic theatre. Indeed, the magnitude of his victory surprised Gustavus himself. His battle-hardened and proficient army handed the German Protestants a powerful new weapon, but as the king had already achieved his aim of pushing the Imperialists back from the Baltic's southern shore, a question mark remained over how next to wield it.

While Gustavus pondered his options, Tilly received a reprieve that allowed him to withdraw beyond the Saale and Weser, and begin rebuilding his shattered army. Meanwhile, Gustavus led his weary men southwest into the rich Catholic lands along the Rhine and Main. Despite Breitenfeld – the first major victory of the war for the Protestant cause – the Swedes were no more successful in attracting the support of substantial rulers. Some who would have preferred neutrality felt obliged to side with Gustavus as his hard-bitten horde drew ever closer to their territories. Such lukewarm 'allies' provided the supplies that sustained Gustavus's swollen army. While far from popular with Germany's Protestant rulers, elsewhere Gustavus enjoyed celebrity as the bulwark of his religion, fuelling a veritable industry of publications and artefacts commemorating his exploits.

During the winter of 1631/2 the Imperialists regained their balance. In the northwest, Pappenheim raided Swedish communications, while Tilly shifted to Bavaria to raise forces for a fresh campaign. Now aged 73 and plagued by pessimism, in March 1632 Tilly precipitated events when he ejected the Swedes from Bamberg. Gustavus's response was brisk and brutally effective: within a month he moved south with a formidable army of 37,000 men to counter Tilly's 22,000. Covered by an intensive barrage from seventy-two heavy guns, on 5 April a pontoon bridge was constructed across the River Lech at Rain, enabling his troops to smash Tilly's Bavarian army. Tilly died of his wounds, Bavaria lay helpless and the Catholic cause seemed at its nadir. In this crisis situation, in April 1632, it was decided to reinstate Albrecht von Wallenstein, a lapsed Protestant whose cynicism and greed were remarkable even by the standards of seventeenth-century commanders, as the only man capable of raising and leading a viable Imperial army.

Acutely aware that the Imperial cause now depended upon the survival of his army, Wallenstein campaigned cautiously. In July 1632 he selected a heavily fortified position adjoining an old castle called the Alte Feste, just outside Nuremberg. On 24 August Gustavus instigated a bloody and futile effort to dislodge him, his determined assaults baffled by a tenacious defence and rugged terrain. Weakened by heavy casualties, disease and desertion, in October the Swedes finally withdrew towards the northwest. While his subordinates cleared Saxon forces from Bohemia and Silesia, Wallenstein personally overran Saxony itself. On 1 November Leipzig once again fell to the Imperialists.

For two weeks Wallenstein kept his troops together. Then, on 14 November, he dispersed them to winter quarters. This was a costly decision. Next day, when intelligence reported that the Swedes were converging upon his head-quarters at Lützen, he was unable to concentrate his detach-ments. Despite his summer losses, when Gustavus met Wallenstein on 16 November, their armies were evenly matched, with 19,000 men apiece. As Swedes and Imperi-alists alike employed the new formations that had triumphed at Breitenfeld, the battle degenerated into a brutal slugging match, fought under a masking mist until both armies were exhausted. That evening, after tallying his 6,000 casualties, the disheartened Wallenstein resolved to withdraw, not only abandoning his artillery and baggage, but relinquishing his Saxon conquests and retreating to Bohemia.

Although now technically the victors, the Swedes had little to celebrate: their losses were likewise heavy, and Gustavus himself had been killed. Spurring into the cavalry mêlée on his white charger, Streiff, he had been shot in the arm and back, unhorsed and dragged along with one foot entangled in a stirrup. As he lay face down in the mud, a bullet in the head from some anonymous soldier finished him off. Stripped by looters, the king's body was only identified after the fighting was over.

Reports of Gustavus's death were hard to credit. That December, courtiers in London were willing to wager £200 that the news was false. The loss of Gustavus, and Lützen's indecisive outcome, ended the spectacular upsurge of Protestant fortunes in Germany. The king's death left a vacuum; his heiress, Queen Christina, was just 6 years old, so affairs remained in the capable hands of Gustavus's trusted collaborator, Oxenstierna. His guidance, combined with the battlefield talents of commanders who had learned their trade in the Polish wars of the 1620s, ensured that Sweden maintained the prestigious new position won by the military prowess of Gustavus and his devoted soldiers: when the Thirty Years War ended at the Peace of Westphalia in 1648, their territorial conquests were confirmed, elevating Sweden to Great Power status.

COUNT TILLY

1559–1632

JOHN CHILDS

TILLY WAS AMONGST THE LAST of the great condottieri *who combined managerial, political, financial and military acumen to raise and lead* ad hoc *armies on behalf of princes. Favouring well-established tactics rather than the innovative styles of his opponents, Tilly is renowned for his efforts on behalf of the Imperial and Catholic forces during the first half of the Thirty Years War. He knew that battle could deliver decisive results and would fight whenever the odds were favourable. His high reputation declined after the sack of Magdeburg and his defeat at Breitenfeld, where his antiquated approach failed before the new methods of Sweden's Gustavus Adolphus.*

Born in February 1559 in the Château de Tilly, Brabant, about 30 miles southeast of Brussels, he was a younger son of Martin 't Serclaes, Count Tilly, and Dorothea von Schier-städt. During his youth he saw his homeland ravaged by Dutch Calvinists, and developed a hatred of Protestantism reinforced by attendance at the Jesuit seminary in Cologne. However, he did not take Holy Orders but turned instead to the profession of arms, the traditional alternative occupation for junior offspring of the aristocracy, joining the Walloon regiment in the army of Ernst von Bayern, Prince-Bishop of Liège, in 1574. He served in Germany and the Netherlands, including the capture of Antwerp in 1585, and in France when the army of Flanders intervened in the Wars of Religion. Following transfer into the cuirassier regiment of Count Adolf von Schwarzenburg he was successively governor of Dun-sur-Meuse and Villefranche in Lorraine. In 1594 Tilly entered the Imperial army engaged in the 'Long War' against the Turks in Hungary (1593–1606), fighting at the capture of Stuhlweissenburg, 9–14 October 1601, and receiving promotion to major-general before purchasing the colonelcy of a Walloon regiment in 1602. For his role in the successful defence of Gran on the Danube in 1604 he was raised to the rank of general of cavalry. Elevation to Imperial field marshal followed in 1605.

As the religious and political compromise established in Germany in the 1550s deteriorated and princes looked to their defences, in 1605 Duke Maximilian I of Bavaria appointed Tilly lieutenant general at a monthly salary of

4,000 florins. Tilly led the Bavarian forces, mostly mercenaries and militia, when they occupied the Imperial free
city of Donauwörth on 17 December 1607. Bavaria founded
the Catholic League in 1609 and the following year Tilly
became commander of the League's army (effectively that
of Bavaria). Although he spent much time training the
Bavarian militia, there were few permanent troops apart
from some garrisons and guards: in the event of war, the
army had to be filled with trained officers and recruits. Here
Tilly proved his worth in managing the military enterprisers,
most pre-engaged to the Bavarian government, to produce
a professional force. He subsequently grew rich through
salary, commission, plunder, booty, contributions and the
sale of protections.

Early successes in the Thirty Years War

When Protestant Bohemia rebelled against the Holy Roman
Empire in 1618, the Catholic League pledged its support
to the emperors Matthias (r. 1612–19) and Ferdinand II
(r. 1619–37). Accompanied by the Imperial army under
Charles de Longueval, Count of Bucquoy, Tilly led the League
army through Austria into Bohemia. In less than an hour
on the morning of 8 November 1620, across the slopes of
the White Mountain outside Prague, Tilly and Bucquoy with
25,000 soldiers annihilated the 15,000-strong Bohemian
army. While the army of Flanders attacked from the west,

Tilly invaded the Rhenish territories of the Elector Palatine and now-deposed king of Bohemia, Frederick V, who was defenceless until another professional soldier, Count Ernst von Mansfeld, his pockets stuffed with English and Dutch gold, reactivated the 21,000 troops of the dissolved Protestant Union. Mansfeld withdrew towards Alsace to link up with another Protestant mercenary corps under George Frederick, Margrave of Baden-Durlach. They advanced north to prevent a junction between Tilly and 20,000 men from the army of Flanders under Gonzalo Fernández de Córdoba. This objective was achieved and they successfully repulsed an attack by Tilly on their rearguard south of Heidelberg on 27 April 1622. Mansfeld did not pursue and Tilly was able to combine with Córdoba. Mansfeld and Baden-Durlach sought to combine with the 12,000 troops of Duke Christian of Brunswick, who was approaching the right bank of the River Neckar.

Mansfeld and Baden-Durlach separated their corps in the hope that Tilly and Córdoba would do likewise. Mansfeld crossed the Neckar near Heidelberg while Baden-Durlach marched eastwards along the Neckar intending to cross at Wimpfen. Tilly and Córdoba did not oblige by dividing their forces and pursued and overtook Baden-Durlach's 12,700 soldiers on 6 May near Wimpfen, on the left bank of the Neckar north of Heilbronn. Trusting that Mansfeld would march down the right bank, cross at Wimpfen and come to his aid, Baden-Durlach deployed defensively along a low, horseshoe-shaped ridge outside the village, his front covered by a wagon-laager (*wagenburg*). Tilly and Córdoba's 18,000 men made little impact on the wall of wagons until a cannonball hit a powder-cart which had been positioned too close to the front line. The resultant explosion ripped a hole in the defences and Baden-Durlach's army disintegrated under a general assault, only 3,000 escaping to reinforce Mansfeld.

Numerically inferior, Mansfeld was in a vulnerable position on the right bank and hurried to unite with Christian of Brunswick at Höchst on the River Main, a junction that Tilly and Córdoba intended to thwart. They intercepted Brunswick at Höchst on 20 June while he was bridging the Main. Although surprised and outnumbered by nearly two to one – 28,000 to 15,000 – Brunswick established a bridgehead which he successfully defended against heavy musketry and artillery fire. At a cost of 2,000 men and nearly all his baggage, Brunswick held off Tilly and linked up with Mansfeld. Tilly exploited his success by besieging Heidelberg, the capital of the Palatinate, which fell on 19 September following a siege of eleven weeks.

Having dismissed Mansfeld and Baden-Durlach on 13 July, Frederick of the Palatinate retired into exile at The Hague. After wintering in East Friesland, Christian of Brunswick, an arrogant, rash, one-armed adventurer of questionable judgement known as the 'mad Halberstadter', took

15,000 men into Lower Saxony through the Weser–Elbe corridor in March 1623. Deprived of Mansfeld's anticipated support, Christian found himself isolated deep in Catholic territory with no possibility of reinforcement. Tilly had learned of Brunswick's expedition and marched 25,000 men to intercept before he could reach shelter in the Dutch Republic. Encumbered by loot, Brunswick squandered a three-day lead and was forced to stand and fight on 6 August at Stadtlohn, 10 miles short of the Dutch border. Taking position on a low ridge, with his infantry deployed in Dutch-style battalions, Brunswick's 15,000 troops withstood several assaults from Tilly's four tercios, which went into action directly from column of march, until both wings of cavalry were swept away. Trapped between a bog on their left and the River Berkel in the rear, Brunswick's infantry lost 6,000 killed and 4,000 prisoners. Stadtlohn ended the Palatinate Phase of the Thirty Years War.

Tilly's successes of 1620–23, which had resulted in the suppression of the Bohemian revolt and conquest of the Palatinate, were attributed to the quality of his army, which was better trained, drilled, commanded and organized than the hastily raised hordes of Mansfeld, Baden-Durlach and Christian of Brunswick. Tilly was raised to the status of Count of the Holy Roman Empire.

The war with Denmark

Tilly and the Bavarian army of the Catholic League had fought the lion's share of the Palatinate War, allowing Emperor Ferdinand's Austrian forces to operate in Hungary against Prince Bethlen Gabór of Transylvania. During the winter of 1624–5, Bavaria asked for Imperial assistance and the Catholic forces in Germany were reorganized. Already chafing at the political constraints imposed by his reliance upon Tilly's League army and anxious to possess his own German army, Emperor Ferdinand turned to Albrecht von Wallenstein (1583–1634), who quickly raised 24,000 men at his own expense in return for permission to 'recover' expenses and appoint his own officers.

Christian IV of Denmark, who hoped to acquire the bishoprics of Verden, Bremen and Osnabrück but saw that partial Spanish and Imperial occupation of northern Germany threatened his ambitions, now advanced across the Elbe in July 1625 with 17,000 men, a mixture of mercenaries and militia cavalry, heading for Hamelin on the Weser. Tilly, whose troops were cantoned in Westphalia, successfully parried the Danish advance in a series of minor actions before capturing Calenburg (3 November) and defeating a Danish relieving force at Seeze on the following day. However, at The Hague on 9 December 1625, Denmark, England, the Dutch Republic and Frederick of the Palatinate, supported by France, Bethlen Gabór and his suzerain, the Ottoman sultan Murad IV, formed a loose alliance against the Catholic League and Imperialists. Funded by the English and Dutch, Christian IV undertook to attack Lower Saxony; Christian of Brunswick agreed to assault Tilly in Westphalia and the lower Rhineland; and Mansfeld, the coalition's generalissimo, would engage Wallenstein and advance along the Elbe to ravage the Habsburg lands before combining with Gabór against Austria and Moravia.

The plan was both ludicrously complex and took insufficient account of Wallenstein's new Imperial army, and led to disaster for Christian. On 25 April 1626 Mansfeld was checked by Wallenstein at Dessau Bridge on the Elbe and lost one-third of his force, but after regrouping, on 30 June he marched southeast for Silesia with 10,000 men, pursued by Wallenstein with 30,000. Meanwhile Christian IV of Denmark, assuming that Tilly's Catholic League army – deployed far to the west in Westphalia – had been weakened by the need to quell a peasant revolt in Upper Austria, now sought him out. Tilly lured him to fight at Lutter on 17 August, and destroyed his army for good.

Lutter-am-Barenberg

Tilly's greatest and most professional battle took place when he faced Christian IV of Denmark as part of the three-pronged Protestant assault on the Catholic armies in 1626. Christian, seeking Tilly out, marched south with 21,000 men from Wolfenbüttel along the valleys of the Innerste and the Neile between the Hainberg and the Oderwald. Having received 8,000 reinforcements from Wallenstein, Tilly slowly withdrew, skirmishing with the Danish vanguard, until the arrival of a further 4,300 reinforcements under Count Nicolas Desfurs made him strong enough to risk battle.

Christian, aware that he now faced superior forces, began to retreat back to Wolfenbüttel on 24 August in pouring rain through close, heavily wooded country, his rearguard constantly harassed by Desfurs and Croatian irregulars. At Lutter-am-Barenberg the road narrowed into a defile, which was already blocked by the baggage train. On 27 August Christian had no option but to take up position behind the Neile River and stand and fight, with 21,000 men against Tilly's 24,500. Christian adopted a Nassau-style deployment, arranging his infantry in 1,200-strong battalions in three, echeloned lines: cavalry stood to either flank. Tilly's infantry comprised five old-style tercios with cavalry also deployed on both wings.

Tilly first attempted to cross the Neile through the village of Rohde and create a bridgehead on the Danish left but was successfully counter-attacked by cavalry. This encouraged the Danes to launch a disorganized general assault over the Neile on Tilly's main infantry position, but they were thrown back and cut to pieces by artillery fire and disciplined musketry from the tercios. When Desfurs finally brought his detachment forward through Muhle to outflank the Danish right and debouch into their rear, the victory was complete. Christian lost about 8,000 men while Tilly suffered only 700 casualties. The remains of the Danish army straggled north to form a defensive front along the Elbe.

Tilly and Wallenstein swept through Saxony in 1627, occupied the Jutland peninsula and drove the Danes into the islands. Wallenstein defeated Christian's remaining forces at Wolgast on 24 August 1628. Tilly and Wallenstein were now established along the Baltic coast and had reconquered Germany on behalf of the emperor and the Roman Catholic faith.

The Peace of Lübeck, on 22 May 1629, ended the Danish War. Christian of Denmark was restored to his possessions provided that he supported the Spanish and Imperial ambitions to control the Baltic through the creation of a navy based at Wismar, terms that he was happy to accept because they incommoded his principal enemy, Sweden.

War with Sweden

Emperor Ferdinand now dismissed Wallenstein, who was beginning to allow personal ambition to override his duty to the emperor, and when Gustavus Adolphus of Sweden landed with 13,000 men at the mouth of the Oder in 1630, the emperor appointed Tilly to command both the Imperial and Catholic League armies. The general was now over 70 years of age, increasingly prone to misjudgements and mistakes and unable to control his headstrong subordinates: in the opinion of Lieutenant General Count Gottfried von Pappenheim, he was rapidly descending into senility. To contain Gustavus within his Pomeranian bridgehead, Tilly blockaded Magdeburg, Sweden's principal German ally, a key bridging point on the Elbe commanding the roads from Pomerania into Lower Saxony and Thuringia.

At the end of March 1631 Tilly upgraded the blockade of Magdeburg into a formal siege. In an unsuccessful attempt to draw Tilly away from Magdeburg, Gustavus struck southwards and seized Frankfurt-an-der-Oder on 13 April, but the bait was refused and Magdeburg was stormed, looted and burned on 20 May: only 5,000 out of 20,000 inhabitants and garrison survived.

Across Europe, the sack of Magdeburg was represented as a deliberate slaughter of Protestants by the Roman Catholic forces of the Holy Roman Empire. Tilly, who already had a considerable and justified reputation for permitting barbarities and atrocities against Protestants, explained that his soldiers had reacted to months of deprivation in flooded siege trenches, and that the unwritten laws of war permitted the pillage of towns that offered over-enthusiastic resistance and caused the attacker to suffer unnecessary casualties. In fact, neither Tilly nor Pappenheim personally sanctioned the massacre and they tried to intervene, but their men were beyond control. The impact was immense: the Lutheran and Calvinist states began to reconsider their tacit support for the emperor and support grew for the new Protestant hero and talisman Gustavus, the 'Lion of the North'.

Tilly moved northwards from Magdeburg but could make no impression on Swedish field fortifications at Werben. After losing a small cavalry engagement at Burgstall (27 July), he withdrew on 29 July. Tilly demanded that Elector John George of Saxony disband his army, but when he refused Tilly, short of supplies, invaded Saxony, storming Merseburg and Leipzig in September. Gustavus concluded an agreement with John George on 2 September that added 18,000 Saxons to his 23,000 Swedes. Gustavus then pushed down the Elbe from Werben and encountered Tilly's twenty-seven field guns and 31,000 men on 17 September at Breitenfeld, a village on the northern edge of modern Leipzig (see also pp. 41–3). Gustavus's army comprised two separate forces: the Saxons on the left under Hans George von Arnim and the Swedes in the centre and right. The Imperial infantry deployed in twelve tercios, the Swedes and Saxons in 500-man battalions, six ranks deep. Tilly first attacked the Saxons and drove them from the field before turning on the exposed Swedish left. Exploiting the flexibility of the battalion organization, Johan Banér and Gustav Horn formed a new front to the left, ordered up reserves from the third line and launched a series of vigorous counter-attacks against Tilly's tercios which were tired and disorganized after their exertions against the Saxons. Once Pappenheim's cavalry on the right – he made a total of seven charges – had eventually been held and defeated by the Swedish horse, Horn and Banér crushed Tilly's tercios in a fury of musketry, cannon-fire and hand-to-hand combat.

Despite having moved some way towards the new Dutch methods during the 1620s by increasing the numbers of musketeers in the tercio and thinning the ranks of pikemen from thirty to fifteen, Tilly's outmoded deployments had been exposed. In response to Breitenfeld, Wallenstein experimented with shallower infantry formations, which he put into effect with some success at Lützen in 1632. However, Tilly's conservatism was based on sound practical considerations: the tercio allowed the military enterprisers to give lightly equipped, raw recruits a minimum of instruction before pushing them into the rear ranks, whereas the Dutch–Swedish systems required extensive drill. Similarly, Tilly's cavalry employed the 'caracole', an equally antiquated tactic of riding forward, firing pistols and then wheeling around and returning to the lines to reload, but one which could be performed adequately by relatively untrained troopers and horses.

Tilly now withdrew and scraped together reinforcements from amongst the Imperial garrisons in north

Germany, incorporated the corps of Duke Charles IV of Lorraine and then retreated into northern Bavaria, taking winter quarters around Ingolstadt. Having captured half of Germany in the wake of Breitenfeld, in March 1632 Gustavus moved south with 37,000 men from Nuremberg to Donauwörth, intending to beat Tilly before advancing on Vienna. Elector Maximilian I of Bavaria brought reinforcements to Tilly at Ingolstadt, raising his forces to 22,000 men. Tilly entrenched behind the River Lech, close to the town of Rain, confident that Gustavus would be unable to force a crossing. On 5 April, a portion of the Swedish infantry, covered by an artillery barrage and the smoke from burning straw, threw a bridge of boats over the river and succeeded in establishing a bridgehead despite furious counter-attacks from Tilly's foot. In the interim, the Swedish cavalry moved 6 miles south of Tilly's position, crossed the Lech unopposed and was marching rapidly into the open left flank and rear of the Imperial League army when Tilly was badly wounded by a cannon shot. He was carried into Ingolstadt and his army rapidly withdrew, thus unintentionally thwarting the Swedish plan. Tilly lost 3,000 men and the Swedes about 2,000. He died in Ingolstadt on 30 April and was succeeded in command of the Bavarian/Catholic League army by Johann von Aldringen.

OLIVER CROMWELL

1599–1658

ANTONIA FRASER

OLIVER CROMWELL IS PROBABLY UNIQUE among the great commanders of the world in that he had no proper military training nor any military experience until he was well over 40. The most famous soldiers among his contemporaries – Gustavus Adolphus of Sweden, Marshal Turenne, the Prince de Condé, Rupert of the Rhine – were all vigorously engaged in warfare from their youth. Yet as a general Cromwell was in effect undefeated. Certainly the few minor reverses he did endure were very small in contrast to the swingeing victories that enabled him to charge at full gallop down the path of British history. And by these victories Cromwell undoubtedly changed the course of the nation.

During the two English Civil Wars – of 1642 and 1648 – to say nothing of Cromwell's campaigns in Ireland and

Scotland, the Royalist side was well supplied with generals, many of them trained and experienced soldiers who had commanded troops in the wars which had raged across Europe since 1618. Militarily speaking, the odds were never loaded in favour of the Parliamentary side, rather the reverse, hence the inestimable value of Cromwell's personal contribution. It is no wonder that the twentieth-century paladin Field Marshal Montgomery called Cromwell one of the great 'captains' – his preferred term – of history. And the novelist John Buchan, a serious military writer and author of many campaign studies, called him 'the first great soldier of the new world' who would not be matched until Marlborough half a century later.

The making of a great leader

Oliver Cromwell was born in Huntingdon in 1599; he was thus two years older than the man who would succeed the first Stuart monarch, James I, as King Charles I in 1625. There was no princely magnificence in his own background: he came of a minor branch of the gentry, originally Welsh, and received the conventional upbringing of his class, a brief spell at Cambridge University followed by education in the law. By the time the king raised the standard at Nottingham in August 1642, Cromwell had enjoyed a career from which it would have taken a remarkable feat of prophecy to predict future greatness. He sat in parliament for his native Huntingdon in 1628 and during the eleven years of the king's 'personal rule' retreated to Ely, becoming a convinced Puritan. When the issue of taxation obliged the king to call parliament once more, Cromwell was twice elected as MP for Cambridge in 1640, both in the Short Parliament and the Long Parliament, which was still sitting at the outbreak of the war.

Military character

There were elements, however, in this apparently obscure life which were to be enormously influential in his future career as a soldier, even if it is easier to discern this with hindsight. First Cromwell had a passion, verging on an obsession, for horses. Later foreign ambassadors realized that horses as gifts to the Lord Protector were a sure way of gaining favour. This passion extended to days spent hunting and hawking, a kind of amateur military training of a sort – and the nearest Cromwell got to studying the elements of a cavalry charge. Cromwell's interest in the physical welfare of his horses (a novel idea, surprising as it may seem) would pay dividends for parliament, as the Royalists were originally so much better endowed with cavalry resources. And there was a human parallel in his local concerns for those small-scale peasant farmers in East Anglia whose livelihood was being destroyed by Fenland enclosures.

Thus by the arrival of war, Cromwell had an excellent territorial base of local support. The building of the army of the Eastern Association, as this territorial group became known, and later the New Model Army benefited from this cohesion between some of the local gentry and smaller landholders.

His instinct for leadership of men (and animals), together with an emphasis on the materials of war, was to prove vital almost at once in the battles in which Cromwell was involved. But it was a kind of leadership which deplored disorder, let alone anarchy. The inspirational, wild and wonderfully reckless courage of, for example, Cromwell's opponent Prince Rupert was in direct contrast to Cromwell's emphasis on discipline. He expected of his men not the freebooting style of the Cavaliers but the decent restraint of 'a russet-coated captain that knows what he fights for', as he once remarked. He rated military order with God's order: if the battle was won (as it nearly always was) then clearly God approved of the winners and their agenda. His battle cry was 'The Lord of Hosts' and his motto 'Seeking Peace Through War' (*Pax Quaeritur Bello*). So the man who became Cromwell the Commander combined from the start messianic fervour with a strong materialist grasp of the need for proper supplies and well-trained men. It was to prove a lethal combination.

Civil war leader of men

Cromwell fought as a captain at Edgehill on 23 October 1642. It was, however, at the Battle of Marston Moor in the Vale of York on the evening of 2 July 1644 that his outstanding quality was first displayed with results that turned a prospective defeat into something more like a victory.

The Parliamentary forces were intending to besiege the northern Royalist fortress of York. Sir Thomas Fairfax was in overall command, Lord Manchester was in general charge of the cavalry, and Lord Leven led the large contingent of Scots. However, the arrival of the intrepid Prince Rupert to relieve York's commander, the Marquess of Newcastle, caused the Parliamentarians to draw back from the siege; the day of 2 July was spent in sporadic fighting. By the evening the prospective forces were drawn up facing each other, according to the custom of the time, ready for what would prove to be the largest battle ever fought on British soil. According to modern reckoning, about 22,000 allied (Parliamentarian and Scots) forces faced 18,000 Royalists. Both armies consisted of cavalry, dragoons (mounted infantry) as well as foot soldiers and artillery.

As was customary, the foot were placed in the centre, flanked by the cavalry, including dragoons, on both wings. Close by Long Marston, on the Parliamentarian right, were Fairfax's forces, including 2,000 horse and a further reserve of Scottish cavalry. On the left were 3,000 cavalry of the Eastern Association under Cromwell's personal command, interspersed with platoons of infantry musketeers, some Scots dragoons and a further reserve of Scots cavalry under David Leslie.

Facing Fairfax was the bulk of the Royalist cavalry under Lord Goring; opposite Cromwell was drawn up the cavalry of Lord Byron. Both sides showed their mettle: the Parliamentarians with psalm-singing, the Royalists with banners which caricatured their opponents as little beagles yapping 'Pym, Pym, Pym' (the Parliamentarian political leader who had died in December).

At about six o'clock in the evening, as the Royalist commanders ate supper, the allies took the dramatic decision to attack. Cromwell with his loyal men of the Eastern Association charged on the left: this was a rapid but controlled exercise, the men riding short-reined and short-stirruped, close together at something like a fast trot rather than the modern gallop. The careful pace meant that they did not lose contact with their infantry firepower. The whole line moved forward 'like so many thick clouds', wrote Manchester's chaplain, an eye-witness. This ferocious yet disciplined charge 'in the bravest order and with the greatest resolution that ever was seen' went extremely well, scattering the enemy opposite them; the allies' infantry in the centre also fought doughtily. Unfortunately Fairfax on the right, with marshy ground to hamper him, was soon in trouble.

Two hours into the battle the situation was chaotic. Not only was Fairfax in trouble but Cromwell may have been lightly wounded, leaving David Leslie and his Scots cavalry to come to the rescue. There was at least the strong possibility of a Parliamentarian rout. It was at this point that the recovered Cromwell and his stalwart men of the Eastern Association, held 'close and firm together in a body', proved themselves to be the one coherent force left on the battlefield. Conventional wisdom of the time might have been to plunge on and strike at York. Instead, Cromwell used his 'lovely company' like a hammer, to assault the Royalist centre, and most surprising of all, strike from behind at Goring, whose exhausted cavalry was not expecting an attack that evening and from that quarter. The Royalist cavalry scattered and at least 3,000 Royalists were killed with only 300 of the allies, although there were many wounded on both sides.

'Truly England and the Church of God hath had a great favour from the Lord in this great victory given unto us,' wrote Cromwell characteristically afterwards. It was true. Marston Moor cost the king his northern army and indeed the north. For those who sought a more human explanation, it was Cromwell's disciplined use of cavalry which was the single element that had saved the day.

One year later – at Naseby in Northamptonshire on 15 June 1645 – Cromwell was able to lead the recently developed 22,000-strong New Model Army to a decisive victory over the king's forces; after this there was never any question of the Royalists winning the war. Marston Moor had done more than consolidate Cromwell's military reputation: it also called attention to his potential as a leader. In the intervening months the removal of the Parliamentarian aristocrats and Presbyterians from army command, in the so-called Self-Denying Ordinance, left the religiously 'Independent' Cromwell as the military strongman under Fairfax's command. Naseby was not won without a struggle, though the Parliamentarians enjoyed a huge numerical superiority of 11,000 to around 7,500 Royalists. At first Prince Rupert's brilliant, successful cavalry charge seemed to assure another of his daring victories, but then his troops scattered for pillaging, while Cromwell's men held firm. This allowed them to overwhelm the Royalist right flank as the army which the Royalists had derided as 'the New Noddle' showed its calibre. Even in success Cromwell did not allow his men the fatal indulgence of plunder that had effectively ruined the Royalist triumph earlier in the day. As a result Cromwell was full of 'holy glee', according to contemporaries. That particular emotion, a kind of manic elation at God's apparent favour, might hold an ominous message for the future, in contrast to his usual emphasis on discipline both of himself and his troops. Cromwell's persistent references to his victory at Naseby led to rumours after his death that he had actually been buried on the battlefield.

Preston: Second Civil War

Cromwell passed – for the time being – into civilian and political life with the ending of the First Civil War. He was not seen in action again until the beginning of the Second Civil War in the spring of 1648. By this time the military defeat of the king had merely exposed crucial divisions between parliament and its army. This renewal of warfare, about which Cromwell felt extremely bitter – he called it 'a great mischief'– was the result of the collusion of English and Scottish Royalists. Nevertheless it included one of Cromwell's most spectacular victories. When 20,000 Scots under the Duke of Hamilton invaded northern England, the natural reaction of a competent commander would have been to fall back and protect the capital. Cromwell, however, decided on the risky gambler's throw of marching northwest himself – and then attacking the Scots from their own rear. His reasoning was that if he defeated the Scots in battle, he would rout them completely, leaving them no opportunity to withdraw to Scotland and regroup. After nine days of constant fighting in late August 1648, during which he covered 140 miles – a prodigious feat – Cromwell routed the Scots at Preston in Lancashire with 8,500 troops. He was in fact vastly outnumbered, but as Cromwell wrote later: 'It was thought that to engage the enemy to fight was our business.' The results were catastrophic for the Scots, and led to the end of the Second Civil War much as Naseby had led to the end of the First.

General in Ireland

During the various stages of political strife which now led up to the trial and execution of Charles I on 30 January 1649, Cromwell's position was at all points strengthened by his hold over and popularity with the army, especially when Fairfax withdrew from the judicial proceedings in disgust. It was thus Cromwell whom parliament, as the sole authority in the country after the death of the king, dispatched to Ireland in the summer of 1649: he was to blast the resistance of that intractable (and of course mainly Catholic) island. Opposition in Ireland, consisting of a number of disparate forces in favour of royal rule, could never be taken lightly given the geographical position which made it a convenient launching-pad for England's foreign enemies. Nevertheless it was in Ireland that Cromwell irrevocably stained his reputation with the massacres of Drogheda and Wexford on 11 September and 11 October 1649 respectively.

How far is this staining justified? To estimate it, we must divide the military from the humanitarian. The seventeenth-century rules of warfare, as carried out all over Europe during the Thirty Years War and earlier, were indeed ruthless, even chilling. But they were generally recognized. The commander of a fortress had to make a decision, when officially 'summoned', whether to surrender or not. If he refused to do so, and the city was successfully stormed, then his soldiers and other combatants might be killed out of hand and the rest of the civilian population – women and children – would be subject to the unrestrained looting and rapacity of the besiegers. This provision was based on the harsh physical conditions of the attackers, in their camps, compared to the comparative ease of those within the town, endowed with shelter, water and provisions. It was naturally in the best interests of any fortress to procrastinate – unless there was a strong motive to do otherwise. Nor was Drogheda, where around 2,800 troops and several hundred priests and civilians were massacred, an easy target: as one saying had it, 'He who can take Drogheda can take Hell.'

But if Cromwell, desperate to pacify Ireland and to establish a solid armed presence before winter set in, had a military justification for the massacres which followed the sieges (they certainly presented a clear message to the rest of Ireland), the same cannot be said of his personal attitude to the native inhabitants. Here was a kind of scornful xenophobia, a sense of a holy crusade in which religion justified everything, singularly lacking from the disciplined

Cromwell of England and Scotland. Once again but in a more marked form, 'holy glee' is evident in Cromwell's attitudes to these victories; furthermore at Wexford (where a similar number died as at Drogheda, though a higher proportion were civilians) his soldiers, encouraged no doubt by the rampaging atmosphere, even broke out and pillaged, something that was elsewhere expressly forbidden.

Dunbar and Worcester

We are on less controversial ground with Cromwell's two last fighting engagements. These were at Dunbar in Scotland against the Presbyterians under the young King Charles II on 3 September 1650 and at Worcester exactly a year later: in a letter to Parliament Cromwell called this the 'crowning mercy', since he had defeated Charles and thus brought the nine years of wars to a conclusive end. In both cases Cromwell showed himself a daring strategist and a cool calculator: no manic streak was visible here, illustrating the truth of Machiavelli's maxim: 'In war, discipline can do more than fury.' At the coastal town of Dunbar, apparently hemmed in, he lured the Scots, with twice his own numbers, down from their superior position on the hills. He was thus able to break their flank, and so drive them 'like turkeys'. There were 3,000 Scots' casualties to a few hundred English. Heading for Worcester, Cromwell showed an astonishing turn of speed, marching parallel with the young king as he attempted to raise English support. Not only that, but apart from planning a successful, two-pronged attack with his generals John Lambert and Charles Fleetwood, he led his own men in the assault, at the age of 52, with great personal courage. However, there is some evidence that Cromwell, normally eager for the sudden sally, actually delayed the action to coincide with the date of 3 September, his 'most auspicious day': it is always interesting to be reminded of the other semi-mystical side to 'Old Ironsides' (as he was nicknamed, just as his men were known as the Ironsides).

After that it was forward to what the poet John Milton, saluting Cromwell, called 'peace's victories'. Cromwell's career as Lord Protector (from 1653) meant that the man who had killed a king played a virtually royal role before his death in 1658, also on 3 September – another coincidence? His tortured attempts at a godly rule, unable to manage either with or without parliament, are another story. Nevertheless it is impossible to consider his political career realistically without the knowledge that he had gained this position in war – even if he had been seeking 'peace through war'. Cromwell had shown himself a military genius, a leader of men, and by that means had reached the highest position of state. It was the perfect example of another Machiavellian principle, by which war 'not only maintains those that are born Princes but many times raises men from a private fortune to that dignity'. Unfortunately the qualities which made him a great soldier – daring, the capacity to innovate, courage, a steely nerve – worked much less well in the complex world of politics, where his legacy is, to say the least, controversial. Lucy Hutchinson, whose husband John had been one of those who signed Charles I's death warrant in 1649, described Cromwell in her memoirs as having 'much natural greatness'. It is easier to agree with her unequivocally in the military rather than in the political sphere.

VICOMTE DE TURENNE
1611–75

JOHN CHILDS

LOUIS XIV'S GENERAL TURENNE possessed one of the outstanding military minds of the seventeenth century. Always prepared to adapt and improvise, he became thoroughly expert in tactics, strategy and manoeuvre. Having served his apprenticeship during the Thirty Years War, he reached professional maturity in the 1650s and, following Louis's creation of a powerful French army in the 1660s, his most masterful campaigns occurred during the final two years of his life. Although an aristocrat, Turenne had the common touch, enjoying a close rapport with the soldiers whose lives he husbanded.

Initially trained in the military style of Nassau and Gustavus Adolphus, Turenne developed their techniques to such an extent that they became instrumental in the widespread adoption of linear tactics between 1660 and 1700. Unhindered by preconceptions, he learned from his mistakes, especially in his campaign against the Bavarians in 1645 in the final years of the Thirty Years War. A cautious, circumspect and calculating tactician, Turenne placed great emphasis upon accurate intelligence and could assess situations quickly before acting with dispatch and decisiveness.

From 1667, leading an improved French army, he began to act more offensively. In order to reduce desertion and enable greater freedom of action he encouraged logistical planning, the magazine system and the creation of protected lines of communication and supply. Turenne always aimed to campaign in an opponent's territory both to inhibit the enemy's recruitment and logistics, and to reduce the costs of warfare to France: this was the old Swedish principle of making 'war pay for war'. Contrary to received wisdom, in order to maintain concentration of force he preferred to billet his men in the countryside rather than disperse them into garrisons, a technique that paid handsome dividends during the defence of Alsace against the Imperial forces in 1674–5, the campaign that brought his death.

Into the service of the French king

Henri de la Tour d'Auvergne was born on 11 September 1611, the second son of the Duke de Bouillon, ruler of the semi-independent principality of Sedan, by his second wife,

Elizabeth of Nassau, daughter of William the Silent. The family was Calvinist. A slow developer who enjoyed poor health, Turenne also suffered from a life-long speech impediment. As an aristocrat's younger son, he was destined for a career in either the church or the army and, in view of his physical frailty, the former seemed more likely; but his health improved with physical maturity and in 1625 he entered into a cadetship in the Dutch army commanded by his uncles, princes Maurice and Frederick of Nassau. After a year as a private soldier in Frederick's bodyguard, Turenne was commissioned captain in 1626. During the next four years he learned the modern art of war, the 'Nassau School', and experienced extensive action including the siege of 's-Hertogenbosch in 1629.

In 1623 his elder brother Frederic Maurice had succeeded as Duke de Bouillon, and the statesman Cardinal Richelieu, ever keen to strengthen the authority of the French state, began to seek to reduce the independence of the principality of Sedan. Elizabeth and Frederic resisted these overtures, but Turenne was withdrawn from the Dutch army in 1630 and sent to Paris as an unofficial hostage for Sedan's political loyalty. Richelieu formed a favourable impression of the young man and appointed him colonel of an infantry regiment. Turenne returned to the Dutch army for short secondments but after 1635 devoted his career wholly to the French monarchy.

Apprenticeship

Whilst serving under a fellow Huguenot, Marshal Henri de la Force, at the siege of La Motte in Lorraine in 1634, Turenne's courage and determination during the final assault earned a field promotion to *maréchal de camp* (major-general). In 1635 Turenne fought under Cardinal de la Valette, raising the Imperial siege of Mainz on 8 August. For want of provisions, Valette had to retire to Metz. During the retreat, Turenne, in command of the rearguard, tangled with General Matthias Gallas. He was seriously wounded in the successful storming of Saverne in 1636, but returned to action in 1637. During 1638, under the command of Bernhard of Saxe-Weimar, he directed the siege of Alt-Breisach, which fell on 17 December. In 1639 he was transferred into the army of the Comte de Harcourt in northern Italy, where distinguished service resulted in promotion to lieutenant general in 1640. He commanded his own corps in Italy in 1641 and Roussillon during 1642.

Marshal of France

Politically suspect because of his Protestantism and family connections with the principality of Sedan, in 1642 Turenne's position was compromised by his brother's involvement in the conspiracy of the Marquis de Cinq Mars to bring down Richelieu. However, Turenne continued to demonstrate his personal loyalty to the French crown, whilst

his increasing proficiency at his job guaranteed employ-
ment. In 1643 Richelieu entrusted him with an independent
command in northern Italy under the direction of Prince
Thomas of Carignano. At the end of the campaign he was
promoted to Marshal of France on 9 December 1643 and
appointed to Alsace to command the 'army of Weimar',
the remnants of Bernhard of Saxe-Weimar's corps following
its defeat at Tuttlingen a few weeks earlier. Turenne now
campaigned in Alsace and Germany until the end of the
Thirty Years War, but he enjoyed mixed fortunes: his military
education was incomplete and the French army still
compared unfavourably with the veteran formations available to the Imperialists, Swedes and Bavarians.

In June 1644 Turenne's army of Weimar joined a
French detachment commanded by the Duc d'Enghien,
the future Prince de Condé, who, as a prince of the blood,
assumed overall command. They defeated Franz von
Mercy's Bavarian army at Freiburg-im-Breisgau, then
harassed his retreat in a cavalry action, successes that
resulted in the capture of Philippsburg (between 25 August
and 12 September). The following spring, having received
information that von Mercy's army had been weakened
through sending reinforcements to the Imperialists to
counter a Swedish offensive towards Vienna, Turenne
crossed the Rhine. Mercy had, however, actually received
substantial reinforcements. Turenne was enticed deep into

Swabia, lost contact with his line of communications and was obliged to disperse his troops to find supplies. In this vulnerable position he was surprised and badly beaten by Mercy at Marienthal-Bad Mergentheim on 5 May. Enghien absorbed the remains of Turenne's corps and defeated the Bavarians at the second Battle of Nördlingen (Allerheim) on 3 August.

The following year Turenne, accompanied by a Swedish army under Karl Gustav Wrangel, separated the Bavarian army from the Imperialists, forcing Elector Maximilian I to conclude a separate peace in March 1647 (though this was annulled in September). In a final campaign against the recalcitrant Maximilian, Turenne and Wrangel heavily defeated an Imperial–Bavarian army under Count Jobst Maximilian von Gronsfeld and Count Peter Melander von Holzapfel at Zusmarshausen near Augsburg on 17 May 1648, in one of the last battles of the long and bloody war.

Internal pressures and unrest in France led to the outbreak of civil war known as the 'Frondes' (between 1648 and 1653), and Turenne was central in securing the victory of the young King Louis XIV and his chief minister Cardinal Mazarin. In 1652 Condé, supporting the defeated rebellious French nobles, led a Spanish invasion of France. The resultant Franco-Spanish War, between 1653 and 1659, witnessed the flowering of Turenne's martial abilities as he led the French armies into the Spanish Netherlands and defeated the Habsburg forces at the Battle of the Dunes, near Dunkirk, on 14 June 1658.

Turenne had proved a most able and devoted servant of the French monarchy. He was created Marshal General of France when Louis XIV assumed his majority in 1661, but came under pressure to cement his loyalty by converting to Roman Catholicism. Perhaps understanding that the Catholic Church was one of the principal pillars of the French crown whilst the Huguenot faith encouraged division, localism and fragmentation, he finally renounced Protestantism in October 1668.

Franco-Dutch War, 1672–3

In the 1660s Louis, aided by Michel le Tellier and his son the Marquis de Louvois, both of whom served as secretary of state for war, built an army and navy capable of dominating the Habsburgs and the Dutch Republic. With it Turenne led 80,000 men across the border with the Spanish Netherlands on 24 May 1667. The resultant *'promenade militaire'* captured Bergues, Ath, Charleroi, Tournai, Oudenarde, Alost and Lille. Had the Dutch remained loyal to France rather than panicking at French success and joining the English and Swedes in a Triple Alliance in 1668, commented Turenne, the entire Spanish Netherlands would have fallen. Louis now determined to punish the Dutch and in 1672 Turenne advanced along the Sambre while

Condé (rehabilitated and back in the service of the French crown) marched up the valley of the Meuse from Lorraine, the two forces joining at Visé in the Bishopric of Liège. They feinted towards Maastricht, causing the Dutch to denude their Rhineland garrisons to reinforce this key fortress, before turning away through the Electorate of Cologne, crossing the Rhine at Lobith and penning the Dutch army into Holland.

Leaving Condé to contain the Dutch within their 'Water Line', Turenne demonstrated before Maastricht, then on 31 August 1672 marched 15,000 men to the Rhine. He proceeded south to Koblenz before turning down the Moselle to take winter quarters in Lorraine. He allowed his men to plunder the Rhine and Moselle valleys in order to 'waste' the countryside and ensure that Imperial forces would be unable to operate in those areas during the next campaign, thus clearing the flank and rear of the French forces in Utrecht and Holland. The peasants removed themselves and their possessions into the afforested hills and skirmished fiercely with the starving soldiers.

The centrepiece of the campaign of 1673 was the siege of Maastricht. Turenne screened the preparations during February and March by threatening the Imperialists and Brandenburg forces along the Rhine whilst the besieging corps of 40,000 men assembled at Ghent. Once Maastricht had been enveloped, Turenne moved west and blockaded the suburb of Wyck on the right (east) bank of the Maas. Maastricht fell on 30 June but the position of the Dutch Republic soon improved following an alliance with Spain on 30 August 1673 and the termination of the war with England on 19 February 1674. What had begun as a short, limited campaign of conquest for Louis XIV had turned into a major conflict against a European coalition.

The defence of Alsace, 1674–5

During 1674 Turenne was charged with preventing a large German–Imperial army from interfering in either the Spanish Netherlands or Franche-Comté. Its general, Aeneas Caprara, had already crossed to the west bank of the Rhine and encamped near Strasbourg. He dispatched Duke Charles IV of Lorraine south along the right (east) bank of the Rhine to threaten Franche-Comté, but Turenne parried the thrust and forced Charles of Lorraine to return downstream. Turenne sought to subsist at the enemy's expense by operating on the right bank of the Rhine; his army contained 6,000 cavalry but only 1,500 infantry so that he could gather supplies from a wide area. In June, he left Hagenau, crossed to the east side of the Rhine on a bridge of boats near Philippsburg and set off to locate Caprara, who was known to be marching northwards to effect a junction with reinforcements approaching from Frankfurt-am-Main under the cautious Duke Alexander de Bournonville. Covering 100 miles in five days, Turenne overhauled Caprara's 7,000 horsemen and 2,000 infantry before they had contacted Bournonville, and brought them to battle at Sinzheim on 16 June.

Although Turenne's preponderance of cavalry had been ideal for rapid marching and widespread foraging, it severely circumscribed the conduct of battle. Caprara, whose army was similarly unbalanced, lined the hedges and gardens along the edge of the village with musketeers but Turenne deployed his foot and dismounted dragoons in small skirmishing parties that drove in Caprara's outposts and forced a passage over the River Elsatz into the village. Behind a fighting rearguard, Caprara withdrew and formed line of battle on the plateau above Sinzheim. The French now had to advance up a narrow defile knowing that the Imperial horse would pounce as they emerged on to the plateau. Turenne, however, took advantage of the new tactical capabilities of the French army by pushing his infantry and dismounted dragoons up the sides of the defile to line the numerous hedges along the edge of the plateau and occupy a castle on the left and a vineyard on the right. The flanks thus anchored, the cavalry moved up the defile and arranged itself in order of battle relatively unhindered. Turenne mingled groups of musketeers amongst the horsemen in the Swedish manner, to provide additional firepower, lengthen the front and disorder any Imperialist attacks. A premature advance by the French right nearly resulted in disaster, but well-aimed volleys from the infantry in the vineyard broke up the counter-attack. Turenne then ordered a general advance and, supported by musketry, the mounted troops steadily pushed the Imperialists back across the plateau. Exhausted and somewhat disorganized, Turenne's soldiers allowed the Imperialists to leave the field in good order. Both sides incurred about 2,000 casualties.

Lacking the strength to exploit his success, Turenne demonstrated towards Heidelberg before recrossing the Rhine to encamp at Neustadt. Early in July 1674, having taken in reinforcements, he returned to the right bank of the Rhine and marched towards the Imperial headquarters at Heidelberg, seeking to force Bournonville to battle. Bournonville, however, refused to be drawn and withdrew north of the River Main. Turenne's troops remained on the right bank, living off the country, commandeering, looting, plundering and levying contributions while the peasants retaliated by attacking isolated parties and murdering stragglers. This 'First Devastation of the Palatinate' continued until Bournonville took 30,000 men over the Rhine at Mainz towards the end of August, threatening Lorraine and northern Alsace. Turenne terminated his maraud and concentrated 25,000 men between Wissembourg and Landau, confident that Bournonville would be unable to feed his troops and have to retire. As anticipated,

Bournonville withdrew to the right bank and marched south to attack Strasbourg with its valuable Rhine bridge, thus separating Turenne from supporting forces in Upper Alsace and Franche-Comté.

Bournonville's 36,000 men stood in the village of Enzheim, west of Strasbourg behind the River Breusch, awaiting the arrival of reinforcements under Frederick William von Hohenzollern, the 'Great Elector' of Brandenburg. Turenne knew that he would have to risk battle in order to reopen his communications with Upper Alsace and prevent a junction between Bournonville and Frederick William. Through an oversight, Bournonville had failed to block all the Breusch crossings and, on the night of 3/4 October, Turenne quietly moved his army over the river and drew up at Molsheim between Bournonville and Strasbourg and attacked at dawn. According to Bournonville, the Battle of Enzheim was 'one of the longest, most obstinate, and artilleryized that have [sic] ever been seen', the French firing 2,500 cannon balls. At the end of a day of crude frontal assaults, both Bournonville's flanks were in danger and he withdrew from the field having suffered around 3,500 casualties. Turenne lost about 3,000 men.

On 10 October Frederick William crossed to the west bank of the Rhine at Kehl with 20,000 soldiers and 33 cannon, passed through Strasbourg and joined Bournonville to create an army of 50,000. Greatly outnumbered, Turenne fell back to Deittweiler, between the fortresses of Saverne and Hagenau, where he received reinforcements sufficient to raise his strength to 33,000 men. Thinking that Turenne had gone into winter quarters, Bournonville and Frederick William settled their men into cantonments on the plain between the rivers Ill and Rhine. Early in December 1674 Turenne left nine battalions at Saverne and Hagenau to cover his rear and marched his troops in a series of small detachments first north and then west. Through snow and heavy frost he then turned south behind the screen of the Vosges before swinging east into the Belfort Gap. Having reassembled his army at Belfort, on 27 December Turenne debouched on to the plain of the Rhine, surprising the Imperialists, who were scattered in garrisons and quarters. Bournonville threw forward his cavalry to delay the French while attempting to concentrate his forces on Colmar and the little town of Türkheim. Driving rapidly north, Turenne broke the Imperial horse at Mulhouse on 29 December and appeared before Türkheim on 4 January 1675. In the interim, Bournonville and Frederick William had assembled 30,000 men between Colmar and Türkheim but their front was over-extended and could not be held in strength along its entirety: Türkheim itself was under-garrisoned. Quick to spot these weaknesses, Turenne denied his opponents the opportunity to improve their deployment by ordering his 30,000 men into line of battle. The French advanced to pin the Imperial left and centre while making their main effort against Türkheim itself. Progress through the town was interrupted when Bournonville committed reserves, leading to heavy fighting in the outskirts.

As more and more French troops were sucked into the fighting around Türkheim, the pressure on Bournonville's left and centre eased, enabling him to swing his line round to face Türkheim and block any further advances. After dark, though, the Imperial army left Turenne in possession of the battlefield and withdrew through Strasbourg and over the Rhine.

Turenne's last campaign and death

For the 1675 campaign, Emperor Leopold I recalled the veteran Italian Raimondo Montecuccoli to command the Imperial forces on the Rhine. He decided to capture the bridge at Kehl-Strasbourg prior to invading Alsace. Leading 35,000 men directly on Strasbourg, he was thwarted by Turenne's 25,000. Next, Montecuccoli feinted before moving north to attempt a crossing at Speyer but again Turenne was able to gain position and block the attempt. True to his principle of operating on the right bank of the Rhine whenever possible, Turenne then passed the river and a campaign of manoeuvre followed during which each side felt for the other's supply lines and communications, seeking a fractional advantage. By the end of July, Monte-cuccoli had been manoeuvred into such a disadvantageous position at Nieder Sasbach that he was compelled to offer battle on terms propitious to the French. Whilst recon-noitring an enemy artillery battery, however, Turenne was decapitated by a cannon-shot on 27 July.

He was buried in the Abbey of St Denis, the final resting place of the kings of France. The tomb was defaced during the French Revolution and his remains stored in the Jardin des Plantes until 1800 when Napoleon ordered their removal to Les Invalides church.

DUKE OF
MARLBOROUGH

1650–1722

CHARLES SPENCER

THERE HAS BEEN no more successful English soldier than John Churchill, 1st Duke of Marlborough. During the War of the Spanish Succession, he won all his battles, and triumphed at every siege. Moreover, Marlborough was simultaneously in charge of overall allied strategy and, as Ambassador-Extraordinary, of high diplomacy. The finer details of military administration, operations and logistics again fell to him. No other British general has ever been burdened with such all-pervading responsibilities.

The future duke came from gentry stock. His father, Sir Winston Churchill, had served as a Royalist cavalry captain in the Civil War, his ill-fated allegiance leading to a large fine that consigned his family to a life of poverty. After a sketchy education at St Paul's, John followed his sister Arabella to court. She became the Duke of York's favourite mistress, while John became his popular page-boy. Although a consummate courtier throughout his life, Churchill's primary ambitions were, from an early age, military.

Baptism of fire

In September 1667 the 17-year-old Churchill gained his first commission as an ensign in the King's Regiment of Foot Guards. He was sent to Tangier the following year, where he received his baptism of fire against the Moors. In 1670 he also saw his first action at sea, blockading the Barbary pirates in Algiers. Two years later Churchill fought aboard the English flagship, the *Royal Prince*, at the Battle of Sole Bay, off the Suffolk coast. The precise nature of his daring against the Dutch that day is unrecorded, but it resulted in a rare double promotion.

Captain Churchill next displayed his valour when fighting the Dutch on land, in the British unit serving as part of Louis XIV's army. During the storming of Maastricht, despite being wounded, he saved the life of the English commander, the Duke of Monmouth. Churchill raised the French standard over an outwork of the city just before it fell. Ironically, given his later stellar career at France's expense, after the taking of the city Churchill was singled out by the Sun King for praise.

The most significant part of Churchill's military apprenticeship now followed. From 1672 to 1675 he served under Marshal Turenne, perhaps Louis XIV's most able general (see pp. 75–89). The fighting was hard: at the Battle of Enzheim, half of Churchill's fellow English officers were killed or wounded. However, Turenne took a personal pride in the potential, spirit and accomplishments of his 'handsome Englishman'.

It was from Turenne that Churchill learnt the importance of infantry firepower; the effectiveness of employing artillery throughout a battle, rather than as a mere prelude; and the desirability of seeking decisive battle, rather than following convention and marching from siege to static siege.

Royal favourite

Churchill was entrusted with command of a new regiment of foot in 1678, and was promoted brigadier general. He had recently married Sarah Jenyns, the girlhood crush of the Duke of York's younger daughter, Anne. The two women's association was to have, in turn, happy and disastrous consequences for Churchill's military career. At this juncture John's links with York and Sarah's with Anne reaped dividends. In 1682 John entered the Scottish peerage as Baron Churchill of Aymouth (Eyemouth), and the following year he became Colonel of the Royal Dragoons.

In 1685 the Duke of York succeeded to the throne as James II. That same year the Duke of Monmouth, an illegitimate son of Charles II, landed in the West Country in an attempt to seize the throne from his uncle. However, Churchill saw that Monmouth was never allowed to settle, snapping at his heels with his terrier force. Worn down, the rebels were eventually provoked into that most high risk of manoeuvres, a night-time attack, which ended in defeat at the Battle of Sedgemoor on 6 July. Although nominally only second in command, Churchill was the architect of victory, directing the royal troops with courage, flair and energy. He was upset not to have his contribution sufficiently recognized.

Fall from favour

When William of Orange landed in 1688, Churchill was again Lieutenant General of the English army. However, this time he sided with the invaders, putting his desertion down to James's increasingly dogmatic Catholicism. After the success of the 'Glorious Revolution', the newly crowned William III granted Churchill the earldom of Marlborough and confirmed him in his military rank, while charging him with the particular task of reforming and strengthening the English army in the wake of James II's defeat and exile; but with the titles came little trust. William's instinct was to rely on his Dutch compatriots, who were allowed to dominate the upper reaches of the English army, and he never forgot the surprising speed with which Marlborough had deserted his previous royal master.

In 1689 Marlborough was dispatched to command the 8,000 English soldiers serving with the Dutch in Flanders. He proved a tireless general, training his poorly regarded men until satisfied that they were fit to fight the French. That same year, Marlborough demonstrated the improvements he had instilled in his men at the Battle of Walcourt. His troops took the brunt of the French attack, before Marlborough led the Household Cavalry in a spirited counter-charge. The veteran allied commander, the Prince of Waldeck, reported to King William: 'Marlborough, in spite of his youth, had displayed in this one battle greater military capacity than do most generals after a long series of wars.'

Marlborough received his first independent command in 1690. In a combined operation by land and sea, he quickly captured the Irish strongholds of Cork and Kinsale from the Franco-Jacobite army. Despite these successes, his career came to a halt when he was among those suspected (correctly) of communicating with the exiled court of James II. Dismissed from all his posts in 1692, Marlborough was briefly imprisoned on false charges in the Tower of London. After his release, his career lay in the doldrums for several years. In 1694 he was suspected of giving information to the French about a secret English attack on Brest. However, the enemy already knew of the plan from other sources.

Redemption

Peace arrived in western Europe in 1697, but William III's distrust of Louis XIV made him think ahead to the inevitable next war. Aware that his own fragile health was on the wane, William identified Marlborough as the man to continue the fight against France during the next reign, and restored him to his army ranks. By the time of William's death and the accession of Queen Anne in 1702, the War of the Spanish Succession – in which the French Bourbon claim to the Spanish crown was challenged by Louis XIV's old enemies – had broken out. Marlborough, the new monarch's favourite, was appointed Captain-General of the English army, and Deputy Captain-General of that of the Dutch. Aged 52 (six years older than both Napoleon and Wellington at Waterloo), he was keen to establish the military reputation denied him in his prime.

Marlborough's aggressive intent was constrained by the constant interference of Dutch field deputies. These civilian representatives determinedly shielded their troops from the risk of open battle. On several occasions they refused Marlborough permission to attack the wrong-footed French, to his intense annoyance. Nevertheless, 1702 was a triumphant year for Marlborough: he swept the enemy out of the 'barrier fortresses' lying along the River Meuse, captured Liège, and was rewarded for an outstanding campaign with the dukedom of Marlborough.

The Blenheim campaign

The year 1703 was marked by further English exasperation at Dutch reluctance to fight. Marlborough decided on an astonishingly bold plan for the following year: he would march from the North Sea to the Danube, and rescue the Austrians from a Franco-Bavarian advance that threatened to knock the Habsburgs out of the war. This rescue mission could only be achieved if neither Louis XIV nor the field deputies guessed the duke's true intentions.

Marlborough's men covered the 250-mile trek, observed from a distance by a succession of mystified French marshals. Discipline on the march was excellent: supplies were paid for with gold provided by Marlborough's friend and ally, Sidney Godolphin, the English Lord Treasurer. The allied troops marched mainly before the sun was at its hottest, arriving at camps that were ready to welcome them with rest and food. At Frankfurt, every man received fresh boots. Marlborough's attention to his men's welfare led to the affectionate nickname 'Corporal John'.

Arriving at the Bavarian frontier, Marlborough led a bloody assault on the Schellenberg, a fortified hill overlooking Donauwörth. Thirty-eight generals were among the 1,500 allies to die that July day. However, 12,000 of the Franco-Bavarian forces were killed, wounded or captured as the Schellenberg fell for only the second time in its 2,000-year history. Albeit at great cost, the allies had gained their crucial bridgehead across the Danube.

Marlborough now began his successful partnership with the hugely talented and charismatic Imperial field marshal, Prince Eugène of Savoy (see pp. 105–19). Both commanders wanted to bring the enemy quickly to battle. Marlborough goaded the Elector of Bavaria to attack by torching his villages, but to no avail. Eventually, on 13 August, the allies launched a surprise dawn attack on the strong enemy position surrounding three villages, including Blindheim (named 'Blenheim' by the British). The French outnumbered the allies by 55,000 men to 50,000. Marlborough's masterstroke was to coop up the bulk of the French infantry inside Blenheim village, annulling the enemy's numerical advantage. The ensuing Battle of Blenheim demonstrated what were to become the signature pieces of Marlborough's generalship: relentless pressure on the French line at a chosen point, which drew the enemy reserves to that sphere of the action, before delivering a body blow elsewhere. Blenheim also vindicated the methods that Marlborough had instilled in his men through rigorous training: allied infantry fire was delivered by platoon rather than in line, which led to more concentrated and controlled fusillades, which in turn led to greater enemy casualties.

Meanwhile Marlborough employed his artillery throughout the battle. When, at one point, the 'Wild Geese' (Irish troops serving Louis XIV) threatened to break through the allied centre, Marlborough hauled some of his guns through muddy marshland and raked grapeshot into the enemy ranks, to devastating effect. Blenheim also proved the superiority of Marlborough's cavalry tactics. He led the steady focused charge that swept the enemy from the field, relying on growing momentum and cold steel instead of the French method – firing pistols and carbines on horseback then retreating to reload.

Blenheim, Louis XIV's first taste of defeat in a reign of sixty years, stunned Europe. Marshal Tallard, the French commander, was among the prisoners: indeed, of the 4,500 Franco-Bavarian officers who fought at Blenheim, only 250 were not killed, wounded or captured. Marlborough's rewards included the principality of Mindelheim, and what was to become Blenheim Palace in Oxfordshire.

The Battle of Ramillies

Arguably Marlborough's greatest victory, the Battle of Ramillies took place in May 1706. Effectively invited by his opponents Marshal Villeroi and the Elector of Bavaria to fight on their chosen battleground, Marlborough eagerly accepted, even though he rated the large enemy army – its front measured 4 miles across – the best he had ever seen.

It was all over in two hours: Marlborough made a strong feint, with his English and Scottish troops, into the enemy's left flank, which Villeroi reinforced at great cost to the centre of his line. The allies pushed hard into the French right, while Marlborough led the cavalry in the centre. Here the fighting was intense, the elite *Maison du Roi* cavalry nearly breaking through. Marlborough himself had his horse shot from beneath him. He was nearly killed soon afterwards, a cannon ball passing between his legs as he clambered on to a fresh mount. Under the steady pressure of increasing allied reinforcements, Villeroi's men buckled, before eventually breaking into a total rout when confronted by Marlborough's final cavalry charge. There were 22,000 Franco-Bavarian casualties, as opposed to Marlborough's 2,500. Total victory brought huge rewards: the enemy lost two-thirds of the Spanish Netherlands in a day, while the duke's reputation for military genius soared yet higher.

The Battle of Oudenarde

Reunited with Prince Eugène in 1708, Marlborough achieved his third great victory at Oudenarde to prevent a French invasion of the Dutch United Provinces. The allies ambushed the more numerous French, Marlborough marching his men 15 miles overnight to surprise a French army that had taken longer to cover just 6 miles. The French had to decide whether to fight the allies before them, or to retreat to Ghent. Marshal Vendôme urged caution, but the Duke of Burgundy, a prince of the blood, overruled his fellow commander.

Oudenarde was predominantly a running infantry battle between two armies of over 80,000 men, the French enjoying the advantage in numbers and terrain. Marlborough risked everything by urging his men to attack across the River Scheldt. It was the duke's cool command, assisted by Eugène's grit, as well as the dissent between the two enemy generals, that eventually led to gradual but total victory. The allies kept pushing more and more men on to the plain where the battle was decided. The result was the double encirclement of the enemy centre and right, and 16,400 French casualties – five times the allies' losses. Marlborough then oversaw the successful (but costly) siege of the supposedly impregnable city of Lille.

Pyrrhic victory

The year 1709 witnessed Marlborough and Eugène's third joint victory, Malplaquet, which Marlborough termed 'a very murdering battle'. Marshal Villars initiated the action, in an attempt to lift the siege of Mons. Some 110,000 allies attacked 80,000 French in woodland, where they were embedded in trenches and earth ramparts. The fighting was furious, and the Dutch advance on the allied left was subject to particularly terrible fire from well-placed French artillery. Marlborough and Eugène suffered 24,000 casualties, to Villars's 14,000, the worst losses in any European battle for more than a century. The day after the engagement, Mons was invested. It fell to Marlborough five weeks later. However, Marlborough and Eugène were later severely criticized for fighting the enemy unnecessarily, when the siege of Mons could have been pursued without such terrible bloodshed. The decision was apparently Eugène's, with Marlborough agreeing to it against his better judgement.

The Marlboroughs had risen through royal whim, and now their careers were crushed by the same capricious force. Sarah's outspokenness and hot temper had placed her increasingly at odds with the queen. Meanwhile the huge losses at Malplaquet had given the duke's enemies ammunition with which to attack him.

Aware of this, and worried by the Whig government's rejection of Louis's peace terms, Marlborough sought personal and career security. He asked the queen to make him Captain-General for life. This ill-judged request played into his detractors' hands: they had long sought to paint Marlborough as a self-interested parvenu. In October 1710, after the Whigs were swept away in a general election, the new Tory ministry conspired to undermine Marlborough's control of the army while fomenting suspicion at the duke's desire to see the war through to total French defeat. Weighed down by the stress of it all, the duke seriously considered resigning his command, but was talked out of this decision by his friends at home and his military allies overseas.

Marlborough's military swansong was a brilliant manoeuvre in the summer of 1711. In early May he began to prod Villars's supposedly impenetrable 'Ne Plus Ultra' defensive lines which ran 160 miles from the English Channel to the Ardennes. The French were confident that, if they could avoid a major engagement with the duke, political developments in London would force his dismissal – a result to place above mere victory in battle.

Marlborough was equally keen to advance into France. In August he tricked Villars into suspecting a frontal attack in the west. The duke then led an electrifying night march that left the French in his wake, before piercing the lines at their centre, at Arleux. News of this success was greeted with astonishment across Europe. He then moved to Bouchain, despite being advised by nearly all his senior officers that this city was impossible to take. He dug 28 miles of earthworks and corridors round the French to assist supplies and attack the garrison, and Bouchain fell to him the following month. This was his last great achievement, in his tenth great campaign as England's Captain-General.

Unbeknown to Marlborough or to Britain's allies, the Tories had been secretly negotiating a peace with France. The duke was now in the way, and he was brought down by a series of attacks on his war expenditure: Marlborough's enemies were determined to have him branded an embezzler. In January 1712 he was dismissed his posts, by a cruel letter in Queen Anne's own hand. She claimed that she had not 'deserved the treatment I have met with' from Marlborough – an accusation that cut him deeply.

Unappreciated at home, he and Sarah spent increasing periods on the Continent. They returned in August 1714 to a new reign: Queen Anne had died that same day. George I's first signed state paper was the restoration of Marlborough to the Captain-Generalship. However, there were to be no more heroics: the ageing duke suffered a disabling stroke in 1716. He died six years later, aged 72. Buried in state at Westminster Abbey, his remains were later interred at Blenheim Palace.

Assessment

Cool-headed, resourceful and focused, Marlborough had a genius for soldiering. At Blenheim, he commanded a British-led army in its first continental victory since Agincourt, three centuries earlier. The painstaking training of his men; the unison and expertise he demanded from infantry, cavalry and artillery; his meticulous logistics; his astonishing calm and decisiveness in battle; the ease of his relationship with Prince Eugène: all helped to forge some of the earliest battle honours of the British army. He also ended Louis XIV's six decades of victory and blocked the Sun King's chances of becoming emperor of Europe. Marlborough was greatly admired by a later French tyrant, Napoleon, who encouraged (and contributed to) the research and recording of the Duke's military accomplishments. If the duke's gifts are less celebrated today than they were, this is the fault of the teaching of history rather than of the man in question: Marlborough is the military colossus of a major war that is now almost forgotten.

PRINCE EUGÈNE
OF SAVOY
1663–1736

CHARLES SPENCER

SMALL, SLIGHT, POCK-MARKED AND BUCK-TOOTHED –
physically, Prince Eugène of Savoy (also known as Prinz Eugen)
makes an unlikely martial hero. However, he was a military Titan
who, in Napoleon's estimation, deserves to be ranked as one of
the seven greatest generals of all time.

It was France's tragedy that the extraordinary talents of
Prince Eugène of Savoy, although home-grown, should
be displayed with such dazzling effect against, rather than
for, Louis XIV. Some of his successes against the Sun King
were achieved when he was in sole command, others in
tandem with the 1st Duke of Marlborough, with whom
he formed one of the greatest military partnerships of
history.

The other principal sufferers, as Eugène wielded his sword for the Holy Roman Empire through thirty-two campaigns, were the Ottoman Turks. Although frequently outnumbered, Eugène was never daunted. He knew his enemy, and made their numerical advantage irrelevant through careful exploitation of terrain, as well as superior discipline and weaponry. His sure touch during the key moments of an engagement, as well as his charismatic bravery, made him a leader of rare distinction. Eugène's Turkish victories, culminating in his delivery of Belgrade, ended the Ottoman threat to western Europe once and for all. It had taken the Holy Roman Empire a century and a half to unearth a soldier capable of such an achievement.

Drive and charisma

Eugène led the Habsburg armies at a time when Vienna was desperately short of money, and the war effort was further hamstrung by the machinations of ministers jealous of the prince. At times it was only the sheer force of Eugène's personality that kept the Imperial war machine functioning. The same could be said of his talismanic presence on the battlefield.

The prince would lead from the front, wearing his simple brown leather jacket with brass buttons. The dowdy clothing was misleading, for Eugène in battle was a blood-curdling sight. In the nineteenth century the English novelist

William Thackeray described, from first-hand accounts, how the prince 'became possessed with a sort of warlike fury; his eyes lighted up; he rushed hither and thither, raging; he shrieked curses and encouragement, yelling and harking his bloody war-dogs on, and himself always at the end of the hunt'. His men worshipped him.

Royal roots

Eugène (full name François-Eugène de Savoie-Carignan) was a scion of the royal house of Savoy. His father was a brave but unspectacular soldier, his mother – a niece of Cardinal Mazarin – a scheming harridan. When she failed in her ambitions to become the queen of her childhood friend, Louis XIV, she resorted to increasingly bizarre tactics, including the use of magic spells, to try to remain in favour. She was eventually exiled, in disgrace, accused of witchcraft.

Eugène's early years were also scandalous. An ugly yet effeminate boy, with questionable sexuality and pitiful personal hygiene, he was known by malicious elements at court as 'Madame l'Ancienne'. Despite appearances, Eugène was passionate about soldiery. To prepare for his vocation, he strengthened his body through vigorous exercise, and improved his mind by devouring biographies of the ancient heroes, as well as mastering mathematics. However, when Eugène asked for a commission in the French army, he was insultingly rebuffed. Louis XIV, accustomed to his generals being cut from more obvious martial cloth, denied Eugène a commission, insisting that he instead join the priesthood. After a final plea to the king was rejected, and with his mother's humiliation still rankling, Eugène left France promising only to return with vengeful sword in hand.

Imperial service

In 1683 Eugène joined the army of Emperor Leopold. Here he would be known as 'Prinz Eugen'. The same year he received his baptism of fire, serving in the Duke of Lorraine's army which lifted the Turkish siege of Vienna. So brave was Eugène that day that Lorraine gave him a pair of golden spurs and command of a regiment. This was the beginning of a startlingly swift rise. A colonel of dragoons at 20, he was appointed major-general at 22, lieutenant general at 24, field marshal lieutenant at 25 and general of horse at 26.

Eugène's military exploits demanded attention. In 1687 he led the decisive cavalry charge that delivered Imperial victory over the Turks at the Battle of Mohács. The prince planted the Imperial Eagle in the vanquished enemy's camp, and carried off their standard, the Crescent. As a reward for his valour, Eugène was given the honour of delivering news of the victory to the emperor.

After the outbreak of the War of the League of Augsburg in 1688 between France and the Grand Alliance, Eugène was active in Italy. His troops were a ramshackle mixture of Spaniards, Savoyards and Piedmontese, confronted by crack French troops with a record of invincibility stretching back half a century. It was Eugène's exceptional leadership, as well as his men's ruthlessness, that made this contest equal. (In 1690 he reported that they habitually castrated prisoners before dispatching them.) From 1694, Eugène was the supreme allied commander in Italy.

Victory at Zenta

In Vienna there was jealousy and resentment at Eugène's success. When in 1697 the Ottomans drove westwards, recapturing cities lost a decade earlier, Eugène was sent to meet them, though with instructions from the Imperial war council not to attack. Eugène, always a man of action, ignored such negativity. He appreciated that the Turks' huge numbers and bravery could not compensate for their often rudimentary weaponry, which included bows and arrows, and that Ottoman hopes of success depended on their ability to maintain forward momentum and strict formation. The prince was confident of exploiting these vulnerabilities.

Eugène attacked the Turks at Zenta on 11 September 1697, and 30,000 of the enemy were killed, including the grand vizier and four of his deputies. Among the booty were 60,000 camels and the Great Seal, the grand vizier's symbol of authority, which had never before been captured. Meanwhile Eugène lost just 300 men.

The prince's immediate reward for this astonishing victory was dismissal by the Imperial war council for disobeying orders. However, popular demand ensured that the emperor quickly restored him. Eugène only accepted his reinstatement on condition that he was given greater independence in future. Zenta eventually led to the conclusion of the war with the Turks.

Fighting the French

The Peace of Ryswick (20 September 1697) ended the conflict with France at much the same time. However, in 1701 the War of the Spanish Succession broke out, after Louis XIV championed his grandson's acceptance of the Spanish crown rather than allow it to go to the Austrian Habsburg claimant. Eugène returned to the Italian peninsula, keen to reverse early enemy strikes, and convinced that this would be the key sphere of the Franco-Austrian conflict. He advanced southwards with just 22,000 men, passing through neutral Venice before beginning a successful guerrilla campaign against Marshal Catinat's forces. Louis XIV castigated Catinat: 'I sent you to Italy to fight a young and inexperienced prince; he has flouted all the precepts of warfare. But you appear to be mesmerized, and let him do as he pleased.' Catinat was replaced by Marshal Villeroi.

Villeroi attacked Eugène and his army in the fort at Chiari. Outnumbered, Eugène was nonetheless confident of success: he had observed that the French were most effective in their initial charge, and tended to be much less successful in subsequent fighting. He ordered his men to lie on their stomachs, and only to stand and fire when the French were close, which caused them to flee in disarray. Villeroi lost 2,000 men, Eugène just 40.

In February 1702, before the beginning of the customary campaign season, Eugène launched an audacious strike. Finding Villeroi in winter quarters at Cremona, Eugène led his forces through an abandoned canal, up into the centre of the French position. Although unable to overrun the city, Eugène took Villeroi prisoner.

Now Louis XIV pitched Marshal Vendôme against Eugène. The Frenchman had 80,000 men, the prince 28,000. In August the two armies met at Luzzara, a bloody battle that ended in stalemate. Eugène's bosom friend, Prince Commercy, was killed during the engagement. After the fighting both armies stubbornly remained facing each other for eighty-two days, rather than withdraw in defeat. Thanks to his exploits and his tenacity, Eugène was now the foremost hero of the Grand Alliance. In 1703 the prince was appointed president of the Imperial war council in Vienna, the controller of the emperor's military affairs.

Comrades-in-arms

The next stage of Eugène's career was inextricably linked with that of the other great military genius of the era. John Churchill, Duke of Marlborough, met Prince Eugène in the summer of 1704, while leading his allied army towards the Danube, in a bid to save the Imperialists from a potentially devastating advance by the Franco-Bavarians. It was the beginning of an extraordinary military partnership.

The duo's first victory was at Blenheim, on 13 August 1704. Prince Eugène led the Imperialists on the right-hand wing of the Allied army, overcoming rough terrain and superior enemy numbers to contribute hugely to the victory. Eugène continued to lead his infantry and cavalry forward, despite repeated repulses. When he spied two of his men deserting, he rode them down and shot them both in the back.

Late in the afternoon, Marlborough led the cavalry charge that destroyed the main French army. Although the junior partner at Blenheim, Eugène's role had been crucial, as Louis XIV suffered his first major defeat on land, after sixty years on the throne (see also pp. 96–8).

Triumph at Turin

In 1705 Eugène returned to Italy. He was attacked at Cassano, another bloody stalemate. In early 1706 his army was overwhelmed at Calcinato before he could reach it. The prince withdrew his forces to the Alps, and the Franco-Spanish thought they had seen the last of his interference in Italy. However, Eugène marched towards Turin, the allies' last major possession in Savoy, which was being besieged. Such was the effect of Eugène's reputation that the French army, poised to strike the city, seemed paralysed by news of his approach.

On 7 September Eugène led the attack outside Turin, capturing the enemy guns and turning them on the French. In the fierce fighting, the prince's page and servant fell beside him, and he himself had his horse shot from beneath him. Later in the day he was wounded in the head. While both sides suffered 3,000 dead and wounded, the French also forfeited 6,000 prisoners. Louis's dreams of Italian domination were over in a day, and Eugène's victory resulted in Austria, rather than Spain, being the dominant power in the peninsula over the next century and a half. Eugène's rewards from the emperor included the governorship of Milan.

Disaster in Provence

The year 1707 started promisingly, when the prince was promoted Imperial Field Marshal. Meanwhile Peter the

Great of Russia proposed Eugène to fill the vacant position of king of Poland. However, the emperor, anxious not to lose his ablest lieutenant, failed to support his candidacy. It was now decided that Eugène, under the nominal command of his cousin the Duke of Savoy, should attack the French naval base of Toulon, and so gain control of the Mediterranean for the alliance. This, it was hoped, would persuade the French to withdraw their forces from Spain.

The viability of the Toulon offensive relied on surprise. However, the Duke of Savoy wasted time waiting for supplies, and by the time Eugène's army, 35,000 strong, set off on 30 June, the French had established his true destination. The prince was now in a race with Marshal de Tessé's force of the same size, which the Frenchman won. Never optimistic about the Toulon campaign, Eugène now grew despondent. On 22 August he admitted defeat and lifted the siege.

Partnership resumed

In 1708 Eugène was reunited with Marlborough. The action was in Flanders, where the Duke of Burgundy and Marshal Vendôme headed an army of 110,000 men, which quickly took Bruges and Ghent before heading for Oudenarde. In a bid to save the city the duke pushed his men to march 50 miles in two and a half days. Eugène, while unable to get his troops to link up with Marlborough's grand army in time, managed to join his colleague.

The Battle of Oudenarde began at 4 p.m. on 11 July. It was a fast-moving engagement, during which Eugène, commanding the allied right wing, was almost swamped by Vendôme. Timely reinforcements allowed Eugene to break Vendôme's first line, before the Dutch all but encircled the French. At nightfall the allies were ordered to cease fire, to prevent them from inflicting casualties on their own. Eugène was not finished, though. He ordered his drummers to sound the French army's retreat, and had his Huguenot officers shout false orders to trick their compatriots into following them. Those duped by the prince were among the 9,000 prisoners taken at Oudenarde. Meanwhile the allies suffered 3,000 casualties, against the French 6,000.

Eugène and Marlborough now tackled Lille, France's second city. With solid and intricate defences designed by Vauban, Louis XIV's great fortifier-in-chief, it was the toughest of propositions. Eugène invested the city on 17 August. Five weeks later, he was hit by a musket-ball when leading an attack. Eventually, on 9 December, Lille fell. Ghent and Bruges soon followed.

The following year, 1709, was more challenging. Eugène oversaw the main army, while Marlborough besieged and took Tournai. When marshals Villars and

Boufflers divined that Mons was the next allied target, they dug in to woodland at Malplaquet, and invited attack. On 11 September Eugène led the allied right wing at the Battle of Malplaquet. His troops were Imperialist, supported by Danish infantry and Dutch cavalry. He took the wood of Sart after vicious fighting, during which the prince was hit behind the ear by a musket-ball. He refused to leave the battlefield for treatment. After a terrible day's fighting, the French withdrew in defeat. They had lost around 14,000 men, but the allied victory was a Pyrrhic one, with 24,000 men killed or wounded. Malplaquet was the last battle in which Eugène and Marlborough would act in concert.

Victim of Villars

Towards the end of 1710, the British government began clandestine negotiations with the French. At the beginning of 1712 the Tory government gained Marlborough's dismissal, and then secretly forbade his replacement, the Duke of Ormonde, from taking part in military action against the French. Eugène was left in the dark and, unsurprisingly, these years of English treachery were the least successful of his military career.

In July 1712 Eugène captured Quesnoy. This initial success persuaded him to venture forward too far. Later in the month Villars, the most able marshal available to Louis for a generation, wrong-footed Eugène and trounced the

Dutch at Denai. After this, the French took Douai. Soon afterwards, with the Dutch field deputies constraining him terribly, Eugène had to surrender Quesnoy, and then Bouchain. In three months the prince had lost a third of his forces and five of his strongholds.

While the rest of the alliance made peace with Louis XIV through the Treaty of Utrecht in April 1713, the emperor continued the struggle alone, sending Eugène to command the Imperial army on the Rhine. With morale low, and Villars in the ascendant, Eugène lost Landau and Freiburg. After this, the prince represented the Imperial interest at peace negotiations with Villars, which resulted in the Treaty of Rastadt (7 March 1714).

The Turks tamed

The Turks now marched westwards, sending an army of 120,000 men under the grand vizier to Peterwardein. Eugène defended this Austrian fortress with 60,000 men and on 5 August 1716 he attacked. The grand vizier headed the list of 6,000 Turks who died that day. Eugène took as a prize the fallen enemy leader's silk and gold tent (so large it required 500 men to erect it) as well as its rich contents. Eugène followed up by taking the fortress of Temesvar. The Turks sued for peace, but Eugène persuaded the emperor to hold out for one more great victory. He had Belgrade in his sights.

The taking of Belgrade in 1717 was the high-point of Eugène's career, ending the Turkish threat to Austria.

Belgrade had been in Turkish hands since the mid sixteenth century. Prince Eugène was eager to recapture it, and to deprive the Ottomans of their principal westward staging-post. He hoped to overrun Belgrade quickly, and then turn on whatever rescue force the Turks sent from Adrianople.

Mustapha Pasha and a garrison of 30,000 men defended the city bravely, their efforts helped by a summer cyclone that destroyed Eugène's bridges over the Danube. The garrison remained defiant, as nearly a quarter of a million men under Halil Pasha arrived to deliver them from the prince. Trapped between two Turkish armies, his army wilting from dysentery and the heat, Eugène resorted to his customary reflex and attacked.

His men advanced in the pre-dawn mist of 16 August 1717. The Ottomans missed an early chance to decide the battle, when they unwittingly isolated the Imperialist right wing. Eugène, alive to the threat, led his cavalry forward, with strong infantry support, then advanced with a disciplined tread, holding his men's fire until within 50 feet of the Turks.

The Imperialists now fell upon the Ottoman enemy with bayonets and swords, inflicting 20,000 casualties. Belgrade surrendered immediately. Western Europe, prepared for news that Eugène had been crushed between two Ottoman armies, learnt instead that the prince had delivered them from the Turkish threat for the first time in 150 years.

Peace followed in 1718. When, fifteen years later, the elective crown of Poland was disputed – by France on the one side, and the emperor, Russia and Prussia on the other – Eugène was recalled to high command. This was a war too far for the frail septuagenarian who had been wounded eleven times in battle. His chest was permanently infected, and his memory was on the wane.

Confronted in 1734 by a French army that outnumbered his by five to one, Eugène looked for victory in Germany to compensate for early Habsburg losses in Italy. He was, however, no longer the confident leader of his prime, and his indecision allowed Philippsburg to fall. In 1735 Eugène undertook his final campaign. He was, by this stage, physically and mentally in tatters. It was a relief to the Imperialists when, that autumn, the Peace of Vienna concluded the War of the Polish Succession and the prince retired. He died in April 1736, aged 72. Despite his Franco-Italian extraction, he is remembered as Austria's greatest soldier.

CHARLES XII

1682–1718

STEPHEN BRUMWELL

CHARLES XII OF SWEDEN has always attracted extreme reactions. Was he a heroic warrior king or a berserker whose belligerence ruined his country? Like Gustavus Adolphus before him, Charles was a bold leader and an astute tactician. Yet as a commander, Charles faced the greater challenges: Gustavus's military career coincided with the rise of Sweden, Charles's with her decline. And while he ultimately failed to save the Swedish Empire, Charles's remarkable campaigns were worthy of 'the Lion of the North' himself.

When Charles XI of Sweden died from stomach cancer in April 1697 his namesake son was just 14 years old. Eager to exploit the young king's inexperience, Sweden's enemies and rivals saw an opportunity to attack her Baltic empire, clawing back territories lost during the previous century. Between 1698 and 1700, a formidable anti-Swedish coalition formed, allying the king of Poland-Lithuania and Elector of Saxony, Augustus II, 'the Strong', with Peter the Great of Russia and Frederick IV of Denmark.

But Sweden's perceived vulnerability was deceptive. The allies underestimated both the resilience of the Swedish empire and the determination of its teenaged ruler. Charles's father had groomed him carefully for kingship, and by his accession he was already well schooled in the theory of diplomacy, strategy and tactics. Such training was mandatory: Swedish tradition decreed that the monarch should not only conduct foreign policy – in conjunction with the expert advisers of his itinerant 'field-chancery' – but also command his troops in person.

Thanks to his father's reforms, Charles XII inherited a formidable army. It was well trained and equipped, and founded upon a reliable system of territorial recruitment, with individual provinces contracted to raise and maintain regiments in peace and war alike. Under the allotment system of conscription, farmers shared the burden of supporting soldiers, who were provided with housing and pay and in return helped with the farm-work when not on military service. This yielded a permanent, native army of 11,000 cavalry and 30,000 infantry. Another 25,000 mercenaries garrisoned the overseas provinces. In the summer of 1700 the streamlined and highly professional Swedish army mobilized for war on three fronts.

The onset of the Great Northern War

The coalition's members did not anticipate a long conflict, particularly as they calculated upon exploiting anti-Swedish sentiment in the Baltic provinces of Livonia and Estonia. In fact, the bitter and bloody Great Northern War lasted for twenty-one years. The allies' first overconfident assaults were uncoordinated, the Swedish response brisk and devastatingly effective. By the time Peter declared war on 20 August 1700, and the Saxons began a siege of Riga in Livonia, Denmark had already been eliminated. On 25 July, in Charles's baptism of fire, a 10,000-strong Swedish army had landed on the Danish island of Zealand and marched against Copenhagen. Blockaded in his capital, Frederick soon caved in, signing the Treaty of Travendal on 18 August 1700.

Meanwhile, Augustus's siege of Riga was also foundering. Contrary to expectations, the Livonian nobles did not rally to the Saxons, and the disillusioned Augustus raised the siege on 29 September. The Russian army, at least 35,000 strong, began bombarding Narva, in Ingria, on 31 October 1700. Charles was already heading to its relief. On 30 November, in the Battle of Narva, the Swedes assaulted the Russian siege-works under cover of a snow-storm. Outnumbered three to one, they nonetheless broke through and routed the enemy. Including fugitives drowned in a frenzied flight, Peter lost 8,000 men. The stunning victory, which reminded commentators of Gustavus Adolphus's impressive debut at Breitenfeld in 1631, gave notice that the Swedes remained a force to be reckoned with.

Charles had played an important role at Narva, and shared in the campaign's planning. Over the next six years, as he gradually gained experience and confidence and took an ever-greater role in command, the young king seemed invincible. In 1701, Charles resolved to deal with Augustus. On 19 July he forced his way across the Dvina into Courland (western Latvia). Crossing the 600-yard-wide river in open boats against determined Saxon resistance was a remarkable feat, aided by a feint to deflect the defenders' attention and a smoke-screen to mask their fire. Along with Lieutenant General Bernard von Liewen, Charles led the first wave of 6,000 infantry. Although the cavalry were unable to cross in time to maximize the victory, the episode demonstrated that the Swedes could prove as effective against the well-trained Saxons as against the less professional Russians.

Charles invaded Poland-Lithuania in January 1702. That July, he destroyed a Saxon–Polish army at Kliszów, southeast of Krakow. Regarded as his finest victory, it was a battle in which Charles himself took the decisive role.

Charles XII comes of age as a commander

Narva has been dismissed as an aberration, scored against an outmoded enemy under fluke conditions; it was a battle in which Charles XII was subordinate to his generals. No such qualifications can diminish his victory at Kliszów, a battle fought in perfect summer weather against a numerically superior and thoroughly modern force arrayed in a formidable defensive position.

Late on the morning of 19 July 1702, Augustus II of Saxony received disconcerting news at his headquarters at Kliszów, south of Kielce. The Swedish army thought to be encamped some 3 miles away had suddenly emerged from the woods fronting his own camp. Augustus immediately drew up his army on rising ground to the north. An extensive swamp protected his left flank, while a stream running through the boggy valley that separated the rival armies discouraged frontal attack. Charles was keen to engage – so eager that he had been prepared to march against Augustus without the 4,000 men under General Karl Gustav Mörner who had only arrived the previous evening. Yet even Charles was awed by the strength of the enemy's position. He was also outnumbered by almost two to one: his 8,000 infantry, 4,000 cavalry and four light 3-pounder cannon faced 9,000 Saxon horse and 7,500 Saxon foot, plus another 6,000 Polish cavalry and no fewer than 46 guns.

Despite the odds, Charles was undaunted. Examining the ground, he ordered an advance. As Augustus was most vulnerable on his right, Charles strengthened his own left wing for an enveloping attack there. After the initial Swedish assault was stymied, Charles's entire army stood on the defensive, withstanding charges by Hetman Lubomirski's Polish hussars on its left, and a Saxon thrust across the valley against the centre and right.

Decisively repulsed at last, Lubomirski withdrew, so exposing the Saxon right flank. Charles swiftly exploited this weakness: in personal command of his main left-wing force of mixed infantry and cavalry, he struck the Saxon flank, while the rest of his army advanced to its front. After hard fighting, the Saxons buckled under the mounting pressure, finally breaking in retreat across the marshes to their rear.

By late afternoon the battle was over. At a cost of about 900 killed and wounded, including Charles's brother-in-law, Frederick of Holstein-Gottorp, who was cut in half by a cannon ball, the Swedes had slain or captured some 4,000 Saxons. Kliszów vindicated Charles's opportunistic brand of personal leadership, and the potency of his army's equally aggressive tactics.

In the brief but hectic interim of campaigning, Charles had matured as a commander, learning on the job: at Kliszów it was the king, not his advisers, who orchestrated events

– with striking results that devastated Augustus and the Saxon army.

In the wake of the Battle of Kliszów, Poland's leading cities fell to Charles, and in July 1704 he presided over the election of his own candidate as king of Poland-Lithuania, Stanisław Leszczyński. Following a crushing victory by his trusted general Karl Gustaf Rehnskiöld over a Saxon–Russian army at Fraustadt in February 1706, Charles invaded Saxony. That September he obliged the Saxon Estates to accept the Treaty of Altranstädt, by which Augustus was to abdicate his Polish throne. Just a month later Augustus, at the head of a Saxon–Russian army, riposted with a victory of his own at Kalisz. However, Augustus had already ratified the Treaty of Altranstädt in secret, and when Charles publicized his duplicity, was shamed into complying with its terms. In November 1706 Augustus left for Saxony: Charles's second opponent had been knocked out of the war.

Charles XII stamped his character upon his army. His fatalistic piety – the belief that divine providence governed all things – was disseminated via the sermons of regimental chaplains, and encapsulated in the watchword, 'With God's help'. The king's frugal lifestyle, which likewise helped to forge a bond of comradeship with the rank and file, also attracted much comment. In an age when generals campaigned with extensive personal baggage, Charles's contemporaries were shocked and fascinated by a soldier-king who disdained such creature comforts, preferred weak beer or even water to wine, ate standing up and buttered his bread with his thumb.

Tall, slim-waisted and with a high, domed forehead, Charles rejected the full-bottomed wig universally worn by men of his class, instead sporting his own hair cropped short. His stark appearance was only heightened by a severely plain uniform of blue coat and elk-skin breeches, with a black taffeta scarf instead of a lace cravat. Charles's Spartan austerity was mocked by his enemies, but admired by many professional soldiers.

A 'Carolinian' way of war

Reflecting Charles's own inclinations and Swedish military traditions alike, his troops employed exceptionally aggressive tactics, calculated to dismay and overwhelm even the steadiest opponents. Such 'gå på' ('go on') techniques bucked conventional tactical trends, but proved remarkably successful. The Swedish infantry fought four deep, the musketeers reserving their fire until the enemy was just 40 yards away before pouring in volleys and rushing on with the bayonet and sword. At a time when other armies were abandoning the pike, the Swedish penchant for cold steel ensured that pikemen remained an important component of infantry battalions. Unlike their counterparts in most western European armies, the Swedish cavalry eschewed pistols and carbines, typically fired while advancing at a stately trot, instead maximizing shock value by charging home sword in hand.

Such uncompromising battlefield tactics were matched by ruthlessness. At times, the Great Northern War was fought with a cold ferocity that prefigured the Eastern Front of the Second World War. The protagonists often proved themselves as unrelenting as the elements; combat was frequently savage, prisoners rarely taken. In Poland, where the Swedes were dogged by guerrilla resistance, brutal reprisals against civilians were common. The fighting between Swedes and Russians was especially pitiless, and included an ugly, racial element: the Russians were treated as sub-human, and as such, undeserving of mercy. After Rehnskiöld's victory at Fraustadt, while Saxon prisoners were spared, hundreds of captured Russians were butchered in cold blood.

Charles XII versus Peter the Great

While Charles was preoccupied with his convoluted Polish campaigns, Sweden's Baltic provinces suffered encroachment from a resurgent Russia. In 1703 Peter the Great seized Ingria, and began to build his new capital, St Petersburg; in the following year he took Dorpat, Narva and Ivangorod. Meanwhile Russian troops streamed into Poland-Lithuania to bolster factions opposed to Charles's puppet Leszczyński.

Whatever his merits as a tactician and battlefield commander, Charles's decision to intervene in Poland in 1701, instead of consolidating the outcome of Narva by marching directly against Peter, casts serious doubts upon his strategic judgement. The Polish interlude not only allowed Peter to make inroads upon Sweden's vulnerable Baltic possessions, but gave his own remodelled army a chance to acquire experience and confidence.

By 1707, however, Charles was resolved to settle matters with his last remaining enemy. He rejected Peter's offer of peace in exchange for the cession of Ingria, and marched his army – now rested and reinforced to about 35,000 men – eastwards in a full-scale invasion of Russia. With hindsight it is all too easy to point to the folly of such an undertaking, a perspective only underlined by the subsequent fates of Napoleon and Hitler. Yet Charles took a calculated gamble. Through a combination of circumstances, it went tragically wrong.

Peter's armies withdrew into Russia, scorching the earth behind them. Until mid 1708 Charles remained in Lithuania while General Adam Ludvig Lewenhaupt amassed supplies. On 14 July, at Hołowczyn – rated by Charles as the best of his battles – the Russians were beaten after an audacious crossing of the Vabich. In September 1708, without waiting for Lewenhaupt, Charles turned south to winter in the

Ukraine, where he hoped to find fresh provisions and support from the rebel Cossack, Hetman Ivan Mazepa. This risky strategy proved disastrous. Peter pounced on Lewenhaupt's isolated corps at Lesnaia on 9 October, mauling his command and seizing the supply train. The Swedes suffered dreadfully in the bitter winter of 1708.

Harried by the Russians, they died in their thousands from cold and disease. With Polish and Russian forces blocking Leszczyński from coming to his aid, Charles was trapped.

Disaster at Poltava

By late June 1709 Peter was ready to give battle outside the town of Poltava, which Charles had been besieging since April. The homesick Swedes were now running low on ammunition and morale. In addition, when the armies met on 27 June Charles was unable to take personal command: ten days earlier, he had been wounded in the foot by a Cossack rifle-ball. Relinquishing battlefield command to Field Marshal Rehnskiöld, the king was obliged to observe events from a litter.

Under these unpromising circumstances, Charles has been heavily criticized for accepting Peter's challenge. Yet the alternatives were scarcely attractive: withdrawing south to the Crimea or back towards Poland, in either case with the Russians snapping at his heels. By contrast, even if it failed to eliminate Peter's army, a victory would alleviate the Swedish supply crisis, strengthen Leszczyński's position, and hopefully persuade the Turks and Tartars to take the field against Russia.

Peter offered battle cautiously, under conditions calculated to blunt the edge of Charles's tactics. Not only were most of his green-clad infantry ensconced within a fortified camp, but the approach was defended by a T-shaped system of manned redoubts, its long 'arm' intended to act like a breakwater and dissipate the force of any assault. When the Swedish infantry attacked, the redoubts served their purpose; while some of Charles's bluecoats surged past towards the Russian camp, others became mired in a bloody and ultimately futile effort to capture them. Crucially, a six-battalion-strong force under Major-General Carl Gustaf Roos became isolated and was forced to surrender.

Meanwhile, Charles had, incredibly, come within grasp of victory: the Swedish cavalry routed their opponents, and the infantry deployed to assault Peter's camp. With Roos's men missing, it was decided to await them before attacking. This was a fatal error. Two hours were wasted – an interval in which the Swedes lost momentum and the Russians regained their composure. Buoyed up by news of Roos's fate, the Russians left their camp to fight in the open. They presented an awesome sight: no fewer than 22,000 infantry drawn up in two lines and supported by sixty-eight field guns. Ranged against them were the pitiful remnants of the

Swedish foot. Now just 4,000 strong, and further winnowed by Russian artillery, they launched a last, desperate attack. This time Swedish aggression was not enough. A breakthrough on Peter's right went unsupported, and a counterattack splintered Charles's army into a mass of fugitives.

Three days later, as the traumatized Charles and his personal escort crossed the Dnepr into Turkish-controlled territory, 17,000 demoralized Swedes surrendered at Perevolochna. Of the 23,000 made prisoner there and at Poltava, just 4,000 returned from captivity.

Exile and death

Charles spent the next five years languishing at Bender, in Moldavia, an increasingly restless and troublesome guest of the Ottoman Turks. During his exile, the coalition he had dismantled between 1700 and 1706 reformed. Within a month of Poltava, Augustus had returned to Poland with a formidable army of 11,000 Saxons; that November, Danish troops invaded Scania, and Tsar Peter besieged Riga. In Charles's absence, the defence of Sweden was conducted by Count Magnus Stenbock. In February 1710 he defeated the over-confident Danes at Hälsingborg, but Sweden's prized Baltic provinces could not be saved. By September 1710 both Livonia and Estonia had fallen to Russia. The indomitable Charles now persuaded his reluctant Turkish hosts to confront the Russians. They defeated Peter at the

Prut River in July 1711, but the wily tsar extracted his army by offering concessions. Although Peter reneged on these, subsequent Ottoman declarations of war were half-hearted. Two years later, the rivals signed a peace treaty.

Charles finally quit Moldavia in September 1714. For two months he travelled incognito across eastern Europe, disguised under a wig and moustache and posing as 'Captain Peter Frisk'. When he arrived at Stralsund in Swedish Pomerania, instead of continuing his journey to Sweden Charles helped to defend the town against a Danish–Saxon–Prussian siege; wounded during a sortie, and aware that surrender was inevitable, he escaped in an open rowing boat on the very eve of the capitulation. In December 1715 Charles set foot in his kingdom once more. True to form, instead of contemplating peace he took the offensive, launching the first of two Norwegian campaigns calculated to knock Denmark out of the conflict. The second came to a sudden end on 30 November 1718, when Charles was shot through the head at the siege of Frederiksten.

Assessment

Like his life, Charles's death remains controversial. Was he slain by an 'honest enemy bullet' or by his own exasperated countrymen? The prime exhibit is Charles's embalmed skull, perforated from temple to temple. The left hole is much larger than the other and, by usual forensic criteria, should designate the 'exit' wound. This has been used to support the contention that Charles was shot from the right – from his own siege lines. A rival school maintains that because he was wearing his hat, with the brim folded up to the left, this double layer of felt would have minimized the exit wound: if this can be credited, the shot entered from the left – presumably from the besieged fortress. Here, as with so much else relating to this enigmatic figure, a conclusive verdict is unlikely.

By the time of Charles's death, Sweden's position had improved; war-weary and mutually suspicious, the coalition was disintegrating. Yet the verdict of the Great Northern War was unequivocal. When Sweden and Russia finally signed the Peace of Nystad on 30 August 1721, Peter's agreement to evacuate Finland gained him Estonia, Livonia and Ingria. Sweden's Baltic empire had been dismantled; her 'age of greatness' was over.

The extent to which Charles XII was personally responsible for Sweden's relegation from first- to third-rate power has generated intense debate, likewise his culpability for culling his countrymen in a succession of bloody campaigns. Modern research has acquitted him on the second count, although the first continues to provoke scholarly argument. Yet Charles XII deserves recognition as an inspirational battlefield commander, a soldier whose leadership propped up an overstretched empire long after it should have collapsed.

MAURICE, COMTE DE SAXE

1696–1750

JOHN CHILDS

NOTWITHSTANDING HIS GERMAN BIRTH and Lutheran religion, Maurice de Saxe commanded the principal armies of France during much of the War of the Austrian Succession (1740–8). His victorious campaigns of 1744–8 constituted the high point of French military achievement between the death of Louis XIV and the Revolution. His reputation has subsequently diminished because his forte lay in strategy and manoeuvre rather than the conduct of battle – the victories at Fontenoy (1745), Roucoux (1746) and Laufeldt (1747) were 'half won' – and he faced either second-rate or inexperienced generals. He never lost a boyish adventurousness which suggested to many critics a greater suitability for subordinate rather than supreme command.

Maurice de Saxe was born on 28 October 1696 in the Imperial free city of Goslar, the result of a casual liaison between Frederick Augustus II, Elector of Saxony and king of Poland, and Countess Maria Aurora von Königsmarck. Aged 12, Saxe served in a Saxon corps in Flanders and witnessed action at the siege of Tournai and the Battle of Malplaquet in 1709 before returning to Dresden in 1711 to receive the title Count of Saxony. Between 1711 and 1715 he fought with the Saxon army against the Swedes in Pomerania and in Hungary under Prince Eugène of Savoy (1717). Bored, restless, dissolute and debauched – these were lifelong characteristics – in 1720 he travelled to Paris. Equipped with his father's money and the patronage of Elizabeth of the Rhine, dowager duchess of Orléans, on 9 August 1720 he was commissioned *maréchal de camp* (major-general) in the French army and purchased a regiment.

From colonel to lieutenant general

Abandoning some of the more adolescent aspects of his unruly personal conduct, Saxe applied himself to the military profession and the *Régiment Saxe* became an exemplar of administration and drill. Although a veteran of eleven campaigns, Saxe knew more about swinging a sabre than the science of war so he studied under the guidance of the leading military writer and theorist, Jean Charles de Folard. In 1725 he was proposed for the vacant dukedom of Courland but his candidacy buckled under Russian pressure. By 1732 he had served in the French army for twelve years but remained only a colonel and *maréchal de camp*, his prospects hampered by his German birth and Protestantism.

The first indications of potential for higher command occurred during the War of the Polish Succession (1733–5). In 1734 the advance of Charles Louis Auguste Fouquet, Duc de Belle-Isle, along the Moselle was delayed at Traben-Trarbach by 20,000 Imperialists occupying Grevenburg castle and the ruined Vauban fortress of Mont Royal. Saxe led two unsuccessful assaults on 27 April before the position fell on 2 May. Saxe then joined the corps of Adrien-Maurice, Duc de Noailles, in front of the lines of Ettlingen. Leading fifteen companies of grenadiers in a night attack on 3 May, Saxe broke through the outpost zone but Noailles's caution prevented further progress. The remainder of the campaign was consumed by the French siege of the fortress of Philippsburg (7 June – 17 July) during which Saxe's direction of an assault on 14 July impressed both Noailles and Claude François Bidal, Marquis d'Asfeld. On 1 August Saxe was promoted to lieutenant general. During the uneventful campaign of 1735, he guarded the Rhine above Mannheim.

War of the Austrian Succession

Another period of boredom and frustration ended when France declared war on Austria in 1741. In alliance with

Elector Charles Albert of Bavaria, the French intended to march on Vienna to place him on the Imperial throne. Departing in late summer 1741 with Saxe leading the van, by mid October the Franco-Bavarian army had reached St Polten, only 30 miles from Vienna. At the insistence of the Elector, who wanted to annex Habsburg lands, they turned south into Bohemia, appearing before Prague early in November. Saxe thought the difficulties of siege warfare overrated and decided, with minimal reference to his superiors, to surprise Prague. He quickly assembled four companies of grenadiers supported by 2,000 infantry and 1,200 dragoons and, in a daring *coup de main*, during the night of 26 November 1741 seized the Charles Gate and forced the city to surrender. This feat made him famous throughout Europe, but greatly increased the animosity and jealousy felt towards him by many senior French officers. Nevertheless, François-Marie, Duc de Broglie, charged him with the task of besieging the Austrian fortress and magazine of Eger, which fell on 19 April 1742.

Prussia now deserted the alliance with France, leaving Broglie and Belle-Isle stranded in Prague. Saxe attempted a relief but was unable to make progress and Belle-Isle broke out on 16 December with 15,000 men, only half of whom reached the safety of Eger ten days later. France had been humiliated, and defeat by the Anglo-Hanoverian 'Pragmatic Army' at Dettingen, on 16 June 1743, raised the spectre of invasion. In the spring of 1743 Saxe assisted Broglie in Bavaria but envy and dislike led to his replacement by Louis-François I de Bourbon, Prince de Conti. However, the new minister of war, René-Louis de Voyer, Marquis d'Argenson, appreciated Saxe's qualities and appointed him to direct the corps at Speyer. Following the failure of his counter-offensive into Bavaria, Broglie withdrew into Alsace and handed over his entire army to Saxe.

The Austrian commander Prince Charles of Lorraine occupied Alt-Breisach and prepared to cross the Rhine; Saxe moved to Neuf-Breisach, the fortress on the opposite bank, and made clear his intention to fight. During the summer, Saxe blocked all Lorraine's attempts to force a crossing. The crisis past, Saxe was superseded by Marshal François Franquetot de Coigny and relegated to a subordinate command in Noailles's army. Nevertheless, when he returned to Paris in November 1743 he was fêted, welcomed to Versailles by Louis XV and offered grudging admiration by his French colleagues. His cousin and France's ally, Frederick the Great of Prussia, advised Versailles to make Saxe commander-in-chief.

Marshal of France

On 13 January 1744 Saxe was ordered to Dunkirk to prepare 10,000 men for an invasion of Great Britain in support of the anticipated landing of Prince Charles Edward Stuart

(Bonnie Prince Charlie) but this enterprise was postponed indefinitely on 11 March. Saxe was promoted to marshal of France on 26 March and placed in command of the forces in Flanders. He determined that the best way to ease Austrian pressure along the middle and upper Rhine was by attacking the Austrian Netherlands, where a French advance into west Flanders would also separate Great Britain from its allies Austria, Hanover and Prussia; threaten the Channel ports endangering British supply lines; and overawe the Dutch Republic. While Saxe directed the covering army, Noailles quickly reduced Menin and Ypres, menacing the key ports of Nieuport and Ostend. The commander of the allied army, George Wade, fell back behind the Scheldt and was looking over his shoulder towards Antwerp when news arrived that Charles of Lorraine had invaded Alsace. Louis XV and Noailles drew substantial reinforcements from Flanders and departed for Alsace, leaving Saxe with 55,000 men to face 22,000 British, 16,000 Hanoverians, 18,000 Austrians and 40,000 Dutch – 96,000 men in all. Wade remained encamped behind the Scheldt and the campaign concluded: Lorraine eventually withdrew to deal with an invasion of Bohemia by Frederick the Great, who had meanwhile concluded a secret alliance with France against Austria.

Fontenoy, 1745

Saxe's health deteriorated during the winter of 1744/5 – contemporaries described the condition as 'dropsy', probably oedema resulting from congestive heart failure – and he conducted the 1745 campaign from a padded chariot. By besieging Tournai, Saxe hoped to draw the allied commander, the inexperienced William Augustus, Duke of Cumberland, into battle early in the season before his forces had fully concentrated. Leaving Brussels on 23 April, Cumberland marched towards Tournai. Cumberland's slow progress across country and along bad roads allowed Saxe nearly two weeks to prepare the battlefield at Fontenoy, modelling his dispositions on those of Villars at Malplaquet and Charles XII at Poltava. Cumberland attacked on 11 May and his frontal assault was unexpectedly successful, driving the French centre towards the Scheldt, until finally halted by enfilade fire from flanking infantry and redoubts. At a cost of 7,000 French and 10,000 allied casualties, Saxe obliged Cumberland to withdraw, but it was not a resounding victory. Tournai fell on 22 May and Saxe sent his principal lieutenant, Marshal Ulrich Löwendahl, to seize Ghent by a *coup de main* on 11 July: Bruges, Oudenarde, Albert, Dendermonde, Nieuport and Ostend then succumbed in quick succession. Ath, in Hainault, surrendered to Saxe on 8 October. In three months Saxe had realized his strategic objectives in taking the major Channel ports and driving the British north and away from Germany and the Austrians.

Saxe remained in Ghent with his army during the winter of 1745/6. While British attention was distracted by the advance of Charles Edward Stuart's Jacobite army to Derby and rumours of a French invasion force gathering at Calais, in January 1746 Saxe drew 22,000 troops from their cantonments and marched for Brussels. Halle, Louvain, Malines and Vilvorde fell without a shot fired and on the night of 30 January the Brussels suburbs were occupied and the city surrounded. The governor Count Wenzel Anton Kaunitz had a garrison of 12,000 men, plentiful provisions and anticipated the arrival of a relief force from Antwerp. Instead of Brussels falling to a surprise attack, Saxe had to conduct a formal siege in the depths of winter. Losing hope of relief and with the French poised to storm, Kaunitz surrendered on 20 February. In just two campaigns, Saxe had overrun the Austrian Netherlands.

From Roucoux to Maastricht

Diplomatic progress towards peace caused Saxe to abandon the intended invasion of the Dutch Republic in 1746. Instead, the 200,000-strong French army further secured its recent gains by capturing Antwerp (May) and Mons (July). Anticipating that Saxe's next goal would be Namur, exposing Liège and Maastricht, the allied forces – comprising the British under General Sir John Ligonier, the Dutch under Karl August Friedrich, Prince de Waldeck, and the Austrians commanded by Charles of Lorraine – marched down the Maas in an effort to beat Saxe into Namur. Saxe, hampered by the open insubordination of Conti, increasing ill-health and the strategic limitations imposed by the French government, was slow to respond and lost the race. Although the allies' position was strong, their logistics were vulnerable and a series of French attacks on their lines of communication, culminating in the seizure of Huy on 29 August, obliged them to leave their powerful encampment and move north, enabling Saxe to capture Namur (6–19 September).

His next target was Liège. Lorraine tried to protect both Maastricht and Liège by throwing his 80,000 men across the roads from Tongres and St Trond, but Saxe executed a neat flank march and took up a position with 120,000 men between the two roads on 10 October. Liège, which anchored Lorraine's left flank, was betrayed to Saxe by its citizens on the night of 10/11 October, necessitating a rapid readjustment and weakening of the allies' position. A series of infantry frontal assaults levered the British out of the villages of Lier, Varoux and Roucoux (which gave the battle its name), while a flanking assault drove back the Dutch on their left. In good order, the allies left the field behind Ligonier's rearguard and retired across the Maas via the bridge at Visé. Saxe was promoted to marshal general of France in January 1747.

Saxe led 136,000 soldiers into the field at the end of April 1747: Cumberland commanded the 126,000-strong allied army assisted by Field Marshal Karl Batthyány and Waldeck. Saxe began by sending two detachments under Louis George Érasme, Marquis de Contades, and Löwendahl across the southern border of Zeeland to draw the allies away from Maastricht and threaten Cumberland's communications with Great Britain. Contades seized Fort Liefkenshoek, northwest of Antwerp, whilst Löwendahl took Sas-van-Ghent, Ijzendijke and Eeklo. Despite Cumberland's best efforts, Löwendahl then moved east to invest and capture Hulst and Axel. Both sides manoeuvred during May and June until Saxe sent a detachment under Louis de Bourbon-Condé, Comte de Clermont, forward to Tongres, 12 miles south of Maastricht. Sensing an opportunity to defeat Clermont's corps, Cumberland slipped south. Clermont was about to retreat rapidly when Saxe, who had anticipated and shadowed Cumberland's march, appeared in support.

On 30 June 1747 the Duke of Cumberland found himself facing Saxe and the full French army on a plain 2 miles west of Maastricht. Sir John Ligonier commanded the British cavalry standing against the River Geer (or Jaar) behind the villages of Wilre (Wolder) and Kesselt, while the Duke of

Cumberland commanded the British infantry in Laufeldt (the village that would lend its name to the battle) and Vlijtingen; the Dutch, Hanoverians and Bavarians covered the swampy ground opposite Grote-Spaeven; and the Austrians occupied the right flank behind a ravine west of Kleine-Spaeven. Saxe was bound to attack the allies' left and centre to prise them away from Maastricht. Cumberland, whose line of battle was 4 miles long, initially intended to stand behind the line of villages, but was eventually persuaded by Ligonier to occupy them as redoubts to break up the French onslaught.

Cumberland's dithering – the villages were occupied, evacuated and reoccupied three times until they were finally garrisoned just one hour before the French attacked – convinced Saxe that he was about to withdraw across the Maas through Maastricht. Saxe decided to follow as closely and quickly as possible and sent forward Clermont's grenadiers, the heads of their columns masked by a host of light infantry and skirmishers, to take the supposedly deserted village of Laufeldt, only to be thrown back by musketry and enfilading artillery. Saxe then committed more infantry against both Laufeldt and Vlijtingen to force the allies' centre. In a series of crude frontal assaults, French infantry charged down the slopes from the Heights of Herderen: four times they took the rubble of the two villages and four times were forced out by the British and Germans under Landgrave Frederick II of Hesse-Cassel.

Saxe had to continue – he committed a total of forty battalions – or accept defeat whilst Cumberland was able to relieve and reinforce the garrisons from his second line and even bring nine battalions of Austrians around from behind the ravine. After four hours' fighting, Saxe led forward another twelve battalions which gained footholds in both Laufeldt and Vlijtingen. Saxe then charged towards Vlijtingen with his cavalry and Cumberland ordered the Dutch horse from the right to take them in the flank, but they turned and fled, riding down their own infantry. Cumberland's centre had been fractured, the garrisons of Laufeldt and Vlijtingen were isolated, and French infantry started to feed through the gap.

Saxe turned to Louis le Tellier, Comte d'Estrées, to lead 140 squadrons of cavalry down the road into Wilre to turn the allies' left and drive it into the fire of twenty field guns already positioned on either side of Laufeldt. Aware of the developing situation, Ligonier brought sixty British squadrons from behind Laufeldt and Vlijtingen and charged d'Estrées in the flank before his horsemen had gathered momentum. Ligonier's charge provided the defeated infantry with space to reorganize and leave the field in reasonable order. But he realized that if d'Estrées rallied, charged and broke through his shield, then the retreating infantry would be massacred. Ignoring Cumberland's order to disengage, he launched a second charge that was initially successful. He advanced too far, however, and his men were driven back by entrenched French muske- teers and Ligonier himself was captured. By the time that Saxe had reorganized the French forces, Batthyány had moved some Austrians to screen the retreating infantry. Saxe lost 14,000 killed and wounded: the Allies 6,000. Although Saxe was the technical victor of the battle of Laufeldt he had neither taken Maastricht nor destroyed the allied army.

Demonstrating greater skill in strategy and manoeuvre than in directing set-piece battles, Saxe launched Löwen- dahl from Tirlemont with 35,000 men against Bergen-op- Zoom, 63 miles distant. His intention was to draw Cumberland back to the north and thus uncover Maastricht. Furthermore, the capture of Bergen would close the entire length of the Scheldt to allied shipping and alarm the Dutch. On 16 September, following a long siege, Löwendahl stormed Bergen but lost control of his troops and a massacre ensued: overnight, Saxe and Löwendahl were transformed into mercenary Protestant barbarians. Strategically, too, the plan failed because Cumberland did not leave Maastricht.

Maastricht remained the target for 1748, the French needing both a major victory and an expensive bargaining counter to sell at the peace conference. Saxe left Brussels on 20 March 1748 for Antwerp, where he managed to persuade the allies that he was about to attack Breda.

Meanwhile, Löwendahl had secretly assembled a second French army in six towns in southern Luxembourg before concentrating at Verviers. Saxe then turned the main army south and hurried for Maastricht while Löwendahl encircled the right-bank suburb of Wyck. Maastricht fell on 10 May, in the last major engagement of the War of the Austrian Succession.

The war was formally concluded by the Peace of Aix-la-Chapelle on 18 October 1748. Saxe retired to the Château de Chambord on the Loire, where he died on 30 November 1750 from a 'putrid fever', probably a stroke, following a long visit by several court beauties and various 'dancers'. He was buried in the Protestant city of Strasbourg on 8 February 1751.

Saxe's art of war

Saxe had recorded his thoughts on the art of war in 1732 when recovering from a serious lung infection, but *Mes Rêveries* was only published, posthumously and unedited, in 1757. *Mes Rêveries* was the work of an immature soldier who had yet to experience high command and, during the War of the Austrian Succession, Saxe frequently failed to practise what he had earlier preached: for instance, although he said that he distrusted infantry fire and preferred cold steel, he ended his life an admirer of Frederick the Great's system of musketry, field artillery and drill. He argued for the vigorous pursuit of a beaten enemy, advocated the use of skirmishers at a time when they had temporarily gone out of fashion, and was the first to emphasize the importance of morale. He also suggested that all males between the ages of 20 and 30 should be conscripted for a period of five years because it was natural and just that men should participate in the defence of their state.

FREDERICK
THE GREAT
1712–86

GILES MACDONOGH

FREDERICK II OF PRUSSIA'S CONTEMPORARIES dubbed him 'Frederick the Great' and the title went unchallenged until 1945. After the war, though, Frederick the Great was confined to the doghouse of history, and it has only been in the past twenty years that pen-portraits of him have been painted uncoloured by the notions of Prussian 'militarism' or Nazism. As a general, Frederick was very much a man of his time. His campaigns were short on strategy and big on politics. Campaigns were seasonal; during the Seven Years War, when the frosts melted and the spring flowers bloomed, Frederick knew it was time to fight. When the days grew short and snow covered the ground, he withdrew to winter quarters and wrote poetry.

Frederick was no militarist. He called his uniform a shroud. Wearing uniform was a tradition introduced by his father, Frederick William I, who had created a great fighting machine and programmed his son to use it in Prussia's interests. At Frederick's accession as 'King in Prussia' in 1740, he may have appeared more interested in staffing his academy and opera house, but he was also adding to his regiments. The cue was to be provided by the death of the Holy Roman Emperor, Charles VI, in October 1740. He had no sons and in 1713 had made the German vassal states accept the 'Pragmatic Sanction', which allowed his eldest daughter, Maria Theresa, to inherit the Habsburg lands.

Frederick knew that Prussia had a claim to Habsburg Silesia, as Liegnitz, Brieg and Wohlau were meant to revert to Prussia on the death of the last of the Polish Piast princes, which had occurred in 1675. Unfortunately, Frederick William, the 'Great Elector' and Frederick's great-grandfather, had renounced his rights, but Frederick considered that re-asserting them would be acting in the interests of the Protestant majority in Lower Silesia; and it would be a fitting revenge for the way that the emperor had treated his father over the duchies of Jülich and Berg, which Frederick William believed were his by right but which his grandfather had renounced in exchange for Imperial approval of his adopting a royal title in 1701.

There was a further incentive: glory. This was what the young Frederick, as much as an intellectual as a warrior, hankered after most. It seems shocking now to risk subjects' lives for glory, but it was no less than he had read in the works of his favourite authors, the French neo-classical dramatists Corneille and Racine.

Reforming the balance of power in central Europe had long preyed on his mind. To his brother-in-law, Charles of Brunswick, he had said that the emperor's death 'will plunge Europe into bloody combat'. It was merely a question of 'putting those plans into action which I have been hatching so long in my head'.

There was also a nagging feeling that the Bavarians or the Saxons might move first. Maria Theresa's husband Francis Stephen was seen by many German princes as a French pawn, and undesirable as Holy Roman Emperor. Frederick could count on a certain amount of support in Protestant Germany, as well as Great Britain.

The First Silesian War

In 1740 Frederick began his occupation of Silesia, and its major towns and cities fell easily into his hands. It was not until 10 April 1741 that he had to prove his mettle. He surprised an Austrian force led by Graf Wilhelm von Neipperg at Mollwitz. Prussian morale broke when Neipperg's troops scattered their right flank and Frederick panicked.

Taking advice from the Blenheim veteran Curt Christoph von Schwerin, he fled. It looked as if the Austrians would win, but Schwerin rallied his 'moving walls' – the Prussian infantry – and carried the day. Frederick was cowering in a mill and only heard of his first success the following morning.

It had been the Prussian cavalry that had failed at Mollwitz, and Frederick set about reforming it. He consolidated his power in Silesia while the Austrians, faced with a deep Bavarian incursion into their flank, tried to buy him off. Austria relinquished Lower Silesia and Neisse with the Treaty of Klein Schnellendorf of 9 October 1741, giving Maria Theresa time to deal with the French and Bavarians, whose Prince-Elector Charles Albert was elected Emperor Charles VII in February 1742. The Austrians, however, swiftly invaded Charles's electorate of Bavaria and deposed the new emperor, leaving them free to clamour for Silesia again.

The Battle of Chotusitz took place on 17 May 1742. Modern commentators have labelled it a draw, but politically it was carried by Frederick. It went badly at first, with the Prussian cavalry again failing to make its mark, but the infantry set to work and broke the Austrians, whose losses were marginally higher. At the Peace of Breslau in June, Frederick was confirmed in the possession of all Silesia barring a small pocket around Teschen.

The Second Silesian War

The Second Silesian War of 1744–5 was fought by Prussia to find a land for Frederick's ally, the ousted Emperor Charles VII. Frederick made for Bohemia, where he hoped the new kingdom might be situated. He briefly took Prague, then abandoned it, exposing his army to terrible harassment on its retreat towards Silesia, which was already flooded with Hungarian soldiers.

On 20 January 1745 Charles died, leaving Frederick without a *casus belli* and Silesia threatened by its old Habsburg masters. It was not until 4 June that he was able to gain his first great victory, on the boggy ground of Hohenfriedberg. Hohenfriedberg is often compared to Leuthen (1757), Frederick's greatest triumph in the field. Continuing to observe the lessons from Mollwitz and Chotusitz, he had strengthened his cavalry, which was locked in a bitter fight at first until General Zieten found a ford that enabled him to bring up reinforcements and carry the day. It was the first time that Frederick attacked using an 'oblique order', concentrating the bulk of his forces on one flank of the enemy line yet spreading his troops all along it. Having prevailed at the point of attack, his armies could then 'roll up' the enemy from the chosen flank. On this occasion the attack did not go entirely according to plan, but Frederick showed admirable pragmatism on the field of battle. The Austrians and Saxons were routed. Unusually, enemy casualties were three times as great as his.

The Battle of Soor on 30 September was a blow to Frederick's self-esteem. The Prussians were caught in their blankets. The Austrian forces managed to take possession of a vital hill, but Frederick was able to rally his men. Once again it was the cavalry that carried the day, with considerable carnage. Soor counted as a victory for Frederick as the Austrians made their escape at midday, their casualties double the Prussians'; even so, Frederick was disconsolate: he had lost not just men but his favourite dogs, flutes, snuff-boxes and ciphers.

After Soor, Frederick wondered whether he needed to 'box the Austrians' ears' yet again. The final drubbing was administered at Kesseldorf on 14 December, not by Frederick himself but by his general Leopold of Anhalt-Dessau, known as the *Alte Dessauer*. He made a 'ferocious frontal assault' against superior numbers, inflicting losses on the Austrians and Saxons of between a third and half of their army. The peace was signed in Dresden on Christmas Day 1745. Frederick was confirmed as ruler of Silesia and he in turn recognized Francis Stephen as Holy Roman Emperor. The Prussians hailed their king as 'Frederick the Great'.

The Seven Years War: Prague to Kolin

More than a decade passed before Frederick went to war again, but he continued to think about ways of making his army even more effective. In 1748 he privately published his *Principes généraux de la guerre*, in which he made various plans to attack Saxony, combined with some musings on the philosophy of war that prefigured the more famous work by Carl von Clausewitz.

In his *Principes généraux*, Frederick showed that war needed to have an important political objective. Money was a problem for Prussia, and Frederick sought the best army at the lowest price. He reformed the hussars so that they would be a match for the fierce Austrian Pandurs (a force of irregular troops) and created a modern officer corps with promotion based on merit – he was prepared to sack even his brothers if they performed badly. Consequently, his generals were in the main first-rate, unlike some of their earlier Austrian counterparts.

Frederick understood the need for draconian discipline. Punishments were frequently meted out for pillaging or desertion. There were whippings and hangings as well as 'running the gauntlet' – where the miscreant was beaten with rods by other soldiers from his regiment. After the Seven Years War (1756–63) a number of cowardly generals were given short sentences of fortress detention, and one colonel was taken out to be shot, but was pardoned at the post. (It should be borne in mind, however, that the British shot Admiral Byng for losing a battle in 1757.)

Frederick knew Maria Theresa wanted Silesia back. With this in mind, in January 1756 he and his uncle, George II, King of Great Britain and Elector of Hanover, signed the Convention of Westminster, which drove the French, who had begun their colonial war with Britain the year before, back into the Austrian camp. Meanwhile the Austrians and their clever chancellor Wenzel Kaunitz set about raising fears of Prussia in St Petersburg: if they assisted Austria in retrieving Silesia, the Russians might help themselves to East Prussia. The marriage of Frederick's sister Ulrika to King Adolf Frederick of Sweden added to Russian anxiety, and it did not prove difficult to bring them round.

Frederick was now hemmed in. He was aware that he needed to make a pre-emptive strike in order to gain the advantage and to ensure that the fighting take place far from Prussia. In a much-quoted letter of 26 August 1756, Frederick wrote, 'I am innocent of this war. I have done what I could to avoid it. However great may be my love of peace, one may never sacrifice honour and security … now we must think only of the means of carrying out this war which removes the pleasure our enemies derive from disrupting the peace.'

Frederick divided his army into three and sent one part to face the Russians and another to tackle the French.

He himself led the largest segment, against the Austrians. He planned to knock them out and then deal with the others. The attack he launched on Saxony on 29 August 1756 has become the prototype for all blitzkrieg. He had explained to the Saxon king that his territory needed to be violated to maintain supply lines to Bohemia. The Austrian coalition had already dangled the Duchy of Magdeburg before the Saxon king, which Frederick used as a justification for his aggression, but there is no denying he coveted Saxony: Frederick wanted to make sense of his otherwise straggling lands, which extended from the Lower Rhine to the Russian border. West Prussia was another fruit he hoped might fall into his lap. Like Lower Silesia, the vast majority of Saxony's population were Lutheran, and he could play that card once again, especially as the king was Catholic.

Frederick's first battle in the new war was fought at Lobositz in Bohemia. He decided on a direct attack on a well-defended position. It was a Pyrrhic victory, but the Prussian armies pursued their enemy to Prague; the Austrian army entered the city and closed the gates behind them. On 6 May 1757 Austria and Prussia met for battle. Frederick was suffering from food poisoning, and spent the day being sick. The Prussians made a number of errors: their cavalry was unsupported by the artillery, and the fearsome 'moving walls' were defeated by the marshy ground. Two of Frederick's best generals met their deaths: Winterfeldt and the 73-year-old Schwerin, who had rallied the scattered Prussians by tearing a flag out of a staff-captain's hand and crying, 'All brave fellows, follow me!' He was promptly hit in the head and chest. His example encouraged the men to charge with a cry of 'Revenge for Father Schwerin!' The tables were turned when the infantry found a gap in the Austrian line and poured twenty-two battalions through it. It was, however, General Hans Joachim von Zieten who won the day, scattering the enemy like 'straw in the wind'.

Despite his huge losses, his victory at Prague won Frederick European renown, but strategically it was not promising: it halted the Prussian advance and converted the king's campaign from an aggressive to a defensive one – from now on Frederick would be trying to prevent his enemies from coming together. Nineteenth-century critics pointed out that he had both failed to destroy his enemy and committed the error of not investing Prague. On 18 June the battle was followed by the bitter experience of his first major defeat, at Kolin. Frederick's decision to face a numerically superior enemy from a poorly chosen downhill position cost him dearly in terms of both bloodshed and reputation. He issued the command to attack too early. After the battle he said that he would have managed had he possessed four more infantry battalions. He had begun to believe too heavily in his winning streak. He would have lost more, had it not been for the amazing feats of the Prussian cavalry.

From Rossbach to Kunersdorf

Frederick was close to despair but he was determined to learn. The nineteenth-century Prussian General Staff officer Alfred von Schlieffen, who used to teach his students that 'experience is useless unless it is studied', claimed that after Kolin Frederick immediately set about turning the defeat into the blueprint for the victory he would win at Leuthen. To Schlieffen, Leuthen was Frederick's Cannae, a battle of annihilation; this may have been stretching a point.

Frederick's enemies were closing in: the British ducked out of the Convention of Klosterzeven and the French were within an easy march of Berlin. Far worse, the Russians had arrived in East Prussia, and the Hungarian general Hadik had sacked Berlin.

Frederick badly needed a fillip, and he received it at Rossbach in Saxony. On 5 November 1757 a Prussian army of 21,000 faced a French and Imperial force of nearly twice that number. They walked straight into a trap of Frederick's making. The victory was decided in minutes. The cavalry general Friedrich Wilhelm von Seydlitz was the man of the match, nonchalantly tossing away his clay pipe as a signal to the cuirassiers to charge. When the Imperial units fought back, Seydlitz ordered up eighteen fresh squadrons. This occasioned a rout which ended when fleeing troops crashed into a sunken road. Frederick watched the enemy's confusion from the upper window of a house and ordered his artillery to cut up the advancing French regiments. More than 5,000 enemy troops were killed and the same number taken prisoner; Frederick lost 169 dead and 379 wounded. The French would not suffer as grave a defeat until Salamanca, over half a century later. Rossbach was the Agincourt of the German nation.

The cultural significance of Rossbach was immense, but the Battle of Leuthen, fought in Silesia against heavy odds just a month later, was possibly Frederick's greatest victory, and according to the military historian General Sir David Fraser, 'one of the greatest battles of the century'.

On 3 December 1757, Frederick summoned his commanders at Parchwitz in Silesia and issued a declaration: 'We must beat the enemy, or bury ourselves before his guns'. Two days later he gave battle: 39,000 men against the Austrian and Saxon army of 66,000, which was arrayed along a front some 4 miles long. Here he successfully used his favourite tactic of the oblique order, attacking the Austrian left after a feint towards the right which his enemy thought was a retreat, and which caused the Austrian commander Charles of Lorraine to make the disastrous decision of moving his cavalry to the right.

The Prussian manoeuvre, shielded by the cavalry and a line of small hills, only became evident once the well-drilled infantry had already outflanked the Austrians, which obliged the Austrians to turn their front and negated their superiority of numbers. Despite an attempt to reform the Austrian line (which took more than an hour, a result of the extremely extended original deployment), the Prussian infantry with artillery support continued a relentless advance through the village of Leuthen. In the three hours of the battle the Austrians lost 10,000 dead and wounded and a further 12,000 prisoners; Prussian casualties amounted to around a fifth of their army.

It was, though, the high point of the war for Frederick. For the next six years Frederick would be hounded by a numerically superior enemy while he sought to deliver short, sharp slaps to keep them at bay. The sheer doggedness of the Russians made them particularly hard to shake off. At Zorndorf in Brandenburg on 25 August 1758, Frederick only narrowly avoided defeat, and once again much of his success was down to Seydlitz. The Prussians lost 12,800 men, the Russians a staggering 18,000. Zorndorf was to be the beginning of the backward slide: next came Hochkirch, in October. Once again a Prussian army of 30,000 men was caught napping by a hugely superior Austrian force. Frederick was now outnumbered two to one. He had lost half his officer corps since 1756.

The next blow, in August 1759, was Kunersdorf: the worst defeat of all. A combined force of Russians and Austrians numbering 64,000 men faced Frederick in the Brandenburg Neumark. Frederick had fewer than 50,000. Despite Frederick's personal bravery, his army was routed. He was again saved by the superior idiocy of the enemy: the Russians refused to advance, feeling their losses to be too great.

The rest of the war was an endurance test. Frederick won his battles: Liegnitz, Torgau, Bunzelwitz, Burkersdorf and Freiberg, each one demonstrating the pugnaciousness of the king. To some extent they washed away the stain of Kunersdorf. At the Peace of Hubertusburg of 15 February 1763, the Austrians, Prussians and Saxons agreed to return to the *status quo ante bellum*, and the Seven Years War came to an end.

Old age and assessment

As an old man, Frederick fought one last war, against Joseph of Austria, who had become Emperor Joseph II in 1765. Frederick was able to pose as the defender of German liberties against the Austrians. Even the Saxons were on his side. There was no pre-emptive strike this time and no battle except a sad little skirmish at Habelschwerdt in January 1779. Most commentators agree that it was an old man's campaign. Frederick died peacefully at the summer palace of Sanssouci at Potsdam on 17 August 1786.

Throughout his career, Frederick craved territory, desiring wealth, power and men for his armies. Despite what Schlieffen thought, he had no wish to fight a Cannae, and never thought of annihilating his enemy. Frederick's tactics were Fabian: he fought to keep the upper hand, to hang on to his gains, to exhaust his enemy. His brother Henry helped by rupturing the lines of communication to starve out the lumbering armies that threatened Prussia's very existence.

He fought fifteen battles, winning twelve victories. Some, such as Hohenfriedberg and Leuthen, have gone down as some of the greatest battles in history. Frederick was no coward, and was always to be found where the fighting was hottest. He was unique as a modern soldier king. Napoleon paid him his greatest tribute when, after Prussia's catastrophic defeats at Auerstedt and Jena in 1806, he visited Frederick's tomb in the Potsdam Garrison Church. 'Gentlemen,' he said. 'Were he still alive, we would not be here.'

ROBERT CLIVE

1725–74

ROBERT HARVEY

ROBERT CLIVE – the clerk with the East India Company with no training as a soldier – was hailed as a 'heaven-born general' by William Pitt the Elder. As might be expected, his approach to warfare was unorthodox, based on sudden rapid marches and bold strikes where least expected, often taking on vastly superior odds; the formal eighteenth-century disciplines of lines of battle and standard manoeuvres were largely alien to him. The result was a succession of dazzling victories in southern India and Bengal, victories that resulted in the creation of British India. But Clive was much more than just a fighter. A strategic thinker, he was also a brilliant and decisive administrator and the ruler of millions of people, as well as a political intriguer, a lover of ostentation, an occasionally brutal governor, and, to his detractors, an ambitious and successful self-seeker.

Clive was born into a respectable gentry family on 29 September 1725 at Styche, near Moreton Saye in Shropshire. Something of a young tearaway, with few prospects in Britain, at the age of 17 he was sent off to make his fortune with the East India Company. Working as a clerk in the Company's headquarters in the prosperous British settlement of Madras, he was said to be so homesick and bored that he attempted to commit suicide, but his pistol twice failed to go off. When the French East India Company, under the formidable governor of Pondicherry, Joseph-François Dupleix, suddenly attacked and occupied Madras in 1746, the 21-year-old Clive and three companions escaped disguised as Indians, and made their way to Fort St David, 50 miles to the south.

Clive took part in defending the fort against French attack, and also participated in a failed attack on the French stronghold of Pondicherry; but in 1748 Madras was restored to the British under the Treaty of Aix-la-Chapelle. His first real command came when he was put in charge by a tough professional soldier, Major Stringer Lawrence, of 30 British troops and 700 Indians in an assault on Fort Devikottai; the fearlessness of his attack caused the hostile local Indian ruler to abandon the fort.

The French meanwhile sought to gain control of most of southern India, and to this end, in 1751 some 800 French and 20,000 Indians besieged 60 English and 2,000 Indian troops inside the colourful citadel of Mohammed Ali, the Indian ruler of Trichinopoly. Clive was sent as an aide to an incompetent Swiss mercenary, Captain Rudolf de Guingens, who was in command of a relief force dispatched to Trichinopoly. Contemptuous of de Guingens and impatient for action, Clive persuaded his superiors in Madras to allow him to seize the fortress at Arcot, the stronghold of France's Indian allies, while most of their army was at Trichinopoly.

The siege of Arcot

Clive's modest force, which dwindled to 120 British troops and 2,000 Indians, marched through monsoon thunderstorms to seize the citadel at Arcot, which was abandoned on his approach. With his small force occupying the sprawling fortress, Clive held out against a besieging Indian army of some 15,000 men – many of them fervent Shi'ite Muslims – for seventy-five days.

On 13 November 1751 Clive's exhausted, parched and half-starved men, only two-thirds of them fighting fit, were subjected to a full-scale attack by their besiegers. Just before dawn a large number of men carrying ladders were seen running towards the walls. Behind them elephants with huge protective iron plates on their foreheads charged forward to batter down the gates. Further behind, as far as the eye could see, a torrent of enemy soldiers with muskets and spears surged towards the fort.

Clive, entirely cool in a crisis and apparently fearless, promptly gave orders for his men to shoot at the unprotected flanks of the elephants. The animals, maddened by the pain, reared up and then turned and stampeded into the soldiers following them. The gates remained secure. However, at the same time – spurred on 'with a mad kind of intrepidity' by their religious frenzy – the enemy was mounting attacks in the two major breaches caused by the guns brought up by the French to support the attackers.

Clive had organized his tiny force to fire their muskets and then hand them back to loaders who would promptly pass on another gun, thus making best use of both his active and inactive soldiers. This concentrated fire at last caused the attackers to waver. Meanwhile the defenders hurled grenades from the ramparts at the second line of enemy troops.

Two hours later a relentless barrage of musket and cannon-fire began. This was presumably a softening-up intended to deter his men from manning the ramparts. Clive embarked on his rounds once more, cheering up his men and cajoling them, checking on the defences. After more than four hours the relentless bombardment – which had set all of them on edge – ceased, and a small party arrived under a white flag requesting permission to carry off the dead, who were rapidly putrefying under the intense midday sun. The request was granted.

Two hours later the pounding began again. The exhausted garrison rested as best it could. The relentless bombardment continued for a full twelve hours; Clive imagined the enemy were seeking to exhaust the garrison mentally in preparation for the next assault. When the sun rose a second time there was no sign of the enemy, although their guns and baggage were strewn across the ground before the fort. They had left the city, and the bombardment had been a cover to allow them to retire in good order, in case the formidable enemy within the fort sallied out to attack them.

Two more hard-fought battles ensued, a set-piece encounter at Arni and an enemy ambush at Kaveripak, which Clive skilfully but narrowly won, before he returned to Trichinopoly, which was still under siege. Along with Lawrence, he carried the battle to the French, who were encamped on a narrow tongue of land behind a pagoda complex at Srirangam to the north, protected by the Cauvery and Coleroon rivers. Clive relentlessly bombarded the French and Indian forces while Lawrence closed the trap from the landward side, forcing a surrender. Clive's whirlwind of activity in his first tour of India ended with the decisive capture of two French forts, Covelong and Chingleput, before he returned in glory to Madras, where he married the redoubtable Margaret Maskelyne. Back in England, he enjoyed a hero's welcome. At the age of just

27, Clive was hailed as the man who had saved Britain's southern settlements in India.

In London Clive quickly squandered his new wealth, much of it on an expensive but unsuccessful attempt to enter the House of Commons, and in 1755 he was compelled to return to India to seek his fortune once again. On his journey back he took part in the successful storming of the pirate stronghold at Gheria, near Bombay, before taking up his new post as commander of Fort St David on 22 June 1756 – coincidentally just two days after the Black Hole of Calcutta, the much-exaggerated atrocity that followed the seizure of Fort William, the main British settlement in Bengal, which the governor, Roger Drake, had shamefully abandoned to its fate.

The invasion of Bengal

As soon as the news from Calcutta reached Madras, the British started to organize an expedition to regain the settlement, with Clive as one of three commanders. On 16 October one of the mightiest expeditionary forces ever assembled in the eighteenth century set sail. After a bombardment, the looted and largely destroyed Fort William was retaken. In revenge for the attack on Calcutta, Clive marched upriver and took the town of Hugli, which was also abandoned by the Bengalis. But this provoked the Nawab of Bengal, Siraj-ud-Daula, to march south back to Calcutta. Clive now faced his most formidable foe.

In February 1757 Clive bravely decided, as was his custom, on a pre-emptive attack on the nawab's camp at Dum Dum, outside Calcutta. But for once things went wrong: when a fog lifted he was left exposed to a far superior enemy force and he had to cut his way hurriedly through the Bengali camp to escape, inflicting some 1,500 casualties in the fighting. Siraj-ud-Daula nevertheless retreated further up the Hugli River after this display of British determination, and forged an alliance with the nearby French settlement at Chandernagore. Clive promptly replied by bombarding and taking the French enclave.

Clive now set his sights on total victory over the nawab, and embarked on a policy of duplicity for which he was much criticized later, notably by Lord Macaulay. Yet it is hard to see what else he could have done, in view of the overwhelming force arrayed against him. A British merchant, William Watts, was sent to seek a secret agreement with Siraj-ud-Daula's chief general, Mir Jafar, to betray his master and attach his forces to the British side in any battle. This also involved double-crossing an untrustworthy go-between, the merchant Omichand, with a false treaty promising him huge rewards for his help. But by the time Watts secretly left the Bengali capital of Murshidabad, there was no certainty that Mir Jafar would come to the aid of the British.

In this climate of acute uncertainty, Clive marched upriver and took the enormous gamble of confronting the nawab's army at Plassey, a confrontation which he narrowly won, largely because Mir Jafar's forces stood aside from the battles.

The Battle of Plassey

The Battle of Plassey was one of the greatest gambles in British history, a decisive turning point in which the very fate of British India was held in the balance. Clive, aged only 32 and with an army of only 3,000 men, had marched up the Hugli River to confront Siraj-ud-Daula. At this point, with the waters swollen by monsoon rains and still rising, he ordered his men to cross a tributary, aware that he was cutting off their line of retreat. On the wrong side of the river, they faced massacre if they lost. Clive took up position at the nawab's beautiful hunting lodge at Plassey; to the south there was an immense mango grove, to the west the river.

His position, although a good defensive one, was hardly a fort. He had only 3,000 men. Against him was an army of at least 35,000–50,000 disciplined infantry and 15,000 Pathans, fine fighters and riders from the northwest border. In addition, the nawab had more than fifty cannon, maintained and fired by fifty Frenchmen.

Clive ordered his men well beyond the shelter of the grove, to a position directly in front of the enemy line. He placed three of his small guns on either side, and hundreds of his soldiers in between. Sepoys guarded his flanks. A little further back he placed his two remaining 6-pound guns and howitzers protected by brick kilns. At 8 a.m. the first cannonade from the French guns began, and the British replied. The British fire ripped through Mir Madan's men; but the French had killed ten British soldiers and twenty Indians within half an hour. The two sides continued exchanging relentless fire for three hours. The monsoon clouds, which had been building up for hours, then broke; half an hour of torrential rain soaked every man to the skin. The British had hastily pulled tarpaulins over the ammunition as soon as the downpour started; the Bengali ammunition was drenched. British guns continued to fire throughout, while the enemy ones fell silent.

Siraj-ud-Daula was beginning to panic: Mir Jafar and the other senior commanders had so far taken no part in the fighting, although their flanking move had continued and they were now in a position to attack from the side, and very nearly from the back, cutting Clive off. The nawab sent repeatedly for Mir Jafar, who advised him to call off the attack.

Clive ordered his soldiers to advance to take the forward Bengali positions. Simultaneously, one of the enemy ammunition dumps blew up. Eyre Coote captured the little hill in front of Plassey House, while the French fled the redoubt from which their guns had kept the British pinned down for so long.

Siraj-ud-Daula, hearing that the British were attacking, jumped aboard a camel and fled back with 2,000 horsemen towards his capital at Murshidabad. His huge army now also fled, their panic becoming a rout. Around 500 of the enemy had been killed, compared to just 20 dead and 50 wounded on the British side.

The consequences both for the British in India and Clive personally were momentous. The East India Company and Britain had acquired, at a stroke, effective control of the largest and wealthiest part of the subcontinent. Building on their superiority in the south, they now held nearly a third of its land area: only the central belt (divided between the Marathas and the French), the north (controlled by the Nawab of Oudh), and the wild northwest eluded them. Clive had effectively doubled the British area of occupation, and the Company was now indisputably the major power in India. The foundations for British rule had been laid, a rule that was to endure for two centuries.

Clive of India

Clive himself was in a position of power unparalleled by any Briton in history, before or since. He had a kingdom of 40 million people at his feet, more than six times the number of subjects of the British monarch. There was no effective control over his personal rule from the civilian authorities in Madras or Calcutta.

Clive entered in triumph into Murshidabad. After lengthy haggling, it was agreed that the nawab should pay half of what he owed the British immediately, two-thirds in bullion and one-third in jewels, plate and gold, and the rest in equal instalments over the next three years. Clive visited the treasury himself to satisfy his curiosity. From this was to derive his most famous remark before an inquiry of the House of Commons in 1773: 'When I recollect entering the nawab's treasury at Murshidabad, with heaps of gold and silver to the right and left, and these crowned with jewels, by God, at this moment do I stand astonished at my own moderation.'

Mir Jafar had Siraj-ud-Daula killed and became the new nawab, heavily dependent on the British. Clive, the real power in the land, consolidated the British hold on India, sending armies under Francis Forde and Stringer Lawrence to fend off a determined French attempt to take the Carnatic. Sir Eyre Coote routed the French at the Battle of Wandewash in 1760, and a year later took the French settlement at Pondicherry and razed it to the ground.

A further revolt threatened in northern India under the leadership of the Shahzada, the heir to the Mughal emperor. Clive himself marched forward and defeated the enemy, also indulging in uncharacteristic cruelty in destroying 300 villages in Pulwansing. After the triumph he extracted from Mir Jafar an annual payment of £27,000 – a staggering sum for those days – to be paid from the annual rent the East India Company was supposed to pay the nawab for the lands around Calcutta. Clive's many enemies in England complained of his becoming the recipient of the Company's rents. In the meantime, Mir Jafar – who had already shown his treachery once – was conspiring against the British with the Dutch at their settlement of Kasimbasar. The Dutch attacked the British downstream from Calcutta, but in a 'short, bloody and decisive action' were routed on the Plains of Badaw, with the Dutch losing 320 men for ten British dead.

In February 1760 the absolute ruler of much of India set sail for England, where he attempted to become a significant force in British politics. But this brilliant commander in the field and outwitter of the Indians proved no match for politicians such as the scheming prime minister, the Duke of Newcastle, and he also incurred the enmity of the chairman of the East India Company, Laurence Sulivan, and others jealous of his success. Meanwhile, conditions in India deteriorated steadily, with widespread allegations of corruption on the part of Company officials and their agents and the formation of military alliances among Indian princes against the British.

Clive's third tour

In June 1764 the seemingly indispensable Clive returned to India to restore order. On arrival he set out in a *budgerow*, a luxury houseboat, to Murshidabad, where he formally reduced the new nawab's status to that of puppet monarch. He then moved on to Allahabad, seat of the Mughal emperor and his old but prestigious foe, the Shahzada. Here, in August 1765, Clive forced Emperor Shah Alam II to award him the *diwani*, the right for the British to collect taxes in Bengal, Bihar and Orissa, thus in effect formally recognizing the British right to rule a huge swathe of India.

Clive now plunged into a whirlwind of administrative reform to establish the foundations of colonial government in India, including an anti-corruption drive – an ironic rebuttal of accusations of his own past profiteering. He also aimed to provide secure boundaries for British India, set up a Society of Trade to regulate commerce, proposed establishing a class of salaried civil servants – an idea only adopted under his successor, Warren Hastings – announced a crackdown on extortion, and introduced a new postal system and a land survey of Bengal.

Clive faced down intense local opposition, then a strike by company civil servants, and finally, most dangerously, a full-scale mutiny by his own British officers. Hastening up to the city of Monghyr, the centre of the mutiny, Clive walked into the garrison with only a single escort and ordered the rebels to lay down their weapons. When they did so he said, 'Now I am satisfied you are British soldiers and not, as I was erroneously informed, assassins.' The following year he left India for the last time at the still remarkably young age of 42.

Last years

Back in England, Clive used his own vast wealth to buy and improve a succession of large estates. But his enemies were gathering again, as news came that the warrior Hyder Ali had launched a furious rebellion against the British in India, and that millions had perished in the 1769–70 Bengal famine, which was unfairly blamed on British maladministration. Clive defended himself manfully against these attacks, first in a House of Commons committee, then, in 1774, against a vote of censure on the floor, which he carried by 155 votes to 95. Clive could now be considered for the post of commander of British forces in the seemingly inevitable war with the American colonies.

In November the same year, however, Clive was found in the lavatory of his London home in Berkeley Square with his throat cut. That same night his body was hurried away for burial at the tiny church of Moreton Saye, his family's home in Shropshire. The secrecy surrounding his burial, as well as the fact that he was buried in an unmarked grave, suggested that Clive, often prone to depression and illness, had committed suicide. It was a huge shock, given that this was a man who had survived so many battles – it was as though Field Marshal Montgomery, for example, had taken his own life after the Second World War.

It also seems possible that he was murdered, or more likely sought in an emergency to cut his own throat to remove an obstruction, which was not uncommon in those days – a theory believed by at least one prominent surgeon today. The nation that had so often been grudging about his achievements belatedly granted him real recognition by awarding his eldest son, Ned, the earldom of Powys on the death of the 2nd Earl, whose daughter, Lady Henrietta Herbert, he had married. So perished, in tragic circumstances, one of the greatest British commanders of all time, a man whose qualities included decisiveness, speed, manic energy and a willingness to gamble against huge odds. In Clive there also died the only non-royal Englishman who can properly be described as having founded and run an empire.

JAMES WOLFE

1727–59

STEPHEN BRUMWELL

*GENERAL JAMES WOLFE'S NAME will always be linked with
one momentous event: the victory on the Plains of Abraham before
Quebec in 1759 that cost him his life – and decided the fate of
North America. Remarkably, Wolfe was just 32 years old when
he was killed commanding that crucial campaign. Such precocious
responsibility testified to the outstanding training and leadership
skills that Wolfe had acquired during seventeen years as a British
army officer.*

The reputation of James Wolfe has undergone unusually
dramatic fluctuations. In the wake of his death he was
upheld as an iconic British hero, and this image held sway
until the middle of the last century. As the man who won
Canada for Britain, Wolfe was intimately associated with

the British Empire, but when that institution crumbled after the Second World War, he too fell from grace. Since the bicentenary of Wolfe's death in 1959, both his character and military abilities have undergone assaults from debunking writers. Yet Wolfe was neither the saintly military genius lauded by his devotees, nor the vain, mediocre general vilified by his critics. Without doubt, however, James Wolfe was an unusually dedicated and determined professional soldier, a commander capable of inspiring his men to overcome the most daunting challenges.

Born for a soldier

For James Wolfe, who was born on 2 January 1727 at Westerham, Kent, wearing the red coat of the British soldier was a family tradition dating back to the days of Cromwell's New Model Army. James's father, grandfather and great-grandfather were all army officers, and he was destined to follow their example.

After Britain declared war on Spain in 1739 in what became known as the War of Jenkins' Ear, Wolfe's father, Edward, became colonel of a new regiment of marines. The following year, Wolfe's marines joined an expedition bound for the West Indies, and 13-year-old James accompanied his father as a 'volunteer', or officer cadet. But as the transport ships waited off the Isle of Wight, he sickened and was sent ashore. This was a lucky deliverance:

when it reached the Caribbean the expedition met catastrophe. Wracked by inter-service rivalry and ravaged by tropical diseases, it achieved nothing.

Originally commissioned in his father's marines, in March 1742 Wolfe transferred to a line infantry regiment, the 12th Foot, with the equivalent rank of ensign. The start of Wolfe's army career coincided with the escalation of the War of the Austrian Succession. Soon after, his battalion sailed to Flanders, and from there marched into Germany. On 27 June 1743, when a British–Austrian army defeated the French at Dettingen near Frankfurt, Wolfe underwent his baptism of fire. It was a bloody encounter, with Wolfe's regiment in the thick of the fighting, but the 16-year-old ensign behaved with distinction. By now Wolfe was already serving as regimental adjutant. This willingness to master the intricacies of his profession, allied to his father's cash and influence in army circles, swiftly brought promotion to lieutenant in the 12th Foot, and then captain in a senior regiment, the 4th, or 'King's Own'.

In 1745, with the outbreak of the Jacobite rebellion, Wolfe's regiment was recalled from Flanders. During the scrappy fight at Falkirk on 16 January 1746, when other units fled in blind panic, it stood steady against Bonnie Prince Charlie's Highlanders. Three months later, Wolfe served at Culloden. According to a famous anecdote, as the victorious British government forces ruthlessly scoured the battlefield, he reputedly spurned the order of William Augustus, Duke of Cumberland, to pistol a wounded Highlander.

With the Jacobite rebellion crushed, Wolfe was soon back fighting the French across the Channel. As a major of brigade, he was wounded at the Battle of Laufeldt outside Maastricht, on 2 July 1747. It was a British defeat, but the carnage left the victors eager for peace, which was brokered the following year.

The professional soldier

By 1748 James Wolfe had already served five arduous campaigns and survived four bloody pitched battles. It was a punishing apprenticeship: as he later confessed, those hard years 'stripped the bloom' from his youth. However, Wolfe's conscientiousness had brought steady promotion, and attracted powerful patrons. They included both Cumberland and the experienced soldier who ultimately succeeded him as commander-in-chief, Sir John Ligonier. Peace did nothing to halt Wolfe's rise: in 1749, aged just 22, he was appointed major to the 20th Foot in Scotland. A year later, he became its lieutenant colonel.

Wolfe thrived on action, and the ensuing eight years of peacetime service in Britain were characterized by frustration, boredom, thwarted romance, soul-searching and bouts of illness: from 1751 he was tormented by the 'gravel'

– an agonizing bladder complaint that shortened his temper. Increasingly, Wolfe channelled his energies into professional perfectionism, transforming his regiment into one of the army's most efficient units. A tough disciplinarian, Wolfe balanced this stance with a genuine concern for his subordinates, officers and ordinary soldiers alike. Such paternalism earned him an enduring reputation as 'the officer's friend and soldier's father'.

Wolfe was an avid reader of military history, and the titles he recommended to a younger officer in 1756 are revealing: they embraced Thucydides and Xenophon, an account of the fifteenth-century Hussite leader Jan Zizka, and a 1754 essay on the art of war by the French officer Turpin de Crissé. Keen to keep abreast of the latest tactical thinking, Wolfe was among those officers who pioneered the adoption of the simplified firing drill used by the Prussians, even though this went against official British regulations. Most significantly, the fiercely patriotic Wolfe sought to inculcate an aggressive fighting spirit into his men, firmly grounded upon confidence in their own proficiency as soldiers.

The 1748 Peace of Aix-la-Chapelle was never more than an interval in the Anglo-French duel for global supremacy. Fighting had already flared in North America when hostilities officially resumed in 1756. In the opening rounds of what became known as the Seven Years War, Britain suffered jarring setbacks across the globe. In

September 1757 it retaliated by raiding the French coast. A projected attack on the port of Rochefort in the Bay of Biscay resulted in humiliating withdrawal, but Wolfe, who served as the expedition's quartermaster general, was one of the few officers to urge an attack, and emerged from the débâcle with an enhanced reputation.

That autumn, the war ministry dominated by William Pitt, advised by the commander-in-chief Ligonier, sought fresh young officers capable of stemming the dismal tide of defeat: James Wolfe was among those named to serve in North America.

A transatlantic hero

With the temporary rank of brigadier general, in February 1758 Wolfe joined Major-General Jeffery Amherst's strike against the fortified port of Louisbourg, on Cape Breton. There, on 8 June, he commanded the hazardous amphibious assault that secured a vital toehold on the island. Conducted from open rowing boats in the teeth of heavy fire and pounding surf, this was a remarkable and unprecedented feat. During the siege that followed, Brigadier Wolfe was given a roving, independent command. He played an important role in forwarding the operations leading to the surrender of the fortress on 26 July 1758.

Louisbourg's conquest marked a turning point in a war hitherto dominated by depressing bulletins of defeat.

Wolfe's courage and energy impressed his fellow officers, whose letters appeared in newspapers and made him a popular hero for Britons on both sides of the Atlantic. James Wolfe scarcely looked the part. Although 6 feet tall, he was scrawny, with narrow shoulders; red-haired and blue-eyed, his pale freckled features were dominated by a thin upturned nose. Yet Wolfe's unmilitary appearance was irrelevant to his men: they respected him as a fair and vigorous commander, ready to lead from the front.

In late August 1758 Amherst sent Wolfe north to the Bay of Gaspé, with orders to destroy fishing settlements that were vital to French Canada's economy. He fulfilled the task reluctantly, albeit efficiently, before sailing back to Britain with the fleet. Within weeks, he had been interviewed by Pitt and Ligonier. Wolfe was keen to fight again, preferably in Germany, although he was not averse to serving against the French in Canada. By December, Wolfe had been selected to command the most important campaign of the coming season, against Quebec. This was more than he had bargained for, but he felt duty bound to accept nonetheless. Still only a colonel in the army, Wolfe was given the rank of major-general for the expedition.

Detailed instructions made it clear that Wolfe's campaign and the other major offensive against Canada – which was to proceed via the Champlain valley under Amherst, Britain's commander-in-chief in North America

– were to complement each other by dividing its defenders. Wolfe was promised an army of 12,000 men, and the support of three brigadiers: Robert Monckton, George Townshend and James Murray. All were older than Wolfe. And unlike their commanding officer, who came from a 'middling', if respectable, background, all were aristocrats. Both factors may have contributed to tensions that emerged during the campaign for Quebec.

The Quebec command

In February 1759 Wolfe sailed from Spithead with Vice Admiral Charles Saunders. He took with him a miniature of his fiancée, Katherine Lowther, plus another keepsake – a copy of Thomas Gray's *Elegy Written in a Country Churchyard*. During the tedious Atlantic crossing Wolfe annotated the book, underscoring the last line of one verse: 'The paths of glory lead but to the grave.'

Icy weather delayed the expedition's concentration at the designated departure point, Louisbourg, and it was early June – a month behind schedule – before it sailed for Quebec. The skill of Saunders' sailors made short work of the St Lawrence's navigational hazards, and by 27 June the task force was anchored off the Isle of Orléans, within 4 miles of Quebec.

Wolfe had hoped to land on the low northern shore below Quebec then fight his way across the St Charles

River to attack the city on its weak western side. This plan proved untenable: the whole Beauport shoreline from Quebec down to the Montmorency falls was heavily fortified. In addition, these defences sheltered a large army – no less than 14,000 men – under an experienced and capable officer, the 47-year-old Louis-Joseph, Marquis de Montcalm. Wolfe's own army was significantly smaller than promised, barely 9,000 strong. In a total reversal of military convention, Wolfe was heavily outnumbered by the force he was besieging. Unlike Montcalm's troops, however, Wolfe's were all veteran regular soldiers. If they could be brought face-to-face with the enemy, he was confident that their discipline and courage would prevail.

But how was Wolfe to achieve his objective? With barely three months before the onset of autumn there was no time to lose. In coming weeks, like a wrestler seeking to grapple a wily opponent, Wolfe tried a variety of moves. All were shrugged off. In early July, an attempt to land at St Michel, on the north shore above Quebec, was abandoned because naval support was inadequate. Indeed, while a powerful fleet had transported Wolfe's redcoats to Quebec, its subsequent usefulness was proscribed by broad shoals, a fierce ebb tide and prevailing westerly winds that left few chances to push into the upper river. A brief change in the wind allowed a handful of vessels to pass Quebec on 18–19 July, but they were not enough to change the strategic balance.

When a major British attack was finally launched on 31 July, on the Beauport lines below Quebec, it was decisively rebuffed. Anticipated support from Amherst's army failed to materialize, and by early August the frustrated Wolfe had resorted to ravaging the countryside, in hopes of luring Montcalm from behind his trenches. But the marquis refused to budge.

Since arriving before Quebec, Wolfe had suffered poor health, with his gravel exacerbated by dysentery. But in late August a severe fever left him bedridden. On 27 August, while 'indisposed', he invited his increasingly truculent brigadiers to 'consult' together upon 'the best method of attacking the enemy'. Exploiting a sudden change in the wind that allowed more British ships to move upriver on the night of 27/28 August, they proposed transferring operations above Quebec. Their recommended landing zone stretched for some 12 miles beyond Cap Rouge bay, itself about 8 miles from the city.

Wolfe accepted his brigadiers' advice, although with little enthusiasm. On 5 September the British began moving upriver, and most of the army embarked aboard the fleet, now strong enough to mount a full-scale landing. Wolfe and his brigadiers approved an attack for the morning of 9 September, at an unspecified location 'a little below Pointe-aux-Trembles', but this was cancelled due to heavy rain. The same day, Wolfe made a lone reconnaissance downriver, then rejected the brigadiers' plan in favour of his own objective – the cliff-backed Anse au Foulon, a cove less than 2 miles from Quebec. The attack was scheduled to go in at about 4 a.m. on 13 September.

By landing so close to Quebec, Wolfe's critics argue, he added an unnecessary element of risk. But his plan had important advantages: it allowed him to strike between the enemy's two main forces, under Colonel Bougainville at Cap Rouge, and Montcalm at Beauport, and to concentrate all his available troops, including two battalions left downriver. Suggestions that Wolfe never expected his scheme to succeed, even that it was a face-saving 'suicide mission', do not withstand scrutiny. And although certainly risky, Wolfe's strategy was not reckless, but based on solid intelligence and meticulous planning. Above all, it was calculated to deliver what Wolfe had sought all summer – a stand-up fight with Montcalm's army. It achieved nothing less.

The Amphibious Assault on Quebec

Wolfe's assault on the cove of Anse au Foulon involved a phased concentration of troops: the first wave, consisting of 1,700 men, was to be spearheaded by 400 crack light infantry, commanded by Colonel William Howe. They would be followed by the second division, another 1,900 infantry plus artillery and stores. Once these troops had disembarked, the empty boats were to row directly across the St Lawrence, where two more battalions would be waiting. Success would hinge upon clockwork timing, the professionalism of British soldiers and sailors alike – and a measure of luck. All three factors played a part in the coming operation.

Wolfe's troops began boarding their landing craft at about 9 p.m. on 12 September. Tense hours of waiting followed. Meanwhile, the British batteries at Pointe aux Pères bombarded Quebec. Crucially, around midnight, the boats of Saunders' warships below Quebec assembled off the Beauport shore, as if preparing for an assault there. This feint succeeded in fixing Montcalm's attention away from Wolfe's objective. Finally, at about 2 a.m. on 13 September, as the tide began to run swiftly past the anchorage, the signal to cast off was given.

Following the north shore in a long silent string, the boats of the first wave reached within a mile of their target without incident. Off Sillery they encountered a British sloop, HMS *Hunter*. Her crew gave timely intelligence, communicated just hours before by two French deserters: Quebec expected a provision convoy from Montreal that very night. When Wolfe's lead boats were soon after challenged by sentries on the shore, a quick-thinking Scottish officer, Captain Simon Fraser, fooled them by explaining that they were the convoy. Here, luck came to Wolfe's help:

although the convoy had been cancelled, no news of this reached Quebec; and as no password had been agreed, Fraser's *'Vive le roi'* was sufficient.

Almost exactly on schedule, at just after 4 a.m., Wolfe's leading boats landed at the Anse au Foulon. They overshot slightly, beaching to the right of the path running up from the cove. Undaunted, Howe and his light infantry scaled the shale cliff that loomed directly in front of them. Gaining the summit, they dispersed the picket guarding the path. With the way cleared, the redcoat battalions swiftly disembarked, scrambling up the path and cliff. The ships of the second division arrived on cue; once they too had landed, the third wave of troops was ferried over from the south shore.

By about 8 a.m. a force of 4,500 redcoats, complete with artillery, had gained the heights and stood arrayed on the Plains of Abraham, within a mile of Quebec. Remarkably, all had gone precisely as Wolfe intended. It was a classic combined operation, a triumph of organization, discipline, improvisation – and leadership.

The Plains of Abraham

Montcalm had spent an anxious night watching the shore below Quebec. Rumours that British troops had landed at the Anse au Foulon reached him at about 6 a.m. Bougainville at Cap Rouge only heard the news at 9 a.m.

An hour later, long before Bougainville could intervene, Montcalm attacked Wolfe at the head of 4,500 men.

The French advanced bravely enough but Wolfe's men, with exemplary discipline, held their fire until they were just 40 yards away. Their relentless volleys broke the assault within minutes. Fixing bayonets, the redcoats advanced to clinch their victory. Wolfe had shrugged off two flesh wounds early in the fight, but as he led forward his grenadiers, two more bullets slammed into his chest. Wolfe swiftly bled to death, living just long enough to learn that his men had beaten the enemy.

The clash was short but bloody: the British lost about 660, the French an estimated 1,500, with Montcalm and many of his senior officers slain. Although much of Montcalm's army escaped, the psychological blow was decisive: Quebec surrendered on 18 October 1759.

Apotheosis

Wolfe's final dispatch to Pitt, written on 2 September 1759 and received in London on 14 October, gave little cause to think that Quebec would fall that year. When, just two days later, tidings of victory arrived, they sparked an explosion of rejoicing, given added poignancy by news of Wolfe's death. For Britons still facing the prospect of French invasion, Wolfe epitomized a new mood of patriotic defiance, and a revival of national pride. His prominence in the *annus mirabilis* of 1759, which saw British victories on three continents, was only reinforced by the exploits of his old regiment, the 20th Foot, that August at the Battle of Minden in Germany.

The dramatic events at Quebec inspired outpourings of verse, mostly turgid, but it was the painters who really exploited them. Several had already tackled the theme of Wolfe's death before the young American Benjamin West created a sensation in 1771 with his epic version of the scene. Engraved in 1776, it became one of the era's most popular images, a largely fanciful depiction of martyrdom for king and country that fascinated the young Horatio Nelson.

Wolfe's conduct at Quebec will always generate debate among military historians. A single campaign, however important, is perhaps insufficient grounds upon which to decide whether or not a general merits the mantle of 'great commander'. Yet without Wolfe's determination and leadership, the siege of Quebec would undoubtedly have ended very differently. While James Wolfe's merits as a strategist remain open to question, his status as a fighting soldier and inspirational leader is beyond dispute.

NATHANAEL GREENE

1742–86

STEPHEN BRUMWELL

MAJOR GENERAL NATHANAEL GREENE was never victorious in battle. Yet his remarkable career throughout the American War of Independence provides striking proof that campaigns, not battles, decide wars. In the crucial Southern campaign of 1781, Greene's ability to grind down his enemies through harassment and evasion prefigured the guerrilla strategies of other revolutionary commanders obliged to pit largely irregular forces against the conventional armies of imperial powers.

For a general, Nathanael Greene's background was improbable. He was born near East Greenwich, Rhode Island, on 27 July 1742, into one of the colony's leading families of Quakers, a pacifist sect that eschewed formal education beyond the reading, writing and reckoning necessary for leading a godly existence and to make a living.

The self-taught soldier

The Greenes fared well enough, establishing a farm, sawmill and forge. But young Nathanael had wider interests. Hungry for knowledge, he devoured books, particularly military memoirs ranging the centuries from Julius Caesar to Frederick the Great. Despite his obsession with martial glory, Greene looked set for the unwarlike role of entrepreneur. As he entered his thirties, however, escalating tensions between Britain and her North American colonies intervened, transforming him into a dedicated opponent of British policy.

In 1774, as war loomed, Greene joined a local militia company. When this unit was embodied as the 'Kentish Guards', he assumed that his military knowledge and local prominence would ensure his election to officer. Instead, to his shame and chagrin, Greene's comrades spurned him because his slight limp – the result of a childhood accident – spoiled their parades. Greene soldiered on, and his persistence was soon rewarded: in May 1775, when Rhode Island responded to the outbreak of fighting in neighbouring Massachusetts by raising a 1,500-strong 'army of observation', he was invited to command it.

Within weeks, Greene and his men joined the American forces besieging General Thomas Gage and his redcoats in Boston. Greene missed the bloody clash at Bunker Hill in June, but absorbed its lessons: the British might have 'won' the battle, yet their horrific casualties made it a bitter victory. That month the Continental Congress in Philadelphia adopted the troops surrounding Boston as the 'Continental army', appointing George Washington its commander-in-chief. Greene, who had won notice for the efficiency of his Rhode Islanders, gained the rank of brigadier general. At 33, he was the youngest general in the entire American army.

Washington and Greene first met at Cambridge, Massachusetts, on 4 July 1775. The Virginian planter and New England forge-master could not have been more different in background, yet they shared core ideals and beliefs, above all that American liberty could only be sustained by a professional, long-service army – not amateur militiamen. From the outset, Greene was devoted to Washington, serving him with an unswerving loyalty. Washington reciprocated by trusting Greene implicitly, and giving him ever-greater responsibility. In the grim years to come, they would form a formidable military partnership.

Precarious apprenticeship
The dreary siege of Boston dragged on until March 1776,

when Gage's successor, General William Howe, withdrew to Halifax, Nova Scotia. It was clear the British would return, with New York their obvious destination. Washington ordered Greene there with a brigade, and when he arrived in April gave him command of Long Island. Heavily fortified, this was the key to the defence of New York and the strategically vital Hudson River. Greene's daunting responsibilities brought promotion to major-general, but when the British assault finally came in August, he was too ill to meet it. As Greene battled a 'raging fever', Howe's army mauled Washington's outnumbered troops, forcing them to withdraw to Manhattan.

In early September the recovered Greene advised Washington to burn and abandon New York. Congress baulked at torching the city, but the evacuation went ahead. On 16 September Greene faced combat for the first time at Harlem Heights, acquitting himself coolly. A question-mark remained over Fort Washington, above Harlem on the Hudson's east bank. Washington was inclined to evacuate its defenders, but Greene believed the fort could be held, and reinforced its garrison to 3,000. This was a fatal miscalculation. On 16 November Howe stormed the fort, bagging the entire garrison. Greene's blunder drew heavy criticism, but Washington refused to dismiss him. His fortunes remained uncertain: just days later, while the evacuation of Fort Lee, New Jersey, was proceeding, news arrived that 5,000 British troops under Lord Charles Cornwallis had crossed the Hudson and were closing fast. Greene escaped, but it was not the last time he would find the determined Cornwallis snapping at his heels.

In the coming weeks Washington's dejected army retreated through New Jersey, enduring appalling weather. On 8 December 1776 it crossed the Delaware River into Pennsylvania. Although Washington had been bundled out of New Jersey, British garrisons there were dangerously isolated. Aware that many of his men's enlistments expired at New Year, Washington decided to take the offensive while he still could. A bold plan was agreed: three columns would cross the Delaware on Christmas Day to attack the 1,500 Hessian troops in Trenton. In icy darkness the complex plan swiftly unravelled, and only the main column, under Washington and Greene, reached its target, at 8 a.m. on 26 December. But surprise was total, and the Hessians were routed. An exultant Greene urged a vigorous pursuit. Reluctant to risk what he had won, Washington instead returned to Pennsylvania.

Trenton was a momentous victory, and Greene, who had spearheaded the attack, received a taste of the glory he craved. More was to come. Buoyed up by this timely success, Washington re-crossed the Delaware on 30 December. His reinvigorated army of 5,000 men, with Greene commanding a division, established defensive positions outside Trenton. Soon after, Cornwallis arrived at Princeton, some 12 miles off. Leaving three regiments to hold the college town, he went after Washington with his main force. But the wily Virginian gave Cornwallis the slip, using back roads to strike instead at the heavily outnumbered garrison of Princeton on 3 January 1777. Another victory followed, with Greene once more conspicuous for battle-field leadership.

Its morale restored, the Continental army went into winter quarters at Morristown, New Jersey. For Greene, no less than Washington, the Trenton–Princeton campaign was a turning point, reviving his self-esteem after the igno-minious loss of Forts Washington and Lee.

Washington's right-hand man

In spring 1777 Washington sent Greene to Philadelphia as his representative in talks with Congress. The experience underlined the dichotomy between the Revolution's politi-cians and its soldiers, the talkers and the fighters: frustra-tion with Congress would become a familiar theme in Greene's correspondence.

That summer, Howe's intentions remained unclear. Would he march up the Hudson, to join forces with General John Burgoyne, advancing south from Canada, or strike at Philadelphia? Howe eventually chose the second option, sailing to Maryland and advancing from there on 8

September. Washington prepared to stop him at Brandy-wine Creek, Pennsylvania. Greene was again given a key responsibility, holding the centre of the American line at Chadd's Ford. But when the British attacked, on 11 September, Howe virtually ignored Greene's position, opting instead for a flanking attack on Washington's right. Marching to the crisis point, Greene prevented retreat from escalating into rout.

Howe had beaten Washington yet failed to deliver a knockout blow. Naturally optimistic, Greene was undis-couraged by this setback. Brandywine underlined another Greene trait: eager for recognition and acutely sensitive of his personal reputation, he was disgruntled that Wash-ington's report to Congress had not mentioned his services.

On 26 September 1777 the British occupied Philadel-phia. However, Washington's army remained in the field, and by 3 October was reinforced to 11,000 men – enough to take the offensive against Howe's 8,000. Greene and his colleagues urged an attack upon the main British encamp-ment at Germantown. The plan followed that which had delivered victory at Trenton, with multiple columns mounting a surprise night assault. Greene played a pivotal role, heading three divisions. But the ambitious paper plan soon fell apart on the ground. Conditions were misty, and Greene's column momentarily lost its way. To add to Greene's problems, when he got back on track, one of his divisional commanders, the drunken Adam Stephen, opened fire on his fellows. Regaining their balance, the British counter-attacked, forcing Washington to retreat.

The Americans had been beaten once more but, as before, their performance had been far from despicable, and with a little luck the outcome might have been very different. Other revolutionaries, including leaders of Congress, took a bleaker view of Washington's campaign. Their criticisms of the commander-in-chief and his influential adviser Greene grew more strident when, just days after Germantown, news arrived that the Patriots' northern army under General Horatio Gates had decisively defeated Burgoyne at Saratoga. Perhaps the triumphant Gates and not the seemingly indecisive Washington should assume the chief command?

Washington kept his place, but Congress's opinion of his confidant Greene, was not improved when he voted against their proposal to eject Howe from Philadelphia. Instead, the Continental army broke camp and took up new winter quarters, north of Philadelphia, at Valley Forge.

Quartermaster general

During the winter of 1777–8, the Continental army faced other enemies than the British. A crisis of supply and transport demanded the attentions of a competent quartermaster. Washington pleaded with Greene to take the job. First and foremost a fighting soldier, Greene was loath to exchange his place in the line for such an inglorious and onerous role. He finally accepted the office – but solely from loyalty to Washington.

The Valley Forge winter was not wasted. While the Prussian officer Friedrich von Steuben overhauled the Continental army's drill, Greene placed its logistics on a firm footing, establishing strategically placed supply depots. Heartened by news that the French had signed a treaty of alliance with the fledgling United States, Washington's long-suffering soldiers faced the approaching campaigning season with renewed confidence.

Discredited by Burgoyne's fiasco, William Howe had been replaced by Sir Henry Clinton. With the French in the war, British strategists believed that the occupation of Philadelphia was no longer viable. In mid June, Clinton's army began a sluggish withdrawal into New Jersey, bound for New York. Washington's remodelled army pursued, its progress expedited by Greene's reforms.

Despite his administrative duties, Greene badgered Washington for a combat role – and a vigorous move against Clinton's rearguard. On the stiflingly hot 28 June 1778, 5,000 men under General Charles Lee attacked the British near Monmouth Courthouse. Lee was soon in trouble: Clinton's rearguard had been bolstered by elite troops led by the ubiquitous Cornwallis. Greene was ordered to support the first assault, but on learning of Lee's repulse fell back to reinforce Washington's main position. He buttressed the American right, facing and rebuffing his old rival, Cornwallis. Washington's line held, and the bloodied British continued on their way to New York.

In military terms, Monmouth Courthouse was a draw. Yet the psychological victory lay with the Americans, who gained a further fillip with the arrival of a French fleet off New Jersey, under Admiral Charles d'Estaing. The war's first Franco-American offensive, against British-held Newport, Rhode Island, was to be commanded by General John Sullivan. Greene, who orchestrated the operation's logistics, obtained leave to join the campaign in his home state. The attack was scheduled for August, but the allies soon fell out. When d'Estaing's fleet suffered storm damage that forced a refit in Boston, Sullivan raged at this 'betrayal'. Irate himself, Greene nonetheless knew the alliance was paramount, and worked to smooth ruffled French feathers.

By early summer 1779 the war's northern theatre was stalemated: the British held New York and Newport, while Washington's troops occupied Boston and Philadelphia. That autumn, however, the conflict's mainland axis shifted. In October the British took Savannah, Georgia, rekindling hopes that the Lower South would host a victorious drive north through Virginia.

Clinton and Cornwallis sailed south to exploit the situation. By contrast, Washington and Greene stayed focused on the Hudson valley, fixing their winter quarters on familiar ground at Morristown. There, quartermaster general Greene kept the kernel of the Continental army fed and clothed through an exceptionally severe winter. With money scarce, supplies ran perilously low. By May 1780 the famished troops were poised to mutiny. This crisis was only compounded by bleak tidings from the South: the 6,000-strong garrison of Charleston under General Benjamin Lincoln had fallen to Clinton's siege. This was Fort Washington writ large, the worst Patriot defeat of the war. Horatio Gates was sent south to take command. But the hero of Saratoga soon made a bad situation worse. On 16 August, at Camden, South Carolina, he rushed into battle with Cornwallis and was routed, losing both his army and his reputation.

As if these dire tidings were not enough, one of the Revolution's best fighters, Greene's close friend, Benedict Arnold, defected to the British. Luckily, Arnold's plot to betray the vital Hudson stronghold of West Point – in Greene's words 'treason of the blackest dye' – misfired when his British contact Major John André was captured. After a court martial presided over by Greene, André was hanged as a spy on 2 October. Less than two weeks later Greene, who had finally resigned as quartermaster general, was appointed Congress's new commander of the Southern Department.

Commander in the south

Greene's first independent command seemed a poisoned chalice. Not only was he obliged to restore the morale of a demoralized army, but he must also browbeat the war-weary and apathetic southern states into recruiting, feeding, clothing and arming replacements for the men squandered at Charleston and Camden. Wary of sharing the fate of Gates, Greene resolved to avoid a battlefield confrontation with the aggressive Cornwallis, and instead to wear his opponent down by a rambling winter campaign across the south's punishing terrain, aided by Patriot partisans already seasoned in a vicious civil war with local Loyalists.

On 2 December 1780 Greene assumed command at Charlotte, North Carolina. Two weeks later he boldly divided his army in the face of the enemy. Greene marched south-east, into South Carolina, camping near Cheraw Hill on the Pee Dee River. Meanwhile, a detachment of 600 men, under Brigadier General Daniel Morgan, moved southwest to distract Cornwallis's left flank. Morgan achieved much more: on 17 January 1781, at Cowpens, he eliminated a British force under the ruthless Colonel Banastre Tarleton.

Enraged, Cornwallis followed the retreating Morgan into North Carolina, determined to destroy both him and

Greene. To speed his pursuit he jettisoned all excess baggage, including the soldiers' tents and even their cherished rum. Learning that Cornwallis had been reinforced to 2,500 men, Greene sought to reunite his own forces. The rendezvous was fixed at Salisbury, yet the pace of the chase forced a switch to Guilford Court House, deeper within North Carolina. Cornwallis was gaining swiftly, but unlike Greene, who was moving ever nearer to his supplies in Virginia, he was daily marching further from his own logistical base in South Carolina. Cornwallis nonetheless believed he had trapped Greene against the Yadkin River. But Greene's stint as quartermaster general had served him well: flatboats were waiting to ferry him over in the nick of time.

On 9 February 1781 Greene and Morgan linked up as planned. With just over 2,000 men, Greene had a choice: stand and fight, or retreat another 70 miles to the Dan, crossing that river into Virginia. North Carolina was conceded, but Greene still had to out-distance Cornwallis, now just 35 miles away. On 10 February Greene again split his command, detaching 700 men under Colonel Otho Williams as a screening force. Cornwallis was convinced that Greene was heading for the Dan's upper fords. But Greene had boats waiting downriver, and Williams delayed Cornwallis long enough for him to reach them first. On St Valentine's Day 1781, Greene's army crossed the Dan, concluding a model strategic retreat.

Denied his prey, the frustrated Cornwallis marched his weary men 60 miles back to Hillsborough. There, he issued a victory proclamation. But the words rang hollow.

Re-supplied, rested and reinforced, Greene returned to North Carolina on 22 February. Knowing that Cornwallis was ground down by the futile 'race to the Dan', Greene determined to engage him in battle. Cornwallis eagerly accepted the challenge. They met on 15 March 1781, at Guilford Court House. With 4,400 Continentals and militia, Greene outnumbered his opponent by more than two to one. Undaunted, the bullish Cornwallis launched his veterans in a frontal assault. After savage fighting, the earl held the field, but with 25 per cent casualties, his was a Pyrrhic victory. The exasperated Cornwallis turned north, bound for Virginia – and disaster.

Following his exhausting campaign and costly victory at Guilford Court House, Cornwallis's shattered little army limped off to Wilmington, and thence to Virginia, leaving British posts in South Carolina vulnerable to Greene's forces. While Patriot partisans ranged widely, Greene decided to confront Britain's next commander in South Carolina, Lord Francis Rawdon, who headed 1,500 men at Camden. On 25 April, at Hobkirk's Hill, Greene sustained another tactical defeat but once again scored a strategic victory, inflicting casualties that obliged Rawdon to retreat to Charleston. By July 1781 British forces in the Lower

South were hemmed within a coastal band between that port and Savannah.

As crown influence waned, Greene sought battle with Rawdon's successor, Lieutenant Colonel Alexander Stewart. In a confused encounter at Eutaw Springs on 8 September, Greene was denied outright victory, although here, too, the British sustained losses they could ill afford. Thereafter the war wound down, with Greene's army watching Charleston and Savannah until the British evacuated in 1782. By then, the Revolutionary War had already been decided in Virginia. In July 1781, after two months of inconclusive manoeuvring, Cornwallis dug in at Yorktown. A British fleet failed to reach him, and the inexorable tightening of American–French siege lines forced his surrender on 19 October 1781.

Preoccupied elsewhere, Greene did not witness the culmination of his efforts. Ironically, the self-taught soldier who had done so much to secure American liberty had scant opportunity to reap the rewards and recognition that he had earned from the new Republic, or to enjoy his young family. Mired in debt and hounded by creditors, Greene died suddenly at his Georgia plantation in June 1786, apparently from heatstroke. He was just 44 years old.

The decisive battlefield victory that Greene hankered after eluded him, yet his contribution to the winning of American independence was unquestionable, second only to that of the man to whom he was devoted. Indeed, of the American generals created at Boston in 1775, only Greene and Washington remained in service by the time of Yorktown. During those years, Greene learned his soldiering through hard experience, demonstrating flexibility, leadership, an instinct for guerrilla warfare, and, above all, an unrelenting belief in the ultimate victory of his cause.

NAPOLEON BONAPARTE

1769–1821

PHILIP DWYER

NAPOLEON HAS GONE DOWN IN HISTORY as one of the most successful generals of all time, and the reputation is, on the face of it, deserved. In the twenty-year period in which he commanded French revolutionary armies and then the imperial Grande Armée, he fought in eleven campaigns, personally conducted more than sixty battles (the vast majority of which he won) and defeated every major European power, except Britain. At the height of his power in 1807, at the age of 38, he ruled over a territory comparable to that of Charlemagne; that is, almost all of western Europe. Napoleon was much more than a general, however. He was also one of the most successful politicians of all time, combining a skilful use of propaganda and reform to create a legacy that is still felt today.

Born in Corsica on 15 August 1769, one year after the French occupation of the island, into a family of local notables, Napoleone di Buonaparte was the second surviving child of Carlo and Letizia (*née* Ramolino). He spent his youth on the island until, at the age of 9, he was sent to Brienne in the north of France to get a French military education. In 1784, at the age of 15, he was sent to the École Militaire in Paris, where he graduated the following year as a second lieutenant in the royal artillery.

Embarking on a military career

Napoleon's first posting was to La Fère Regiment in Valence, considered one of the best, if not the best, artillery regiment in France at the time. Over the next few years Napoleon would move between Corsica and France, torn between loyalty to his island and a career in the French army. With the coming of the French Revolution in 1789, Napoleon became deeply involved in Corsican politics. He and his brothers attempted to ingratiate themselves with the leading Corsican politician of the time, Napoleon's childhood hero, Pasquale Paoli. The Buonapartes also aligned themselves with the radical Jacobin faction in France. It was partly as a result of this, and partly as a result of the clan-based nature of Corsican politics, that the Buonapartes eventually fell out with the Paolist faction on the island.

Things became so bad that the family was obliged to flee for their lives in 1793.

The Buonapartes landed as political refugees in the south of France in June 1793. Napoleon's fate would now be tied to that of France and the Revolution. His first big break came a few months later when he took part in the siege of Toulon, a port town that had been captured by the British (among other allies). It was there that Napoleon first came to the notice of some powerful men, including Augustin Robespierre, the brother of Maximilien Robespierre, the head of the Committee of Public Safety, and Paul Barras, a deputy to the Convention, who would go on to become the leading politician in France under the Directory. It was as a result of his performance at Toulon that Napoleon was promoted to brigadier general.

Nevertheless, in the mercurial world of French revolutionary politics, in the blink of an eye political leaders and incompetent generals could find themselves staring into a basket waiting for the blade to drop. Thus Napoleon, after the arrest and execution of Robespierre in July 1794, briefly found himself in prison because of his Jacobin political associations. He was released, but 'purged' from the artillery and ordered to the west of France to take part in suppressing the revolts there. Napoleon baulked, staying in Paris in the hope that something better would turn up. It did, in the form of an uprising by royalist sympathizers in Paris known as the Coup of 13 Vendémiaire (5 October 1795), because of the revolutionary month in which it took place. Barras remembered Napoleon from Toulon and employed him to protect the Convention and to organize the artillery. It set the scene for the famous 'whiff of grapeshot' story that has Napoleon ordering cannon to fire on the crowds, but there is no proof that he either gave the order or was present – if indeed the event ever took place at all.

The rise to power

Nevertheless, as a reward for his role in suppressing the coup, Napoleon was promoted to general of division, and named commander-in-chief of the Army of the Interior, probably the most influential military position in the country. It was around this time, in October 1795, that Napoleon met Rose de Beauharnais, better known to history as Joséphine, and started courting her. They married on 9 March 1796. He was 27, she was 33. Two days later Napoleon rode off to take control of the Army of Italy. He had been harassing his political masters for an army command for some time, and they had finally relented.

Napoleon's military experience up to that point had been limited. He had helped put down a few riots, partic-ipated in a disastrous expedition to take Sardinia, taken part in the siege of Toulon and accompanied the revolutionary army into northern Italy in 1794, but that was the extent of it. Most of his military ideas came from books, not battle-field experience, and a good tactician does not always make for a good general. In Italy, Napoleon was to discover some-thing that perhaps even he did not suspect: he was a bril-liant strategist. In a series of battles fought throughout 1796 and into 1797 – Montenotte, Millesimo, Mondovi, Cherasco, Lodi, Castiglione, Arcola and Rivoli – Napoleon defeated first the Piedmontese and then a number of Austrian armies. It was here that Napoleon put his ideas into practice, perfecting strategic ideas and battle techniques he had largely inherited from others. It was also during this period that he learned how to govern conquered peoples, creating a number of nominally independent sister republics that were in fact subordinated to France. Finally, he learned how to manipulate the media of the day to his own advantage. The military campaign was also a political campaign, which ended in October 1797 with the Treaty of Campo Formio. Britain was now the only power still at war with revo-lutionary France.

When Napoleon returned to France in December 1797 he briefly considered, but dropped, the possibility of an invasion of England. Instead, Napoleon and the then minister for foreign affairs, Charles-Maurice de Talleyrand, persuaded the French revolutionary government, the Directory, to consent to sending an expeditionary force to Egypt. It was justified as an indirect means of attacking Britain (possibly through India) as well as a scientific expedition that gave it the veneer of a 'civilizing mission'. Napoleon successfully evaded the British fleet under Nelson in the Mediterranean and landed in Egypt at the beginning of July 1798. After a painful march across the desert, the French made short shrift of the Mameluke army at the Battle of the Pyramids and entered Cairo. Nelson's victory over the French fleet at the Battle of the Nile (2 August) left Napoleon with a limited number of options, one of which was to pre-empt a Turkish counter-attack on Egypt by marching into Syria at the beginning of 1799. The most notable episode of this phase of the campaign was the massacre of Jaffa, not only of the towns-people but also of thousands of prisoners. The French advance was stalled at St Jean of Acre; lack of siege artillery and the presence of the plague did not help, but nor did the actions of Sir Sidney Smith, who helped organize if not galvanize the defence. Napoleon decided to return to Egypt in a retreat that resembled in many respects the long march from Moscow twelve years later. He returned in time to defeat a Turkish army that had landed at Aboukir Bay (25 July), almost one year to the day since he had entered Cairo. Shortly afterwards, Napoleon took the decision to leave (or abandon) the army in Egypt and return to France.

His landing in the south of France caused a sensation, coinciding as it did with news of the victory at Aboukir. He was soon approached by a number of conspirators, disaffected politicians who wanted to overthrow the notoriously corrupt government and to introduce a new constitution. They needed a 'sword' that would lend military support to the coup they intended carrying out. Napoleon, however, hijacked the whole process and imposed himself on the conspirators. On 9 November 1799 the coup of 18 Brumaire, as it became known, nominally brought Napoleon to power along with two other consuls, but it was evident from the start that only one consul counted.

The conquest of Europe

Napoleon quickly established his position both within France and without, firstly by introducing a series of reforms that consolidated the gains of the Revolution and which culminated in a concordat with the Catholic Church and the introduction of the Code Civil (commonly known as the Napoleonic Code), and secondly by quickly bringing the War of the Second Coalition to an end. Napoleon's second Italian campaign was marked by the closely fought Battle of Marengo (14 June 1800), which once again saw the Austrian army withdraw from Italy. The Treaty of Lunéville with Austria (1801) and the Peace of Amiens with Britain (1802) reinforced Napoleon's reputation as a peacemaker.

For the first time since the outbreak of war in 1792, France was at peace. It allowed Napoleon to conduct a plebiscite that named him consul for life in 1802, a major step on the path towards the foundation of a new dynasty and an empire. The Empire was duly proclaimed in May 1804, and in December Napoleon placed the imperial crown on his own head in Notre Dame de Paris.

The Peace of Amiens was, however, short lived. Within eighteen months a third coalition had formed against France, in part because of Napoleon's expansionist behaviour, and in part because neither Britain nor Russia could tolerate French hegemony on the Continent. Between the renewal of hostilities in 1803 and the actual resumption of land operations in 1805, Napoleon and the bulk of the French imperial army were camped in the environs of Boulogne on the French coast, poised to invade Britain. It was only after learning that an alliance between Alexander I of Russia and Francis I of Austria was forming against him, in association with Britain, that Napoleon decided to act. Rather than wait for the eastern powers to strike, Napoleon pre-empted them by marching east from the coast of France into southern Germany. This led to the battles of Ulm (20 October 1805) and Austerlitz (2 December) and the defeat of the Austro-Russian armies.

Austerlitz is recognized as the ultimate Napoleonic battle, but myth and propaganda play just as much a role as the actual battle itself in establishing Napoleon's reputation as one of the greatest military commanders of all time. Much of the campaign that preceded the battle was improvised, and therein lay Napoleon's brilliance.

The battle, sometimes called the Battle of the Three Emperors because of the presence of Tsar Alexander I, Francis I of Austria and Napoleon himself, took place on the Pratzen Heights, about 15 miles east of Brünn (present-day Brno in the Czech Republic), on 2 December 1805 on the first anniversary of Napoleon's coronation. To the south of the heights were two shallow lakes. Prior to the battle, Napoleon abandoned the heights, thus giving the impression that he had made a mistake. And not only did he not occupy the high ground, he was also clearly outnumbered – around 66,000 French troops and 139 cannon compared with 89,000 allied troops and 278 cannon – but a *corps d'armée* of about 6,000 men under Davout was on its way.

The plan was for the French right wing to feign retreat and to hold the bulk of the allied army, which would descend the Pratzen Heights in order to attack and thus leave its strong position. Most of the French cavalry, Oudinot's grenadiers, the Imperial Guard and Bernadotte's corps were concealed on the French left wing. At the right moment, Napoleon would give the order for the French left wing to attack and take the heights. The battle went according to plan. At about 7 a.m. the bulk of the allied army did indeed attack the French right, and were held off, although with difficulty, strengthened by the arrival of Davout. By 9 a.m. Napoleon, correctly thinking that the heights had been abandoned by all allied troops, ordered his centre and left wing to attack. By 3.30 p.m. the French had occupied the heights and were firing on the enemy below, now sandwiched between two French forces. An attempt to extricate the allied troops turned into a rout. Some troops tried to escape across an icy lake, but it broke under a French bombardment. As many as 2,000 died in this way.

Napoleon's strategy at Austerlitz was a calculated risk that could have just as easily not worked. If the battle had been fought only a day earlier, Davout and Bernadotte would not yet have arrived, and the Grande Armée would have faced even bigger odds than it did. A detailed reading of Austerlitz makes it clear that, although an impressive victory for Napoleon, it was a much more difficult battle than is normally described in the history books. Allied casualties were high, some 15,000–16,000 killed and wounded and another 11,000–12,000 taken prisoner, or a third of the allied forces. The French losses were considerably less, some 7,800 killed and wounded and another 500 missing. The next day Francis sued for peace and within a month had signed the Treaty of Pressburg. The Russian forces withdrew into their own territory, leaving Britain the only remaining great power fighting the French. It left

Napoleon master of central Europe, which he began to rearrange by putting an end to the Holy Roman Empire and by creating the Confederation of the Rhine out of a greatly reduced number of states.

Prussia, neutral since 1795, hesitated about joining the coalition against France in 1805, and pulled out at the last minute. With the defeat of its allies, it too was obliged to enter into a humiliating treaty that forced it to occupy Hanover (of which George III of the United Kingdom was prince-elector) and place a blockade on British shipping. The very next year, however, amid rumours of a deal between France and Britain involving Hanover, Prussia delivered an ultimatum to the French to withdraw behind the Rhine. Rather than wait for the arrival of Russian troops, the Prussians acted precipitously and engaged the French at Jena and Auerstädt (14 October 1806; see pp. 244–6). The Prussian army was not what it had been under Frederick the Great; it collapsed, and within weeks French forces had occupied most of the kingdom. Napoleon entered the Prussian capital, whence he issued the Berlin Decrees (21 November), prohibiting all commerce between Britain and the Continent.

The king of Prussia, Frederick William III, was down but not entirely out. His 'friend' and ally Alexander I of Russia lent his support, and Prussian but mostly Russian troops fought two further battles, at Eylau (7–8 February

1807) and Friedland (14 June 1807). After these two defeats, Russia (and Prussia) sued for peace. The resulting Treaty of Tilsit (7 July 1807), signed by Tsar Alexander and Emperor Napoleon on a raft in the middle of the Niemen (with a pitiful Frederick William III waiting to hear the fate of his kingdom on the banks of the river), led to a re-division of the map of Europe: Prussia was reduced to half its size; part of Prussian territory was incorporated into a new Kingdom of Westphalia (ruled by Napoleon's brother Jérôme), and another part became the Duchy of Warsaw. Furthermore, Russia agreed to join France in declaring war on Britain and blockading its goods from mainland Europe (a blockade known as the Continental System).

Downfall and exile

Tilsit is regarded as the zenith of Napoleon's power. He now ruled over a territory that stretched from the River Oder in the east to the Atlantic Ocean in the west, and from the Baltic Sea in the north to Sicily in the south. However, a series of errors in which Napoleon overplayed his hand, beginning with the Continental System – which led, as tradition would have it, to Napoleon's intervention in the Iberian Peninsula from 1807, the invasion of the Papal States in 1808 and even the invasion of Russia in 1812 – ultimately led to his downfall. In Spain, Napoleon overthrew the Spanish branch of the House of Bourbon and placed his brother Joseph on the throne, but soon faced a full-scale revolt. The combination of guerrilla fighters and the landing of a British army to help the Spanish regulars would tie down 200,000–400,000 troops per year and cost almost a quarter of a million casualties. Napoleon briefly intervened in Spain personally, but was distracted when in 1809 a recalcitrant Austria, financed (as was now usually the case) by British money, once more went to war with France. In the campaign that followed, Napoleon suffered his first real loss, at the Battle of Aspern-Essling, against Archduke Charles (May 1809). However, Charles made the mistake of not following up his advantage quickly enough and he was defeated the following month at Wagram. In 1810 Napoleon sealed an alliance with Austria by marrying the 16-year-old princess, Archduchess Marie-Louise, having divorced the childless Joséphine earlier that year.

If relations between France and Austria had been mended, relations with Russia went from good, after Tilsit, to bad (at Erfurt where the two emperors met in 1808), to very bad. Much of this was Napoleon's fault. By 1810 both sides were moving towards war. It nevertheless took another two years before Napoleon crossed the Oder in June 1812 with one of the largest land armies yet seen in Europe. The ensuing campaign was a disaster from beginning to end. Contrary to popular belief, Napoleon lost most of his men to desertion, disease, battle (Smolensk, Borodino;

see pp. 261–3) and the Russian heat well before the Grande Armée reached Moscow. It is debatable whether the Russians deliberately drew Napoleon ever deeper into their heartland, thus extending the lines of supply, but the wisdom of retreating from Moscow back along the same route over which they had come was questionable (see pp. 265–7). Figures vary greatly, but it is likely that Napoleon lost about 400,000 troops, of which less than a quarter would have actually died in battle. As few as 20,000 men survived the ordeal.

The defeat showed just how precarious was Napoleon's empire. He was now forced to fight a rearguard action throughout 1813 in order to hold on to central Europe, a feat that was hampered by a dire lack of cavalry after the Russian fiasco. Even though Napoleon was able to fend off the combined Russo-Prussian armies with a number of victories before June – at Lützen (2 May 1813) and Bautzen (20–21 May) – they were Pyrrhic victories that cost the French twice as many men as their opponents. The entry of Austria into the war in July 1813 shifted the balance of strength in the allies' favour. With that, to paraphrase the historian Peter Paret, Napoleon was suddenly reduced to being just another competent general. The decisive battle came at Leipzig (sometimes known as the Battle of Nations). In the largest land battle to date, raging for four days, 177,000–195,000 French troops fought 320,000–365,000 allied troops. In the end, Napoleon could not hold out against such overwhelming odds and was forced to abandon central Europe. Leipzig was thus a turning point in much the same way that Blenheim was for Louis XIV, or Stalingrad was for Hitler.

The first few months of 1814 saw Napoleon desperately trying to stave off defeat against an allied army that brought all the great powers together for the first time in the history of the wars against France. Despite some brilliant tactical successes, Napoleon could not prevent the allies from entering Paris. The rest is a footnote in history: a first abdication in April 1814 that led to exile on Elba; his return less than a year later; the Hundred Days that ended at Waterloo on 18 June 1815 (a battle that Wellington described as 'the nearest run thing'; see pp. 230–8); the second abdication later that month. Napoleon passed the last years of his life in exile on St Helena, a remote island in the South Atlantic, where, on 5 May 1821, he died of cancer of the stomach.

DUKE OF
WELLINGTON
1769–1852

ANDREW ROBERTS

*ARTHUR WELLESLEY, 1ST DUKE OF WELLINGTON, was –
along with Marlborough – Britain's greatest military commander.
He was also one of its worst prime ministers. While his premier-
ship was fortunately only short-lived, it was more than made up
for by the splendour of a wartime career in which he fought sixty-
two battles and never lost one, at a time of peril when his country
most desperately needed victories.*

Born in Dublin, the fourth son of the 1st Earl of Morn-
ington, Wellesley hailed from the Anglo-Irish aristocratic
'Protestant Ascendancy' that ruled Ireland from Elizabethan
times until the partition of the island in 1922. Educated
firstly at Eton, where he learned little except perhaps how
to use his fists, and then – probably due to a lack of funds

at his father's early death – in Brussels, Wellesley entered the Angers Military Academy in 1786. Although his mother decried the idea of a military career for him, believing him to have no aptitude for soldiering, he was commissioned as a lieutenant in an infantry regiment in 1787 and became a captain of dragoons five years later.

In the meantime he was elected to a seat in the Irish parliament, but took as little interest in politics as he initially did in soldiering, preferring to idle life away socializing and playing the violin. Indeed he might have spent his life as a wallflower attending the picnics of the Irish Lord-Lieutenant as an aide-de-camp had not the French executed their king in 1793, prompting Wellesley suddenly to take his life and career seriously. He burnt his violin in the grate and became a colonel of the 33rd Foot Regiment, in which capacity he saw action against the French at Boxtel in the Netherlands campaign in 1794 and then again at Geldermalsen the following year.

The campaign, which had been intended to culminate in an invasion of France, was short-lived and disastrous, though no blame attached to Wellesley, who performed well, and the incompetence of the British officers prompted him to take up closer study of the military arts. When his elder brother Richard became governor-general of India in 1797, Wellesley took the 33rd Foot out there and founded a great reputation for himself as a brilliant but also painstaking commander. His victories in Mysore and Seringapatam against the sultan of Mysore and over the mercenary king Dhoondiah Waugh won him promotion to major-general.

Fighting next the Marathas, Wellesley won the famous victory of Assaye in south-central India in September 1803, which he personally considered strategically the finest of his battles. He was knighted the following year and in 1805 returned home, stopping off on the way on the remote island of St Helena in the South Atlantic Ocean. From commanding thousands and subduing sub-continents, he was given the command of a lowly battalion in Hastings in 1806, and the same year was elected MP for the Sussex town.

This time around Wellesley took politics seriously, and became Chief Secretary for Ireland in 1807, largely as the result of the influence of his ambitious and influential family, who were prominent Tory politicians. He also found time the same year to take part in the brief Copenhagen campaign, which was not quite as disastrous as earlier British incursions on Napoleon's continent of Europe had been.

The Peninsular War, 1808–14

In 1808, by then a lieutenant general, Wellesley was at last given an opportunity for genuine glory, when he was – albeit too briefly – given command of the British expeditionary force destined for Portugal. He told a friend that he would not be chased off the Continent as so many other similar forces had been, because he had made a study of French tactics and would not be at any kind of psychological disadvantage to the enemy.

'They may overwhelm me but I don't think they will out-manoeuvre me,' he said. 'First, because I am not afraid of them, as everybody else seems to be; and secondly, because if what I hear of their system of manoeuvre is true, I think it a false one against steady troops. I suspect that all the continental armies were more than half beaten before the battle was begun. I, at least, will not be frightened beforehand.'

It was a brave boast, but fully justified by events.

The Peninsular campaign started off well with victories at Roliça and Vimeiro in August, but soon afterwards Wellesley was superseded in command by two generals, Sir Harry Burrard and Sir Hew Dalrymple, who signed the Convention of Cintra (30 August), an armistice with the French that allowed the defeated enemy safe passage back to France with all their arms, baggage and booty, and even transportation in Royal Navy vessels. Back in Britain there was outrage at the terms of the Convention and an 'Inquiry' (which was effectively a court martial) was heard in the Great Hall of the Royal Hospital at Chelsea. Wellesley, Burrard and Dalrymple were all summoned to it, but after several weeks Wellesley was finally acquitted.

Reassuming command in Portugal in 1809, Wellesley – hugely aided at all times by the Portuguese army and the Spanish guerrillas – proceeded to spend the next five years expelling the French from the Iberian Peninsula. He took not one day's leave as he campaigned to and fro across Portugal and Spain, occasionally being forced to retreat because of the pressure of numbers opposing him, but never losing a battle or even so much as a single cannon. He was almost always outnumbered by the huge French forces that were occupying Spain in the name of Napoleon's brother, King Joseph. The leadership Wellesley showed in the Peninsular campaign was exemplary; he won a reputation of expecting the best, and being a harsh disciplinarian when he did not get it. Yet his troops also knew he never risked their lives unnecessarily.

The Battle of Waterloo

Wellesley – who had been elevated to the dukedom of Wellington in 1814 – had crossed the Pyrenees into France just before Napoleon abdicated, after which he become ambassador to Paris. He was then appointed British plenipotentiary to the Congress of Vienna, which is where he was when, in March 1815, the news arrived that the ex-emperor had escaped from his exile on the island of Elba. Pausing only to declare Napoleon an international outlaw, Wellington went to take up command of the Anglo-Allied army in Brussels. He defeated Napoleon in the only battle the two men fought against one another.

If genius is in part the ability to take infinite care over details, then Wellington showed genius at Waterloo on Sunday, 18 June 1815. A master of topography, he personally sited every battalion in his large, polyglot army of 68,000 men, an ungainly mélange of different British, Dutch, Belgian and German formations, a large proportion of which were raw recruits. It was far removed from the seasoned army Wellington had moulded into a crack fighting force during the Peninsular War.

On 12 June Napoleon had suddenly left Paris and marched north into present-day Belgium, making for Brussels. The speed with which he gathered his force of 120,000 men, crossed the Sambre and Meuse rivers and simultaneously attacked the Anglo-Allied army at Quatre Bras and the Prussian army under Field Marshal Prince von Blücher at Ligny on 16 June, suggested that he was back on the form he had shown in the brilliant campaigns of spring 1814. He defeated the Prussians at Ligny and only bad staff work by his Chief of Staff, Marshal Soult, prevented him from utterly routing them.

Wellington was forced to retreat on 17 June to the defensible slopes of Mont St-Jean, 3 miles south of his headquarters at the village of Waterloo. Only 3½ miles wide, the battlefield was protected by woods and villages on both flanks and two well-defended farmhouses – Hougoumont and La Haie Sainte – in the centre. As in so many of his victorious battles in the Peninsular War, Wellington had chosen his ground with an expert eye. Napoleon, meanwhile, made a cardinal error in splitting off a large proportion of his troops under Marshal Grouchy, with orders to prevent the Prussians joining up with Wellington's Anglo-Allied force.

Heavy rainfall on 17 June meant that Napoleon had to wait until about 11.30 a.m. the next day for the muddy ground to firm up enough for his Grand Battery of eighty-four guns to be deployed and begin cannonading Wellington's line. This loss of time proved crucial because, unbeknownst to him, the Prussian army had evaded Grouchy and was marching in force upon his right flank.

Wellington meanwhile ordered some of those regiments in the direct line of fire of the French cannons to lie down behind the ridge, thus minimizing casualties. He used to say that soldiering was largely about guessing accurately what was 'on the other side of the hill', and his seasoned feel for the unusual ground of Waterloo – with its dips, folds and minor escarpments – served him well.

Wellington had invested Hougoumont with some of his best troops – including the light companies of the Foot Guards – because he knew that the loss of that strategic point would allow Napoleon to operate one of the extravagant flanking manoeuvres at which he was expert. The struggle for the farmhouse became a battle-within-a-battle, lasting all day and sucking in some 9,000 French troops, but although a small number of them did enter the court-yard at one point, and the roof caught fire at another, its 3,000 defenders nonetheless held out.

The next great assault on Wellington's position came at 1.30 p.m. when General Comte D'Erlon's huge corps of 16,000 men marched against Wellington's centre-left, in an attempt to punch through Wellington's force, split it in two, and roll each side up on itself. They were at first held back by the accurate musketry of the Anglo-Allied regiments facing them, and then put to flight by a bayonet charge led by Lieutenant General Sir Thomas Picton, who was killed just after it began.

At just the right psychological moment, a cavalry charge of the Union and Household Brigades under the overall command of Wellington's second-in-command, Lord Uxbridge, then turned D'Erlon's fighting retreat into a rout. Two of the four French eagle standards captured that day were taken then. In one of the few tactical errors made on the Anglo-Allied side, much of the cavalry went too far, and were badly mauled by Marshal Ney's lancers. Wellington severely admonished Uxbridge for this.

No-one knows to this day why (or even if) Marshal Ney ordered his huge cavalry assault against the centre-right of Wellington's line at 4 p.m., and there are even indications that it was entirely accidental. It was launched without the infantry and horse artillery support that might have led to its success. Wellington ordered his infantry to form thirteen or so squares, none of which was penetrated by the French cuirassiers. Instead the cavalry rode round and round them, churning up the already muddy fields and exhausting itself, but not finding any way into the self-protective formations of infantrymen bristling with bayonets. Wellington himself took refuge inside one of the squares during this part of the battle.

It is estimated that the duke rode 20 miles that day on his horse, Copenhagen, and he was always directing the most important part of the battle at great personal danger. Almost every member of his immediate staff was either killed or wounded during the battle, so far forward in the line were they at times. Wellington kept a very close and immediate control of every aspect of the struggle against the determined assaults of a veteran, homogeneous French army of 72,000 men.

At about 4.30 p.m. Prussian units of General von Bülow's corps began debouching on to the battlefield from the east, in accordance with a promise that Blücher had made Wellington early that morning. Having successfully evaded Grouchy, they began arriving in ever greater numbers, staving in Napoleon's right flank and forcing him as the battle progressed to divert more and more troops – including parts of his elite Imperial Guard – away from attacking Wellington and towards defending his exposed positions. The question as to whether Wellington would have won the battle without Blücher is an illegitimate one, since he would not even have fought had he thought that no reinforcements were arriving. (Grouchy, by contrast, ignored the cannon-fire to his west and continued to obey the emperor's by then woefully out-of-date orders.)

The crisis came at about 6.30 p.m. when, after much heavy fighting, the farmhouse of La Haie Sainte finally fell to Marshal Ney. The King's German Legion which had been courageously defending it – 90 per cent casualties were incurred within its high walls – finally ran out of ammunition and so had to concede the building to the French besiegers. Wellington later nobly accepted the blame for not having had a hole cut in the back of the farmhouse wall for ammunition to be passed through.

With La Haie Sainte – which commanded the Charleroi–Brussels road – now in French hands, the whole of Wellington's centre was threatened. Ney brought up horse artillery which poured fire into the Anglo-Allied line at short range. Regiments like the 27th Inniskillings which had formed squares took terrible casualties, but somehow held together. 'Ah,' said Wellington after the battle, 'they saved the centre of my line.'

Ney was unable to exploit this significant but temporary success. After D'Erlon's attack and his own cavalry débâcle, and troops being siphoned off to meet the Prussian threat to the west, and with Hougoumont still under siege, there was simply a dearth of troops available to him. Had Grouchy marched to the sound of guns as soon as he heard the Grand Battery open up before noon, it might have been a different matter.

Wellington, meanwhile, brought up reserves to plug holes in the line, occasionally placing British cavalry regiments behind foreign units that looked on the point of breaking. Putting himself at the head of solid Brunswick troops to close a gap between two British brigades, Wellington showed great bravery. As the contemporary historian General Sir James Shaw Kennedy recorded: 'He was necessarily under a close and very destructive infantry fire at a very short distance; at no other period of the day were his great qualities as commander so strongly brought out, for it was the moment of his greatest peril as to the result of the action.' The line held.

The time had come at about 7 p.m. for Napoleon to unleash his eleven elite grenadier and chasseur battalions of the Old and Middle Guard in a final desperate attempt to break through Wellington's line. As he later observed, Wellington was fighting with the dense Forest of Soignies to his rear, with only one road through it, so any retreat would inevitably have turned into a monstrous rout. The French Imperial Guard had provided the *coup de grâce* several times in battles of the past; now was the chance to exploit Wellington's paucity of reserves, spot a weak point in the line and pour through to snatch victory.

Wellington had about a quarter of an hour to meet this challenge and he used it to reorganize his defences, taking care not to allow units to fall back in such a way that might be misinterpreted as a retreat by other hard-pressed troops further down the line. Thirty cannon loaded with double-grapeshot were manoeuvred into position and he placed his reserve cavalry brigades under Major-General Sir Richard Vivian and Major-General Sir John Vandeleur in the best tactical position to deal with any breakthroughs. 'A black mass of the grenadiers of the Imperial Guard,' wrote a British observer, 'with music playing … came rolling onward from the farm of la Belle Alliance.'

The Anglo-Allied line held against three separate and furious assaults by the Imperial Guard, which nonetheless almost managed to reach the crest of the ridge that formed Wellington's line (it is invisible today owing to the subsequent building of the commemorative 130-foot-high Lion Mound). 'The ground was completely covered with those brave men,' recorded a Briton of the dead and dying grenadiers and chasseurs, 'who lay in various positions, mutilated in every conceivable way.'

Crying 'Up, Guards, ready!', Wellington ordered the 1st Regiment of Foot Guards to rise up from the shoulder-height corn and fire a musket volley at virtually point-blank range into the French ranks. Lieutenant Harry Powell later recorded how, 'Whether it was from the sudden and unexpected appearance of a Corps so near them, which must have seemed as starting out of the ground, or the tremendously heavy fire we poured into them, La Garde, which had never before failed in an attack, suddenly stopped.' Once the momentum had drained out of the attack, it was only a matter of time before the superior Anglo-Allied musketry and artillery firepower of the line prevailed over the columns of French. A brilliant flanking movement by Sir John Colborne's 52nd Regiment against the chasseurs of the Guard completed the rout.

Snapping his telescope shut and riding to the crest of the ridge, Wellington then waved his cocked hat, the signal for a general advance across his whole line, crying: 'Go forward, boys, and secure your victory!' The cries from the French, first of *'La Garde recule!'* and then *'Sauve qui peut!'* and *'Nous sommes trahis!'* indicated that Wellington had won his greatest victory of a long and distinguished military career.

After Waterloo

One month later the emperor abdicated and surrendered to the British, who exiled him to the remote island of St Helena in the South Atlantic Ocean.

Wellington was covered in honours both from Britain and all the European powers, but instead of retiring he entered the Cabinet in 1818, staying there as Master-General of Ordinance until 1827. The following year he became prime minister, and, despite being a reactionary Tory he passed Catholic Emancipation in 1829 with the help of Sir Robert Peel, albeit against his private inclinations. He resigned in 1830 when it became clear that he could not prevent parliamentary reform being enacted.

As commander-in-chief of the British Army from 1827 to 1828 and from 1842 to 1852, Wellington was a force for conservatism, and it has been argued that the lack of reforms in his time led to British ill-preparedness for the Crimean War. Yet even if his political and administrative careers were rather less impressive than his military and diplomatic ones, nothing can detract from his untarnishable glory as the conqueror of Napoleon and, along with Marlborough, as one of the two finest commanders Britain has ever produced.

LOUIS-NICOLAS
DAVOUT
1770–1823

ANDREW UFFINDELL

LOUIS-NICOLAS DAVOUT was not the most charismatic of Napoleon's famous twenty-six marshals, for that distinction lay with more colourful but mercurial colleagues, men such as Lannes, Murat and Ney. Where Davout shone was as a consistently professional, competent and just soldier, and as one of the most intelligent and educated of the marshals. He was more than just a heroic combat soldier, and performed some of his most outstanding services off the battlefield. A capable organizer, administrator, logistician and trainer of troops, he was also adept at collecting and evaluating intelligence. The rigour with which he did his duty and his strictness, even harshness, in upholding standards won him respect and resentment in equal measure.

Davout was born on 10 May 1770 in Burgundy in eastern France, and came from an old noble family with a tradition of military service. 'When a d'Avout is born,' it was said locally, 'a sword springs from the scabbard.' After a good education at a royal military school at Auxerre and then at the École Militaire in Paris, Davout joined the Royal-Champagne cavalry regiment in February 1788 as a sub-lieutenant. His out-spokenness and fervent support for the Revolution that broke out the following year contributed to a turbulent period of service and six weeks in a military prison. He then took extended leave, and used the opportunity to study and improve his understanding of his profession.

A military apprenticeship

Davout remained inactive for less than a year. In September 1791 he was elected junior lieutenant colonel of a local battalion of volunteers, and in 1792 saw action against the Austrians in northern France and Belgium. In April 1793 he had his men fire on his own commander-in-chief, Lieutenant General Charles-François Dumouriez, in an unsuccessful attempt to prevent him from deserting to the Austrians.

Despite such notable actions, Davout repeatedly had to overcome setbacks in the early stages of his career. He was promoted to general of brigade in July 1793, but as a former noble he had to resign from the army the following month as the Revolution became more extreme. He and his mother were both arrested and were in danger of being executed until a coup toppled the radical Jacobin faction and ended the Reign of Terror. The episode helps to explain Davout's subsequent support for Napoleon as a strongman who could maintain order and stability. Davout resumed his army service in September 1794, but was captured a year later when the city of Mannheim surrendered to the Austrians. He was exchanged in 1796, and then served in the Rhine theatre until hostilities with Austria ended in April 1797.

During this time, Davout found an influential friend and mentor in General Louis-Charles-Antoine Desaix de Veygoux. It was through Desaix that Davout met Napoleon for the first time and secured a place in his expedition to Egypt in 1798. He repeatedly saw action, particularly when he was detached with Desaix's force to pacify Upper Egypt, and he further distinguished himself during the fighting at Aboukir on the Mediterranean coast in July and August 1799. At one stage he found himself trapped inside a house with about fifteen men, while Ottoman Turks tried to break in. Davout had his men fire through the closed door, killing several assailants, and then, taking advantage of the surprise, broke out with fixed bayonets and reached safety.

Davout returned to France in May 1800 and was promoted to general of division in July. Meanwhile, Napoleon had seized power in a *coup d'état*, and by February 1801 he had secured a peace on the continent of Europe that would last for four years. Davout, who had divorced his first wife in 1794, made a happier marriage with Louise-Aimée-Julie Leclerc in November 1801. Since Aimée was the sister of Napoleon's brother-in-law, Davout became one of the extended Bonaparte clan, and this was undoubtedly one reason for his appointment that same month as commander of the crack *Grenadiers à pied* of the Guard.

When Napoleon established the Empire three years later, Davout was one of eighteen generals to be made marshals. Some commentators have expressed surprise at his selection, not least as he was only 34 years old and the youngest of this first creation. But Napoleon could hardly do otherwise than elevate all four of the Imperial Guard's most senior generals, including Davout, to the marshalate, in order to enhance the Guard's prestige and avoid destructive jealousies among its component units. Napoleon also knew Davout's ability as a soldier, disciplinarian and administrator, and recognized his potential to develop as he assumed higher responsibilities.

Emergence of a great commander
It was Napoleon's campaigns of 1805–9 in central and

eastern Europe that saw Davout emerge as a great battle-field commander. He had already proved himself as a brave and capable subordinate, and had a mixture of experience in both the infantry and cavalry, but had yet to make a name for himself in a large combat command. He was entrusted with the Grande Armée's superb III Corps, a unit he had spent two years training and disciplining in a camp at Bruges, and one that he himself compared with Julius Caesar's renowned Tenth Legion.

On 2 December 1805 Davout played a key role in Napoleon's most famous victory, the Battle of Austerlitz. Summoned northwards from Vienna as Napoleon concentrated his forces for a masterly counter-stroke against the Austro-Russian army, Davout's leading division marched 70 miles in 46 hours. His arrival checked the allied attempt to outflank Napoleon, and made possible the destruction of the allied southern wing (see pp. 218–20).

When hostilities broke out with Prussia in October 1806, Davout helped crush its army with his brilliant but costly victory at Auerstädt, and then took part in a bitter winter campaign against the Russians in Poland and East Prussia. On 8 February 1807 Napoleon was saved from defeat at the bloody Battle of Eylau when Davout arrived with his corps from the south.

Auerstädt was Davout's finest achievement as a commander and the victory from which he took his title when made a duke in 1808. It was a battle won in his own right as an independent commander, without Napoleon's direct supervision.

When war broke out with Prussia in the autumn of 1806, Napoleon advanced northeastwards from southern Germany on Berlin, with his army so disposed that it could turn in any direction and swiftly concentrate once it encountered the enemy.

The Prussians belatedly began to retreat northwards, but were attacked on 14 October in the twin actions of Jena and Auerstädt. Napoleon himself crushed part of the Prussian forces on the heights above the town of Jena, but was unaware that the bulk, 63,500 troops, were in fact 12 miles to the north at Auerstädt, where they faced the 26,000 men of Davout's III Corps.

Auerstädt was an encounter battle, in which both sides unexpectedly ran into each other in thick fog. The fighting developed as Davout's three infantry divisions came into action one after the other, between 7 and 10.30 a.m. For their part, the Prussians generally fought bravely, but failed to exploit their numerical superiority, partly because congestion delayed the arrival of their reinforcements. Even after the fog lifted, they launched a series of disjointed attacks instead of coordinating a general onslaught. Nonetheless, Davout was repeatedly on the brink of defeat, until the arrival of another division enabled him to restore the situation and deliver a further blow.

The confusion on the Prussian side was increased by the dislocation of their high command. The commander-in-chief, Karl Wilhelm Ferdinand, Duke of Brunswick, was mortally wounded, and there was a delay before King Frederick William III could be informed. The king failed to get a grip on the battle and, not realizing that he faced only one corps, decided to retreat. Davout launched a general offensive that overcame heavy resistance and by the end of the day had turned the Prussian withdrawal into a rout.

Napoleon gave III Corps the honour of leading the Grande Armée's entry into Berlin on 25 October. Auerstädt had been a triumph of superior discipline, training, experience and flexible tactics, but, above all, of better generalship. Davout had kept tight control of his corps, skilfully assessed the terrain and the timing of his moves, and personally inspired his men with his coolness under fire. The ability and professionalism of Davout and his famous trio of divisional commanders (Gudin, Friant and Morand) formed a stark contrast to the fumblings of the Prussian generals as they reacted to the French moves. But the cost was high: Davout had lost one in every four of his men.

Following the conclusion of peace with Russia and Prussia at Tilsit in July, Napoleon entrusted Davout with the role of governor-general of the Duchy of Warsaw, a satellite state created from Polish territory previously held by Prussia. Davout was one of the few marshals equal to such important administrative and political roles.

Davout added to his reputation in the 1809 campaign against Austria. He played a key role in the initial phase, the defeat of the Austrian invasion of Bavaria, Napoleon's ally in southern Germany. This culminated in the Battle of Eckmühl on 22 April, where Davout with just 20,000 troops contained the Austrian army under Archduke Charles until Napoleon could arrive and fall on its southern flank. Davout was made Prince of Eckmühl in recognition of his conduct, and he won further laurels in a massive and costly battle at Wagram near Vienna on 5–6 July. As so often, his corps was once again on the right of the line, traditionally the place of honour, and after hard fighting in which he had a horse shot beneath him, Davout drove back the Austrian left wing and contributed to a victory that induced the Austrians to make peace.

The invasion of Russia

It was nearly three years before Davout fought in another campaign. As relations with Tsar Alexander I deteriorated, Napoleon prepared to invade Russia and entrusted Davout with a leading role in assembling an army of over half a million troops. For the actual invasion in June 1812, Davout commanded I Corps, comprising 70,000 men, by far the largest corps and one widely recognized, with its discipline and meticulously organized logistics, as the finest formation in the Grande Armée after the Imperial Guard.

Napoleon failed to trap the Russian armies in the opening weeks of his onslaught, and was instead drawn deeper into the interior as they retreated. It was during these early stages that Davout fought a skilful defensive battle at Mogilev on 23 July, in which he checked a numerically superior Russian army under General Prince Peter Bagration. But it was at Borodino on 7 September that Davout saw the heaviest fighting. Napoleon attacked the Russians head on, and both sides suffered appalling losses. Davout himself was unhorsed, knocked unconscious and wounded in the belly, but refused to leave his command (see also pp. 261–3).

Napoleon occupied Moscow a week later, but found that Alexander I refused to sue for peace. Five weeks after his arrival, Napoleon abandoned the city and was soon in full retreat. Undermined by relentless marching, exhaustion, indiscipline, inadequate supplies and spells of snow and bitter cold, the Grande Armée became increasingly demoralized and began to disintegrate. Davout's corps initially formed the rearguard, but was relieved after being temporarily cut off and mauled on 3 November. A fortnight later, as Napoleon continued the retreat westwards from Smolensk, the Russians again tried to sever the rear-most corps at Krasnoe. Davout was widely blamed when Ney, the popular hero of the retreat, was cut off and given up for lost until he unexpectedly reappeared with just 900 survivors. In fact, Davout could not have done more to support Ney without destroying his own corps, but he had made influential enemies, not least Marshals Berthier and Murat, while his professional and realistic outlook was often seen by more head-strong men as a lack of dynamism and an unwillingness to cooperate.

Hamburg

In the wake of the disastrous invasion of Russia, Napoleon raised a new army in the first months of 1813 with which to defend his empire in central Europe. But he was faced with a coalition that by the middle of August included all the major European powers, and he was short of reliable subordinates whom he could entrust with detached commands. When Cossacks occupied Hamburg in March, Napoleon sent Davout to retake the city, for it was of vital strategic and commercial importance. Davout then used Hamburg as a base for semi-independent operations in northern Germany.

After a massive defeat at Leipzig in October, Napoleon retreated across the Rhine and prepared to defend Paris in the face of an allied invasion of France. This left Davout isolated in Hamburg, and by December 1813 he found himself besieged by an army at least twice his own strength. Despite the numerical odds, he repelled several major assaults. To ensure the city held out, he had to take harsh actions, including the demolition of suburbs to clear his fields of fire and the expulsion of 25,000 civilians who were unable to feed themselves. He was subsequently accused of brutal and arbitrary acts, but was able to demonstrate that he had acted justly – in fact, he had moderated the measures that Napoleon had ordered him to take. He also enforced strict discipline on his troops to try to prevent looting. Not until the end of May 1814, seven weeks after Napoleon's abdication and six months after being isolated inside the city, did the French troops evacuate Hamburg and they returned to France with their weapons and baggage.

Final years

Exiled to the Mediterranean island of Elba, Napoleon escaped in February 1815 and swiftly regained power from King Louis XVIII, but faced the prospect of renewed war against a European coalition. Davout, who had remained unemployed under the restored Bourbon monarchy, now became Napoleon's minister of war and governor of Paris. He would have preferred a field command, and the outcome of the Waterloo campaign might have been different had his wish been granted. But Napoleon needed a strong, feared and capable soldier-administrator to rebuild the French army and control the politically unstable capital.

By 22 June Napoleon had suffered a decisive defeat at Waterloo and abdicated for the second and final time. Davout prepared to defend Paris to enable a provisional government to negotiate the best possible terms with the invading allied armies. He did not want to waste lives in a pitched battle, but was prepared to fight smaller-scale actions to strengthen the French negotiating position.

After an armistice was agreed on 3 July, Davout resigned as minister of war and took command of the French army, which withdrew south of the Loire. By giving the army's submission to Louis XVIII, Davout helped to avert the risk of civil war. He also did his best to help officers who found themselves at risk of being arrested for having supported Napoleon. When the most prominent victim, Marshal Ney, was put on trial, Davout spoke vainly in his defence.

By the end of 1815 Davout was once again a private citizen, and remained out of favour for the next two years. He then returned to public life, but died from consumption on 1 June 1823 at the age of 53.

The iron marshal

Davout was ruthless, ambitious and sometimes brutally sarcastic. Often taciturn, he lacked the charm and easy manner of some of his peers; he was also physically unimpressive, being bald, bespectacled and careless of his appearance. But Davout was brave and incorruptible, and as outspoken with high-ranking colleagues as with his juniors. On one occasion he apologized publicly to a subordinate he had unfairly berated, and he made firm friends as well as bitter enemies. When one of his divisional commanders, Charles-Étienne Gudin de la Sablonnière, was mortally wounded in 1812, he broke down and wept.

Many accounts that portray Davout in a hostile light were in fact written by unreliable witnesses, notably Louis-Antoine Fauvelet de Bourienne and the Duchesse d'Abrantès, who were mentally unstable, intent on making a fortune or keen to win favour from the restored Bourbons. In contrast, soldiers who actually served under Davout often had more positive views. One brigade commander frankly admitted:

> I, too, had arguments with the Prince of Eckmühl, and I asked the minister of war to permit me to leave his army corps before the Russian campaign. I am well aware that he was not always amiable, but I will always be proud of having served under him, of having learned much from him, and if we had to make war again, I would not ask for better than to serve once more under his orders.

Those who serve zealously are sure to obtain his approval. You know that with him you will be well commanded, which is something, and minor disagreements are compensated for by big advantages.

Davout was a lucky general. He did not have to fight in the Iberian Peninsula or face Wellington in battle; nor did he share in Napoleon's final defeats, for he successfully defended Hamburg during the 1813 and 1814 campaigns and served in Paris in 1815. Only in the invasion of Russia did Davout experience disaster, and the damage to his reputation was temporary.

The secret of Davout's success lay in his combination of intelligence, education and strength of character. Dubbed 'the just', 'the terrible' and 'the iron marshal', Davout was not the most flamboyant of Napoleon's marshals, but for sheer competence, moral courage and consistent reliability, he eclipsed them all.

MIKHAIL KUTUZOV
1745–1813

ALAN PALMER

AMONG EUROPE'S OUTSTANDING COMMANDERS Mikhail Illarionovich Kutuzov, 'saviour of the Fatherland in the Patriotic War', is unique in two respects. Although he cracked the legend of Napoleon's invincibility at Borodino, he was never credited with victory in any major battle; and he owes his enduring fame, not to military historians, but to his pride of place in a great novel, Tolstoy's War and Peace, *where he epitomizes the Russian people's spirit of resistance to the invader.*

Kutuzov's generalship showed a mastery of manoeuvre. In 1770–73 he served under Marshal Pyotr Rumiantsev, who believed pitched battles should be avoided unless victory guaranteed the end of a campaign, and Kutuzov absorbed many of his commander's ideas. In an empire as vast as

Russia's, retaining an army in being, ready to inflict a decisive blow on an overstretched enemy, seemed to him a more profitable strategy than retaining territory. His tactics frustrated conventionally minded contemporaries, and more than once Tsar Alexander I deplored his 'inexplicable inactivity' and apparent indolence; but Kutuzov's style of command, his inherent Russianness and contempt for pompous affectation endeared him to the rank-and-file peasantry. In turn, he indulgently called them 'my children'.

From cadet to governor-general

Kutuzov was born in St Petersburg on 6 September 1745, the son of a general with thirty years service in the Corps of Engineers behind him. Almost inevitably the boy followed his father's career. At the age of 12 he entered the military engineering school as a cadet private, working his way through the ranks while showing outstanding intelligence in his studies. He was commissioned in 1761. By the following spring he was in the Volga delta, serving as a captain in an infantry regiment under Colonel Alexei Suvorov, whose empathy with the peasant soldiery had already made him a legendary commander.

In later campaigns Kutuzov became Suvorov's partner against the Turks, but their first acquaintance was brief. Kutuzov went on to serve three years in Estonia as aide to the military governor, and then helped to crush a Polish rebellion in a clash of arms near Warsaw. But in Catherine the Great's reign (1762–96) reputations were made around the Black Sea, and in 1770 Major Kutuzov went south to Moldavia to join Rumiantsev's army in pushing the Turks out of what is now Romania. Three years later he was wounded leading an assault on Alushta, on the southeast coast of the Crimea. A musket ball penetrated the temple, weakening his right eye; recuperation was slow.

A two-year truce in the Russo-Turkish conflict enabled Kutuzov to tour widely. He met Frederick the Great in Potsdam, received eye treatment at Leiden in the Netherlands and visited London and Vienna. But by 1776 he was again in the Crimea, serving Suvorov with such intrepidity that in 1782 he rose to command the crack Corps of Chasseurs. 'He's crafty and shrewd, that one!' commented Suvorov, 'No one will fool him.'

For more than a year (1788–9) Kutuzov led sorties during the siege of Ochakov, the citadel commanding the Bug–Dniester estuary. Again he was wounded in the temple, completely losing the sight of his right eye, but he was back in the field within weeks. The campaign reached a climax with a bloody assault on the fortress of Ismail. 'General Kutuzov commanded my left flank, but he was my right arm,' a triumphant Suvorov reported to St Petersburg.

Under the allegedly 'mad Tsar' Paul I (reigned 1796–1801) Kutuzov saw little fighting. Instead, he proved an able ambassador in Constantinople and Berlin. He therefore missed the famous 1799 campaign in Italy, when Suvorov defeated the French before subsequently extricating his men from a trap in Switzerland by skilfully retreating through the Alpine valleys.

By then Kutuzov was governor-general in Vilna (Vilnius in Lithuania), achieving such success that he was given similar responsibilities in St Petersburg. He was among Tsar Paul's dinner guests a few hours before his murder by officers in a conspiracy that brought his 23-year-old son Alexander to the throne. Kutuzov soon learnt that Alexander, his companion at table, had approved the plot, though on the understanding his father would not be killed. Memory of that night engendered lasting mistrust between Kutuzov and Alexander.

The War of the Third Coalition

War came in September 1805, with Alexander joining Britain and Austria in the Third Coalition against Napoleon. Kutuzov received command of an army to support an Austrian advance into Bavaria, while Alexander (yet to experience his baptism of fire) mobilized a more powerful army to join his ally in Moravia. Kutuzov's vanguard reached the River Inn too late to save Austria's General Mack from humiliating capitulation at Ulm, and with hopes of invading Bavaria dashed he put into practice his modified Rumiantsev doctrine. On 24 October the army began a retreat down the Danube and into Moravia.

The French pursuit was hampered by wintry weather, Kutuzov's cunning, and running battles in which the Georgian general, Prince Bagration, commanded the rearguard with courage and enterprise. Marshal Murat, commanding Napoleon's cavalry reserve, was deliberately tempted to turn aside for what his emperor angrily called 'the petty triumph of entering Vienna'. Bagration won valuable time by a delaying action at Schöngraben (16 November). Three days later Kutuzov's troops joined the Russo-Austrian army in Moravia at Brünn (Brno, in what is now the Czech Republic).

Kutuzov urged Alexander and the Austrian emperor, Francis, to continue the retreat into Galicia. Winter would play havoc with the invaders, he argued, and it was then that the allies should fall on them in a decisive battle. Both emperors rejected this advice, preferring the conventional strategy of Francis's chief of staff, Weyrother, who wished to envelop the French and recover Vienna. Kutuzov was ordered to prepare for battle above Austerlitz, 15 miles east of Brünn, on a snow-covered plateau pitted with frozen lakes. He obeyed, but suspected that Weyrother was playing into Napoleon's hands by proposing an initial outflanking assault that would expose the centre to French counter-attack. (For the Battle of Austerlitz, see pp. 218–20.)

Kutuzov's fears were justified. He could do little to avert disaster. When he sought to delay General Miloradovich's corps from supporting Weyrother's advance, Alexander ordered him to send the troops forward. Within minutes the Russians received the full impact of the French cavalry, and Kutuzov was wounded on the cheek by a glancing shot. He remained in command, alerting Bagration on the left flank to form defensive squares and check the French thrust. After five hours of battle the tsar's brother, Constantine, led a cavalry charge on his own initiative, without orders from Kutuzov. It incurred such heavy casualties that coordinated counter-attack was impossible. The broken Russian troops trudged eastwards while Austria made a separate peace.

Back in St Petersburg no attempt was made to brand Kutuzov a scapegoat; blame was assigned to Weyrother and the Austrians. But with Alexander preferring non-Russian generals such as the Hanoverian Bennigsen and Barclay de Tolly (a Latvian of Scottish descent), Kutuzov was sent to Kiev as military commander and missed the grim campaign of 1806–7, when Napoleon defeated Bennigsen at Eylau and Friedland.

Defeating the Turks, 1811–12

After another term as governor in Vilna, in 1811 Kutuzov received command of the Army of the Danube with orders to bring final victory in the long-running Turkish wars. This task he accomplished within a year by a campaign planned with characteristic cunning. The Turks were lured across the lower Danube near Rustchuk (modern Ruse in Bulgaria) and advanced towards Bucharest. Kutuzov avoided battle in the summer heat, but in September re-crossed the river upstream, surrounding the Turks on the south bank. Rather than incur heavy casualties in a frontal assault, he settled down to a winter siege. In St Petersburg Alexander fumed at 'General Dawdler's' hesitancy and the slowness of peace talks preceding the Treaty of Bucharest (May 1812). But Kutuzov's military and diplomatic skills kept Turkey from alliance with France and enabled the Army of Moravia to move north and tighten the grip on Napoleon in the great retreat later that year.

Commander-in-chief

Napoleon's invasion of Russia on 24 June 1812 found Kutuzov on his estate, in poor health, obese and crippled with rheumatism. It seemed improbable he would see active service again. But as the Grande Armée drew nearer Moscow popular clamour for a 'true Russian' leader to check the invaders induced Alexander to appoint Kutuzov commander-in-chief in succession to Barclay. On 29 August he reached field headquarters near Vyasma; his arrival boosted morale in a weary army.

Relentlessly hot weather took a heavy toll on Napoleon's men, and in ten days he lost one-third of his troops, either through sickness or desertion. Kutuzov realized Napoleon's predicament and prepared for an early clash of arms. He selected a formidable defensive position at Borodino, 20 miles east of Vyasma.

Kutuzov's chosen ground to take on Napoleon's Grande Armée in the late summer of 1812 lay 75 miles west of Moscow around four villages – Borodino itself, Gorki, Semenovskoye and Utitsa. A tributary of the River Moskva, the Kolocha, protected his northern flank. He placed the First Army, under the command of Barclay de Tolly, on the Kolocha's steep south bank, covering Gorki and centred on a redoubt named after its commander, Raevsky. High ground, broken by a rivulet leading to Semenovskoye, extended southwards for 3 miles and was held by Bagration's Second Army. South of the stream *flèches* (fortified earthworks) were dug. Miloradovich's corps formed a reserve, while General Tuchkov covered the birch forest in front of Utitsa in the south. In all, Kutuzov deployed 120,000 men and 640 cannon in a convex 5-mile curve; Napoleon compressed 133,000 men and 590 cannon along 4 miles of front.

A sharp engagement on Saturday 5 September gained Murat an outlying redoubt at Shevardino, 3 miles southwest of Borodino. There followed a lull for regrouping on

Sunday, Kutuzov's 67th birthday. The main battle began at 6 a.m. on Monday 7 September, with 100 French cannon bombarding the centre. Italians in Eugène Beauharnais's corps speedily captured Borodino village and Poniatowski's Polish corps took Utitsa, but the key positions around the Raevsky redoubt withstood wave after wave of assault for three hours. Although concentrated fire from 300 cannon halted a French thrust on Semenovskoye, Murat's cavalry swept forward against the *flèches*, which were taken after Bagration fell mortally wounded, to the dismay and demoralization of his men. By noon Kutuzov had rallied the Second Army, which he regrouped on neighbouring heights. At 2 p.m. Beauharnais threw three divisions of infantry supported by guns and cavalry against the Raevsky redoubt, and after an hour's onslaught it fell; exhaustion prevented the French exploiting their success. A last Russian counterattack was thwarted by Napoleon's reserve artillery.

Around 5 p.m. the fighting died away inconclusively. The French had suffered 33,000 casualties in gaining a mile of hillocks above ruined villages. Kutuzov lost 44,000 men, but his troops were ensconced on a plateau 1,000 yards to the east, well placed to renew battle the next day. They did not; for though Kutuzov had inflicted a grievous blow on the French he had not routed them. To fulfil his strategic doctrine he needed to keep his army in good order and draw Napoleon even deeper into Russia before striking a second time at the increasingly exhausted invaders. Through rising mist at dawn next day Napoleon perceived 'the old fox' had slipped away overnight.

Borodino was the second bloodiest battle of the Napoleonic Wars, surpassed only by the four-day Battle of Leipzig. 'The most terrible of all my battles,' Napoleon was to recall in exile on St Helena. 'The French showed themselves worthy of victory, the Russians of being invincible.'

At first St Petersburg and Moscow celebrated Borodino as a victory. The tsar sent Kutuzov 100,000 silver roubles and a marshal's baton. But on 12 September the Muscovites realized the truth, and in fear began to flee eastwards. Next morning at Fili, 5 miles from the Kremlin, Kutuzov convened a council of war in a peasant's cottage. Three generals urged a battle to save Moscow; three backed their marshal's strategy of continued retreat. 'Napoleon is a torrent which as yet we are unable to stem,' Kutuzov explained. 'Moscow will be the sponge that sucks him dry.' That night the Russian army filed through deserted streets and over-flowed into the emptiness of the steppe. The Grande Armée entered Moscow on 14–15 September to find the city in flames – a massive act of defiant arson had denied the invaders food and fodder. Napoleon expected Alexander to sue for peace, and over the following month sent three conciliatory messages to him, but without response.

The 'old fox' was elusive. He fell back not towards St Petersburg as expected but southeast, later veering west and setting up a fortified camp near Tarutino, 55 miles south of Moscow. There he remained for four weeks, refitting and re-clothing his men. 'I will play for time, lull Napoleon and not disturb him in Moscow,' Kutuzov told an aide. But at the same time he completed a comprehensive grand design, which was sent to Alexander and finally approved, in amended form, on 23 October. Kutuzov proposed a classic pincer movement: he would trail a retreating Napoleon while Admiral Chichagov's Army of Moravia headed northwest to intercept the French between Smolensk and Minsk and General Wittgenstein's First Army Corps swept southwest from St Petersburg to Podolsk and on to rendezvous with Chichagov.

Kutuzov remained convinced Napoleon would soon find his position in Moscow untenable. On 18 October he ordered a surprise descent on Murat's cavalry screen near Winkovo. It was little more than a skirmish, but came as a warning to the French. So too did a light snowfall. Napoleon saw the need to evacuate Moscow before Russian horsemen and the onset of winter cut links with his empire. On 19 October he left the city.

Napoleon turned southwest at first, seeking sustenance from the fertile lands around Kaluga, but at Maloyaroslavets (24 October) General Docturov's corps intercepted his vanguard, Beauharnais's Italians. The town changed hands seven times before the main armies arrived. Neither Kutuzov nor Napoleon was ready to risk an impromptu major battle. Next morning Napoleon was fortunate to avoid capture by a Cossack patrol while reconnoitring the position. A few hours later he took the momentous decision to abandon the march on Kaluga in preference for Mozhaisk and the battle-ravaged road to the west.

Trailing the great retreat

Kutuzov gave chase next day. He headed across country for Vyazma, hoping to outstrip Napoleon, who was shadowed by Miloradovich's corps and Cossacks under their hetman (leader), Matvei Platov. But Kutuzov made slow progress in the open country. When Napoleon reached Vyazma, Kutuzov was still 50 miles away. It was left to Miloradovich and Platov to maul the French rearguard.

On 4 November heavy snow fell. Blizzards enveloped both armies two days later. The French suffered appallingly, neither men nor horses being prepared for such conditions. Kutuzov's troops were better clothed and their horses better shod, able to cover 16 miles a day. But the snow left armies isolated. During the following week Kutuzov came closer to Napoleon's headquarters than he realized, just 2 miles away on 15 November. Next day Chichagov captured Minsk, and Wittgenstein's First Army Corps already held Vitebsk, but Kutuzov had no knowledge of their respective positions. He was still determined to preserve the army for a *coup de grâce*, probably along the main north–south divide, the River Berezina. For this reason he failed to exploit early gains in a three-day encounter with the French near Krasnoe, and on 17 November was surprised by the Imperial Guard and forced to retreat.

Ironically, his caution at Krasnoe robbed Kutuzov of participation in the decisive battle he sought. He was more than 40 miles short of the French rearguard when on 25 November Napoleon approached the Berezina, where three divisions of Chichagov's army already held the west bank and had destroyed the bridges. A feint by Marshal Oudinot drew Chichagov south from Studienka, the one fordable point where Napoleon's engineers hastened to construct pontoon bridges. Fighting continued around Studienka throughout two days. The French fought off the returning Chichagov and countered thrusts by Wittgenstein from the northeast. In crossing the Berezina the French lost 25,000 soldiers and some 28,000 non-combatants, but most deaths were caused by the collapse of the pontoons and their eventual firing.

Kutuzov finally reached the Berezina on the night of 29/30 November. The temperature fell dramatically in the first week of December. 'General Winter' caused more French casualties than any Russian army, with weary half-frozen stragglers robbed and killed by Cossack marauders. Napoleon left his troops on 5 December, hurrying back to Paris. The last fighting soldier of the once Grand Armée, Marshal Ney, crossed the Niemen out of Russia on 14 December, the day after Kutuzov and the main body of his army entered Vilna.

The death of Kutuzov

Tsar Alexander, who rejoined his army on 23 December, lavished praise on Kutuzov, creating him Prince of Smolensk and bestowing high decorations on him. But behind the façade of mutual respect lay deep divisions in temperament and policy. Kutuzov thought the fighting over, now the invaders were expelled from Russia; Alexander believed he had a divine mission to liberate Europe.

Reluctantly Kutuzov remained commander-in-chief. Weary, worn out and fearful of what would happen once Napoleon raised a new army, he accompanied the tsar when he entered Prussian Poland in mid January. Looking ahead he predicted, 'We can cross the Elbe easily enough, but we shall soon re-cross it with a bloody nose.' He was right, but he did not live to see the setback, nor the final victory, at Leipzig. Kutuzov collapsed with exhaustion in the spring of 1813 and died at Bautzen in Silesia on 28 April.

CARL VON CLAUSEWITZ

1780–1831

ANDREW ROBERTS

CARL VON CLAUSEWITZ, a middle-ranking Prussian general who helped drive Napoleon from his country, wrote a single book that was unfinished at the time of his death but through it he can lay claim to have influenced – for both good and ill – the conduct of warfare more deeply and for longer than any other military theorist in history.

Born in Magdeburg in 1780, the fourth son of a retired lieutenant and minor tax official, Carl von Clausewitz came from a family of theologians and professors. His father had served under Frederick the Great in the Seven Years War, and Carl entered the Prussian army in 1792, going off to fight in the French Revolutionary War the following year aged only 13. He rose rapidly in the ranks owing to his courage and intelligence, becoming a major at 30, a colonel at 34 and a general by 38.

In 1801 Clausewitz received his only formal education when he joined the Military Academy in Berlin. It was there that he met and came under the influence of the charismatic Gerhard von Scharnhorst, Prussia's greatest general since Frederick. Scharnhorst, who fought against Napoleon at Flanders, Jena, Eylau and in the war of liberation of 1813–14, became a 'spiritual father', mentor and hero to Clausewitz.

After graduating top of his class in 1803, Clausewitz became adjutant to Prince Augustus of Prussia and the following year penned his first notes on military strategy. In 1805 he wrote a 100-page history of Gustavus Adolphus of Sweden during the Thirty Years War, and can claim to have been as much an historian as a military theoretician, at least in terms of his literary output.

Clausewitz and Napoleon

It was, as with all Prussians of his generation, the catastrophic defeat of his country at the hands of Napoleon in 1806 that was to focus, energize and radicalize Clausewitz, and the thirst to avenge the humiliation was to give his life meaning. He fought with a grenadier battalion during that disastrous campaign and was forced to surrender, going into French captivity with Prince Augustus.

The total defeat of the Prussian army at Jena-Auerstädt in October 1806 (see pp. 244–6) was followed by widespread French rapine and pillage in Prussia, and although the monarchy and government were forced to accept Napoleon's humiliating peace terms, Prussian nationalists, patriots and especially the army from then on lived and worked solely for eventual revenge. Clausewitz wrote that the Prussian army was ruined 'more completely than any army has ever been ruined on the battlefield' at Jena. He refused to recognize the Napoleon-dictated armistice, writing to his beloved wife Marie: 'I shall never accept the peace which brings submission. If I cannot live in a free and respected state and enjoy the golden fruits of peace in your arms, then let peace depart forever from my heart.'

Prussia's Reform movement, which looked forward to a coming 'war of liberation', was intended to create a state that could one day turn the tables on Napoleon. The coming war against the French Empire, the Reformers vowed, would see a very different Prussia in the field, a nation in arms.

After his release from France in the spring of 1808, Clausewitz rejoined Scharnhorst – who had been wounded at Auerstädt – and served as his private secretary. In that capacity he drafted many of the Reformers' papers, and became involved in every aspect of the movement. He also got to know (and hugely admire) Graf August von Gneisenau, a key military figure in it.

Military education was an important aspect of the Reform programme, and in 1810–11 Clausewitz taught guerrilla warfare at the War Academy. From 1810 to 1812 he also tutored the crown prince in military affairs. In the spring of 1812, when the Prussian government agreed to supply Napoleon with a Prussian army corps to fight against Russia, Clausewitz decided to leave the service of the king and join the Russian army as a staff officer. It was a hard decision for a proud Prussian patriot to take, but he justified himself thus:

> Formerly ... war was waged in the way that a pair of duellists carried out their pedantic struggle. One battled with moderation and consideration, according to the conventional proprieties ... There is no more talk of this sort of war, and one would have to be blind not to be able to perceive the difference with our wars, that is to say the wars that our age and our conditions require ... The war of the present time is a war of all against all.

Or at least all against Napoleon, and if King Frederick Wilhelm and his 'dishonoured' government would not fight it, then Clausewitz would.

It was in the capacity of a staff officer – although more of an observer since he spoke no Russian – that Clausewitz took part in the war of 1812. In the last days of that fateful year, Clausewitz acted as intermediary when General Hans David Yorck, commanding 30,000 Prussians, changed sides from the French to the Russians.

During the ensuing war of liberation that began in 1813, Clausewitz devised a plan for organizing the East Prussian militia. He also advised both Scharnhorst and Gneisenau. Although Scharnhorst died in 1813 of a wound received at the Battle of Grossgörschen, Gneisenau appointed Clausewitz – who showed great bravery in 1814 – as chief of staff of one of the Prussian corps that fought in the Waterloo campaign. After fighting at the Battle of Ligny in June 1815, Clausewitz was present at the vital rearguard engagement at Wavre two days later that prevented Marshal Grouchy from arriving to aid Napoleon at Waterloo (a battle that Clausewitz always called 'Belle-Alliance').

After Napoleon

The following year Clausewitz became chief of staff to Gneisenau, and from 1818 to 1830 he held the important post of Superintendent (administrative director) of the War Academy, which gave him time to develop his theories and write his masterpiece, *Vom Kriege* (*On War*). When the Bourbons were overthrown in France in 1830, Gneisenau became army commander-in-chief and again chose Clausewitz as his chief of staff, but the sense of national danger proved a false alarm after the Orléanist Louis-Philippe was crowned king of France and settled down to a generally pacific foreign policy, at least in Europe.

In August 1831 Gneisenau succumbed to the cholera epidemic that was sweeping through Eastern Europe, and then on 16 November Clausewitz himself, weakened by mild cholera, died of a heart attack. At the time of his death, Clausewitz was thought of as a respectable Prussian general of intellectual leanings who had been a conscientious if middle-ranking figure in the Reform movement that had revolutionized Prussia in time for the war of liberation. He was certainly not considered then, as he generally is today, the most important military theorist who ever lived.

On War

The year after his death, Clausewitz's widow Marie published his masterpiece, *On War*, which sold fewer than fifteen hundred copies in its first twenty years. It was 1867 before the third edition came out. He had not wanted the book published in his lifetime, and was very substantially rewriting and revising the theory at the time that he died. Its many internal contradictions might have been ironed out had he not succumbed to his heart attack, but they should not detract from what is a monumental work of history, scholarship, military theory and occasionally philosophy.

Although he published little between hard covers, Clausewitz wrote extensively on education, politics and art and had a large, wide and varied correspondence. *On War* represents a distillation of thoughts over a lifetime of fighting, teaching and writing, and is presented in the direct, no-nonsense style one might expect from a Prussian general of the Napoleonic Wars. Much of it is very much of its time, with limited application to later ages using very different weapons under very different circumstances. Nonetheless, there are some generalizations that Clause-witz makes – particularly in the fields of morale, genius and chance – that still hold good today.

Although Clausewitz himself dismissed *On War* as a 'shapeless mass of ideas' in its early drafts – and there are undoubtedly many banalities and contradictions to be found in its pages – it is still the greatest work of military theory ever written, and therefore justifies its author's inclusion in a survey of history's great commanders, even though Clausewitz himself never exercised significant independent command.

His two central themes are firstly that war cannot be disentangled from the greater political issues that cause it – hence the well-known formulation 'War is nothing but the continuation of policy with other means' – and secondly that Total War (such as the Napoleonic Wars) constitutes a very different beast from the kind of limited dynastic or territorial wars that had constituted the European norm before the French Revolution.

Yet as well as those two major themes, Clausewitz had a great deal to say about how his country's greatest enemy, Napoleon, managed to impose his will on so much of Europe for so long. Annihilation of the enemy's main force, willingness to accept high levels of casualties, concentration of effort at the decisive point – the *Hauptschlacht* (major battle) which was 'the true centre of gravity of the war' – these were some of the messages Clausewitz imparted.

As one would expect from a long-serving superintendent of one of the world's greatest military academies, Clausewitz prized leadership above all else. In his editor and translator Sir Michael Howard's words, Clausewitz placed great 'emphasis on the creative power of the individual', concentrating in particular on the role and nature of genius in military affairs. Commanders needed to show freedom of thought, initiative, self-reliance. Of course Clausewitz's principal source of inspiration was the genius of Napoleon, whom he hated and sharply criticized but nevertheless called 'the god of war'.

In the Clausewitzian universe, military leaders were not intended to control state policy, since military strategy needed to be subordinated to greater political desiderata.

Having personally witnessed Napoleon's nemesis in the retreat from Moscow, Clausewitz appreciated that ultimate success depended on knowing when and how to stop fighting. It was a message that his admirers in the Prussian High Command were to ignore during the First World War. Everything in war is political, Clausewitz argued, even strategy and tactics.

Having taken part in many campaigns in the French revolutionary and imperial wars over twenty-two years, Clausewitz also well understood the role that unquantifiable factors such as chance could play. Although he looked to history for examples of what happened in battle, he did not believe history was subject to patterns that could therefore lead to anything being predictable. Because of the crucial role of chance, there could be no dogmatic, universal right or wrong way to go about warfare. In explaining how and why smaller forces sometimes overcame larger ones, he dwelled on the importance of moral and psychological factors such as fear, morale and courage.

Clausewitz's uncompromising theories about Total War led to him being called 'the Mahdi of mass and mutual massacre' by Sir Basil Liddell Hart. Certainly Clausewitz did believe, unlike other contemporary thinkers such as Baron Henri Jomini, that extreme violence, rather than merely manoeuvre, was the very essence of war. Total War, such as the one Prussia fought against Napoleon in

1813–15, could only be conducted successfully through the supreme effort of the whole state, as the Reformers had insisted upon ever since the débâcle at Jena. Since blood must be shed to break utterly the enemy's power and will to resist, Clausewitz was in a sense the link between the Total War that ended in 1815 and the one that started almost exactly a century later.

One of the many aspects of Clausewitzian thought that his German followers ignored in 1914–15 was his emphasis on defence rather than offence. By 1916–17 his lessons about the strategy of attrition, *Ermattungsstrategie*, versus that of annihilation, *Vernichtungsstrategie*, had to be relearned by Hindenberg and Ludendorff. Equally, Clausewitz's almost total lack of interest in both sea-power and economics limited his relevance for his countrymen in a war in which both played important parts.

On War was of its (Napoleonic) time and place, and not particularly applicable to the warfare of the nuclear and terrorist age. That is the way that Clausewitz himself would have wanted it, being a man who decried attempts to codify strict, immutable laws and principles of warfare. Since it is impossible to know how the enemy will react in any given situation, and since a battle is a constant movement of interlocking action and reaction, abstract laws cannot, he argued, be applied to the battlefield.

Clausewitz's legacy

Field Marshal Helmuth von Moltke, Prussian army chief of staff from 1858 to 1888, used to say that, along with the Bible and Homer, *On War* was the only really seminal work that ever influenced him. Although Clausewitz's thought was known to only a small number of people by the early 1860s, Otto von Bismarck's three quick victories against Denmark in 1863–4, Austria in 1866, and France in 1870–71 suddenly placed Clausewitz in the Prussian pantheon, because these stunning conquests were popularly believed to have been won on Clausewitzian principles.

Count Alfred von Schlieffen, the German chief of staff, was another great admirer, and he wrote the 1905 preface to the fifth edition of *On War* at the same time that he was drawing up his notorious Plan to invade France via neutral Belgium. The First World War was in a sense a Clausewitzian struggle on both sides, involving, as Michael Howard lists them, his views concerning 'the scepticism for strategic manoeuvre; the accumulation of maximum force at the decisive point in order to defeat the enemy main force in battle; the conduct of operations so as to inflict the greatest possible number of losses on the enemy and compel him to use up his reserves at a greater rate than one was expending one's own; the dogged refusal to be put off by heavy casualties'.

There was nothing Clausewitzian about fighting a war on two fronts, however, or about politicians being subordinated to the army High Command, or about building a high seas fleet and invading a neutral country, thereby bringing the British Empire into the war against Germany.

Marshal Foch took Clausewitz's strictures about the superiority of defensive over offensive fighting to heart, and Clausewitz's military thought was also debated throughout the 1920s and 1930s in France, Britain and America, as well as in Germany. 'In the realm of war,' wrote Basil Liddell Hart in 1932, 'which has covered so great a part of human activity, and has affected so greatly human life and history, the name of Clausewitz stands out more and is better known to soldiers … than any of the generals of the nineteenth century, save perhaps Lee and Moltke.'

The Nazis eagerly embraced Clausewitz, even though he had died over a century before Hitler's rise to power. His call for a vigorous, inspired, flexible yet resolute commander who showed willpower and understood the power of the daring *coup d'oeil* seemed to presage the leadership of their Führer, and they were only encouraged by the knowledge that it had originally alluded to Napoleon. Clausewitz was also put to use by the Soviets; in November 1941 the Soviet air force dropped leaflets on the Wehrmacht quoting *On War*'s injunction that: 'It is impossible either to hold or to conquer Russia.'

Clausewitz's principles also deeply imbued American military thinking in the 1920s, especially his injunction to attack the main body of the enemy with as much force as possible to win the *Hauptschlacht*, 'the true centre of gravity of the war'. This was taken to heart by General George C. Marshall, US Army chief of staff 1939–45, who insisted that only an early second front in the West could defeat the Wehrmacht, and who consequently pressed for an invasion of northwestern France long before the British were finally persuaded to consent to D-Day taking place in June 1944.

With *On War* still on the syllabus at the Sandhurst, West Point, St Cyr and Voroshilov military academies, Clausewitz's day is not over yet.

SIMÓN BOLÍVAR
1783–1830

MALCOLM DEAS

IN A DECADE AND A HALF of struggle Simón Bolívar freed much of South America from Spanish rule, achieving the independence of what are now six countries: Venezuela, Colombia, Panama, Ecuador, Peru and Bolivia – the last named in honour of Bolívar himself, the man who became known as the Liberator. Bolívar's operations ranged from the mouth of the Orinoco on the Atlantic to Peru and Bolivia in the south, a vast, geographically diverse crescent embracing many different societies, from the Indian communities of the high Andes to black slave plantations on the Caribbean coast.

In comparison with the size of the forces in the North American War of Independence, let alone those involved in the Napoleonic Wars, the armies Bolívar commanded in the field were minuscule: as he said himself, 'Here every trio is an orchestra.' In the early years of the struggle he suffered a number of severe reverses, and those campaigns gained him only what he called 'fruitless laurels'. His strategic sense took some time to develop, and none of his battles was of the sort to win a place in texts on the military art. His great achievement has to be measured against the difficulties posed by time and place: only then can one see behind the formal gold-embroidered uniform an extraordinary improviser of armies and resources, a pioneer of national liberation and a great commander. Without question, Bolívar stands above his rivals as the greatest figure in the emancipation of South America.

Bolívar was born in Caracas on 24 July 1783, a child of the local creole aristocracy. His family was one of the richest in the colony, but both his parents died when he was young. At 15 he was made a sub-lieutenant in the local militia, a social rather than a military distinction, and he had little formal military training. From 1799 he was in Spain and France, remaining until 1802 when he married and returned to Venezuela. His wife died early the next year. He swore never to marry again, and returned to Europe, living there until 1806 when he sailed again for Venezuela via the United States. He had been in Paris when Napoleon proclaimed himself emperor, and in Italy he had witnessed one of the emperor's grand military reviews, a sight he never forgot.

Napoleon and the Spanish Empire

In 1808 Napoleon made the mistake – on St Helena he admitted it was indeed a mistake and a misreading of the Spanish character – of forcing the abdication first of Charles IV and then of his son Ferdinand from the throne of Spain, installing his brother Joseph as king in their place. This not only provoked a national uprising; it also, by decapitating the Spanish Empire, produced throughout Spain's vast overseas dominions an unprecedented state of confusion and uncertainty. This soon evolved into war – to a large degree civil war.

The first reaction of many Latin Americans was to profess loyalty to Ferdinand, now proclaimed Ferdinand VII. Many of these professions were no doubt sincere, as the region had no experience of any form of government other than monarchy, and few of its inhabitants were able to think in other terms. Nor was there at this stage sufficient discontent to produce an immediate rejection of the authority of the mother country. Spanish colonial officials were always apprehensive of conspiracies and the spread of the spirit of liberation, particularly after the United States won its independence and the people of Haiti successfully revolted against the French; but Spanish rule was not generally felt as oppressive, and the intricate imperial system of bureaucratic checks and balances, a policy of administrative divide and rule, made it hard to focus what discontent there was. The potential for conflict between the different elements in these societies was muted, and it took some time to emerge. When it did emerge in Venezuela it was to be particularly violent.

The beginnings of revolt

As Napoleon's armies established their hold in Spain and the return of Ferdinand looked less and less likely, so Spanish authority in the empire was weakened. The colonies were less and less inclined to receive orders from the succession of beleaguered and distant juntas that claimed to rule in the. king's name, and set up juntas of their own, a step that soon led to proclamations of independence. Caracas, in what is now Venezuela, was one of the leaders in this process, and Bolívar figured in the upper-class conspiracy that produced the local revolution of 19 April 1810. He was then sent on a diplomatic mission to London, where he met Francisco de Miranda, an early advocate of independence who had led an unsuccessful small-scale invasion of Venezuela in 1806. They both returned to serve the now independent republic.

Peace did not last long. The claim of Caracas to be the capital was contested by other cities, and strong royalist sentiments persisted. Many elements in society – blacks, mulattos, mestizos, poor whites – felt little deference towards Bolívar's class, and the new rulers had little experience of government, and even less tact. When desultory fighting began, as Caracas sought to impose its authority, it also soon became apparent that neither of the new rulers possessed any relevant military experience. Miranda, who was given command, had been a general in the armies of the French Revolution, and had acquitted himself well in 1793 – his name is on the Arc de Triomphe – but he had no idea how to lead the raw levies of a militarily innocent country.

Bolívar's active military career began with disaster and humiliation. Miranda failed to resist the advance on Caracas of small but disciplined local Spanish forces under Domingo de Monteverde. In March 1812 Caracas was reduced to ruins by an earthquake, and the effect on patriot morale was devastating – though it gave Bolívar the opportunity of announcing to the world from atop a pile of rubble that 'If nature opposes us we will fight her and make her obey' (this sounds too good to be true, but the witness is a contemporary royalist). Placed in command of the key fortress of Puerto Cabello, Bolívar failed to prevent its betrayal to the enemy. He and some of his fellow officers then vented their frustration by handing Miranda over to the victors, hardly an honourable act. Bolívar was then permitted to leave the country.

The struggles for Caracas

Bolívar went to Cartagena, the Caribbean fortress port of the neighbouring Viceroyalty of New Granada, and within a year showed the qualities that led the Spanish to conclude that 'Bolívar in defeat is more dangerous than Bolívar victorious'. He was given a minor command by the patriots of Cartagena, and ordered to conduct operations against royalist detachments along the River Magdalena. Through a combination of élan and persuasiveness he was able in May 1813 to turn this limited mission into an invasion of Venezuela from the west, with around a thousand men and a few pieces of artillery; opposing him, Monteverde commanded royalist forces of around 6,000 or 7,000 in the west and centre of the country. In June Bolívar issued his notorious decree of *Guerra a muerte* ('war to the death'), which promised to guarantee the lives of the native-born and to put to death all Spaniards who did not positively embrace the patriot cause. On 6 August he entered Caracas in triumph, and was proclaimed Liberator, a title that remained his alone.

This remarkable campaign showed Bolívar's talents for rapid movement and improvisation of resources; his declaration of 'war to the death' also showed his ruthlessness and decisiveness, and his taste for heightened, dramatic language. But it did not produce lasting success. From 1813, the year of this campaign, until 1819 Bolívar was obsessed by taking – or retaking – Caracas, and it took him a long time to realize that his native city was not the strategic key to undoing Spanish power.

Monteverde had lost Caracas, but he still held Puerto Cabello, and elsewhere the royalist reaction was not long in coming. It took the form of a rising led by a Spanish-born sailor and smuggler called José Tomás Boves, who now embraced war to the death on the royalist side with an enthusiasm that made Bolívar's proclamation look insipid. Boves roused the lower classes – the masterless cattlemen of the plains of the interior (who proved to be natural lancers), the numerous poor immigrants from the Canary Islands, the free blacks and coloureds, and many slaves. Bolívar's small forces could not hold territory, and Boves inflicted a severe defeat on the patriots in the First Battle of La Puerta. This caused panic in Caracas, and Bolívar took the precaution of executing 800 Spanish prisoners. Boves's hosts continued to grow – they are said to have reached as many as 8,000 – and in the Second Battle of La Puerta he annihilated what was left of the patriot army under Bolívar's command. Bolívar and a tragic column of refugees fled Caracas to the east, and on 8 September 1814 he embarked again for Cartagena.

The wilderness years
Boves died of a wound in December 1814, but the following

year, with the defeat of Napoleon in Europe, Spain was able to send to Venezuela and New Granada some 10,000 veterans under the command of Pablo Morillo. Bolívar had once again been employed in New Granada, and had taken part in the internal conflicts that still divided that country despite the manifest threat of Spanish reconquest. Morillo proved irresistible, and Bolívar had to seek refuge first in Jamaica and then in Haiti.

The desire to retake Caracas and to fight Morillo in Venezuela continued to dominate Bolívar's thinking for the next two years, resulting in little success and much frustration. He had to beg meagre assistance from speculators in Jamaica and Haiti, and the odds on his winning must have looked long. Early in 1816 he landed on the Venezuelan coast from Haiti with some 250 men, but failed to establish a footing. His authority was by no means unchallenged within the scattered patriot remnants, and some other commanders – Mariño, Piar, Páez, Monagas – held sway over solid local fiefs of a sort Bolívar never enjoyed.

It was a time of indecisive defeats and victories for the diminutive, ill-supplied and insecurely disciplined patriot forces. The war to the death seesawed in its intensity; prisoners and deserters were dispatched with a knife or lined up in twos or threes to be economically shot with a single bullet. Nevertheless, despite the strategic confusion, some clarity began to emerge. Bolívar was back again in Venezuela at the end of 1816, this time for good, and he gradually reasserted his authority – crucially by executing the mulatto General Piar, who was reluctant to obey his orders and threatened vaguely racial mutiny. Bolívar found a base in the Orinoco delta town of Angostura: the region had good natural defences, and from there he could gather resources and import arms through the trade with Trinidad. He could also bring to Angostura British and other foreign mercenaries, many of whom were useless, but some had valuable military talents: the British were to fight conspicuously well at Boyacá and Carabobo. They were also loyal to Bolívar personally, and less liable to faction than his fellow countrymen. Bolívar could also pretend to be a government, and early in 1819 at Angostura he called together his first congress. That year also saw Bolívar's greatest strategic feat – leading his men over the Andes to defeat the royalists decisively at Boyacá.

Over the Andes to victory at Boyacá

From his base at Angostura, in 1819 Bolívar abandoned his long-sought aim of retaking Caracas. Instead, he attacked the Spanish forces in New Granada by crossing the Eastern Cordillera of the Andes from the plains of Casanare. The obstacles to this plan looked insuperable, and though Morillo, the skilful and experienced royalist commander, saw that it might be attempted, the Spanish in New Granada thought it impossible: it was the rainy season and the plains were flooded; the passes were few and narrow, the men from the plains would suffer too much from cold and mountain sickness, and would desert or die; the horses' hooves would not withstand the change of ground from the soft plains to the rocks; surprise would not be attained.

These obstacles were all real enough, but they were overcome. Not all the forces painfully assembled in Casanare obeyed the order at the end of June to leave the plains, and José Antonio Páez disobeyed his instructions to make a feint towards Cúcuta. Men were lost, as well as horses and equipment, but 900 or so under Bolívar and his second-in-command, Francisco de Paula Santander, reached the highlands to the northeast of Tunja without meeting significant opposition. Bolívar more than made up for his losses in men by rapidly recruiting replacements, announcing that anyone not answering the call was to be shot.

The first battle with the disconcerted Spanish at Pantano de Vargas was not much more than a draw, but a draw in Bolívar's favour. Morale and momentum were on his side, and his opponent Barreiro was subsequently out-manoeuvred, exhausting his troops in attempting to cut off Bolívar's advance on Bogotá, the capital of New Granada. The two armies met again on 7 August south of Tunja at Boyacá, where Bolívar won his most decisive victory.

By European standards it was a small and unsophisticated engagement – some 2,850 patriots against 2,700 royalists, a cavalry and infantry affair lasting only two hours, and in which (according to one account) Barreiro's artillery managed to get off only three shots. Before long, Barreiro had surrendered, with nearly all his officers and 1,600 men. The viceroy, his officials and numerous Spaniards and royalists fled from the capital, and its small remaining garrison withdrew to the south before Bolívar entered the city ahead of his army on 10 August.

From victory to victory

After Boyacá, Bolívar's military career was by no means over, but whereas before that decisive victory he had lost as many battles as he had won, his armies were henceforth to be consistently victorious. New Granada gave him a base the Spanish could never retake, together with resources to tax and a substantial reserve of infantry. Leaving Santander to run the civil government of the new republic of Colombia – Venezuela and New Granada united – Bolívar turned east to deal with the royalist remnant in Venezuela. The Liberal revolution of 1820 in Spain now ended any hope Morillo had for reinforcements. After making a truce with Bolívar that formally ended the war to the death, he departed. In June 1821, after the truce had ended, Bolívar defeated Morillo's successor at Carabobo, which effectively ended Spanish rule in Venezuela.

Bolívar then turned south. What is now Ecuador was freed by the victory of Bolívar's favourite general, Antonio José de Sucre, at the Battle of Pichincha, fought in the hills around Quito on 24 May 1822. At the time Bolívar himself was bogged down by tenacious royalist resistance around Pasto in the south of New Granada, where the Battle of Bomboná on 7 April was not one of his greatest successes. With superior forces at his back, Bolívar met the Argentine José de San Martín, his only real rival in stature in the emancipation of South America, at a famous and still mysterious interview in Guayaquil. San Martín had been the liberator of Chile, and had half freed Peru, the grand viceroyalty where enthusiasm for independence had been most decidedly muted and Spanish resistance most effective. He now left the field to Bolívar and retired to Europe. Not without difficulty, Bolívar completed the task. On 6 August 1824, now in command of an army of some 9,000, he won the short and silent cavalry action of Junín – one hour long and not a shot fired – and on 9 December that same year Sucre won the Battle of Ayacucho, which finally decided the independence of Peru and Bolivia.

That can be said to mark the end of Bolívar's military career. His political career did not effectively end until his death from tuberculosis at Santa Marta on 23 December

1830, in an atmosphere of profound pessimism and *après moi le deluge*.

More than just a general

One of the best summaries of Bolívar's greatness as a commander was written by the English mining engineer Joseph Andrews, who met the Liberator in Potosí in October 1825:

> As a man, in my view, he had achieved more than Washington. He freed his country without foreign help and with all possible disadvantages. No France offered her assistance in armies and treasure. No Franklin, Henry or Jefferson was at his right hand, nor the inflexible and austere character of New England. The ignorance and complete lack of experience of those around him, in civil and military matters, threw all on to his genius: he dared nobly and he succeeded. His talent in battle and invincible perseverance in despite of all obstacles were matched by his capacity for raising the resources of war and impressing on his countrymen confidence in his ability and respect for his authority as leader of his people.

Bolívar had to be more than just a general; he had to be the civil and military chief, the diplomat, and, above all, the visionary. He also had to create his forces out of scant and recalcitrant materials. In old age his fellow commander, José Antonio Páez, set himself to translate Napoleon´s *Maxims*, and found an 'incontrovertible truth' in number LVII: 'It is very difficult to create an army in a nation that has no military establishments or system.' Bolívar's comments on the societies and politics of his time – his letters are vivid and acute, he was a master of military eloquence and his formal political writing is never dull – show great sociological penetration, and sharp appreciation of the strengths and weaknesses of his subordinates: he alone could fit their awkward shapes together to achieve his ends. None came near him in overall vision, and from his early travels and his reading – he always travelled with books – he had an unrivalled knowledge of the larger world and an aristocratic confidence in dealing with it.

Bolívar was physically brave, described as 'perhaps too fond of combat' and as 'a bold but not a graceful rider' (he was certainly a tireless one, given the vast distances he had to travel). He loved dancing, and marked his progress with fiestas. He shared all hardships, and did not care for wealth, giving away most of his fortune. He could be moved, but had duly hardened himself: 'Good God,' he once ex-claimed, 'were I to weep for every friend I have lost, in future I would be called General Jeremiah not General Bolívar.' As well as possessing the appetite for glory that was part of the spirit of the age, the Liberator had a sardonic wit, a romantic sense of irony that would have appealed to Byron, who named his yacht after him. Here is the generous verdict of San Martín: '… the most astonishing man South America has produced … hardened by difficulties and never defeated by them, however great the dangers against which he hurled his burning spirit.'

SHAKA ZULU

1787–1828

SAUL DAVID

SHAKA KASENZANGAKONA, KING OF THE ZULUS, was arguably the finest black African commander in history. In just ten years his military and political genius transformed his small tribe into 'the most politically sophisticated, administratively integrated and militarily powerful' black state in sub-Saharan Africa. He achieved this by revolutionizing the tactics and weapons of war, and by fighting campaigns of annihilation that enabled him to absorb the survivors into his military system. Like all the great soldier-rulers – Alexander, Julius Caesar and Napoleon – he was a master of all aspects of command: tactics, strategy, and even diplomacy.

Shaka was the eldest son of a minor Nguni chief whose clan numbered fewer than 1,500 people (the Nguni were a sub-division of the Bantu people, several hundred clans strong, which slowly spread across southeast Africa in the sixteenth and seventeenth centuries). Shaka was never recognized as his father's heir because he was born out of wedlock – hence his name, which is a sarcastic reference to the intestinal beetle, or *ishaka*, which the Zulu elders used as an excuse for his mother Nandi's inopportune pregnancy. The stigma of his ill-timed birth led to the 7-year-old Shaka and his headstrong mother being sent to live with her tribe, the eLangeni.

Early years as an outcast

Shaka did not stay long with the eLangeni. A well-developed boy with more than his share of his mother's aggression, he clashed with the chief's son and was packed off to a sub-clan of the Mthethwa, the dominant local tribe whose subordinate clans included the Zulu and the eLangeni.

This disgrace rankled deep within Shaka's breast, as did the harsh treatment of his mother by her own people and his own social ostracism at the hands of his peers. He responded with the single-minded determination of the outcast, practising relentlessly at all martial activities: he became so proficient with the throwing spear, for example, that he could hit a small tuft of grass at thirty paces; and he was unbeatable at stick-fighting, directing his forces in mass combat with the same skill and innovation he would display in actual war.

Revolutionizing tribal warfare

Shaka's martial abilities brought him to the notice of Jobe, the paramount chief of the Mthethwa and, after Jobe's death in 1807, to his successor Dingiswayo. For nine years Shaka served in Dingiswayo's army as it subdued tribe after tribe. It was during his time with the Mthethwa that he devised the ruthless political and military strategy that would transform the fortunes of his father's clan.

Previously, tribal conflict had been little more than a ritual show of force with spears thrown from a distance and few casualties, leaving the 'defeated' clan to restart hostilities at a later date. Shaka changed all this by introducing the *iklwa*, a short stabbing spear with a broad, heavy blade that could only be used at close quarters; its name represents the sucking sound the spear made as it was withdrawn from flesh. He turned the traditional cowhide shield into an offensive weapon by instructing his men to hook its left edge behind the shield of their opponent; a powerful backhand sweep would then expose the left side of the enemy to a spear thrust. And, crucially, he introduced the tactics of envelopment by dividing his regiment (and later army) into three parts: a central column to pin down an opposing force, and two flanking parties to surround it.

As Zulu king he would refine these tactics further into the classic double envelopment formation known as *izimpondo zenkomo* (the 'horns of the buffalo'): a 'chest' to close with the enemy and hold it fast; two 'horns' to race either side of the enemy and, having met, to fight their way back to the 'chest'; and the 'loins', or reserve, which was placed behind the 'chest' and deployed as the situation demanded. Further refinements included the abandonment of cumbersome sandals, giving his men added mobility, and an increase in the size of his warriors' shields from 4 to 6 feet to protect them from top to toe.

In an uncanny echo of history, Shaka's new method of fighting was strikingly similar to that used by the legionaries of ancient Rome. They too would close with the enemy in tight formation, then use their shields to unbalance their opponents and their short swords, the *gladii*, to dispatch them. Shaka, of course, had no knowledge of classical warfare and yet applied the same methods to tribal conflict.

An early indication that his innovations were working was when his regiment, the isiChwe, played a key role in putting to flight the army of the Ndwandwe paramountcy, the Mthethwa's main rivals for control of the Phongolo-Tugela region. Dingiswayo took note of this and marked

Shaka out for rapid promotion. In 1814 he was appointed commander-in-chief and a member of Dingiswayo's inner council.

King of the Zulus

Two years later, on the death of his father, Senzangakona, Shaka used Dingiswayo's support to seize the Zulu chieftainship. His half-brother, the designated heir, was quietly murdered and Shaka installed in his place. He was now master of a tiny polity that covered just 10 square miles, with an army of fewer than 500 men.

Shaka knew he had to expand his lands to survive, and within a month of becoming chief he had called up all Zulu men who could bear arms and organized them into three regiments, according to age: 30–40-year-olds, 25–30-year-olds and 18–25-year-olds. All three regiments were trained in the fighting tactics he had developed for the isiChwe, and they were armed with the new heavy-bladed *iklwa*, Shaka having instructed his blacksmiths to convert all existing spears and to forge new ones from raw iron ore.

Tribe after neighbouring tribe either submitted to or was destroyed by Shaka's war machine, his mother's eLangeni clan being the first to cave in. All those clan members who had tormented him or his mother were impaled on stakes from the cattle enclosure. Perhaps mindful of this, the powerful Buthelezi tribe chose not to submit, and the ensuing battle gave Shaka the first opportunity to deploy his *izimpondo zenkomo* formation. It was a resounding success, and not a single Buthelezi warrior was spared. Their homesteads were burned and their women, children and cattle taken back to the Zulu heartland. Shaka's new concept of total war, *impi embomvu* (literally 'war red with blood'), had had its first demonstration.

Defeating the Ndwandwe

In under a year the Zulu lands had quadrupled in size. But Shaka was still technically Dingiswayo's vassal and had to tread carefully. This all changed in 1817 when Dingiswayo, on the eve of battle with the Ndwandwe, was captured and beheaded. The leaderless Mthethwa army melted away and Shaka, aware that a reckoning with the Ndwandwe was imminent, returned to his capital of kwaBulawayo to build up his army, recruiting many former Mthethwa warriors, including the entire isiChwe regiment.

When the Ndwandwe invaded Zulu lands in early 1818, Shaka was ready and waiting. Like Wellington at Waterloo three years earlier, he carefully chose a site for battle, selecting the gentle slopes of kwaGqokli Hill, which he believed would afford his army the greatest chance of a defensive victory. Through clever planning and superior tactics, he was able to defeat the numerically superior Ndwandwe army, though it was a close run thing.

None of Shaka's many victories illustrates the full panoply of his military talents better than this early success against his great foe, the Ndwandwe. Heavily outnumbered by more than two to one, Shaka knew he would have to use every trick at his disposal to come out on top.

His plan involved leaving part of his force of 4,000 warriors at fords across the swollen White Mfolozi River with orders to hold out for as long as possible, and then to fall back to kwaGqokli Hill, 2 miles to the south of the river, where the bulk of his warriors were in position. A low-lying, rounded hill that rises only a few hundred yards above the surrounding countryside, kwaGqokli could have been a death trap for a less capable commander. But Shaka knew the importance of surprise and was a master of deception. He deployed a portion of his men in a series of rings around the hill and hid the rest, as a reserve, in a shallow depression behind the southern summit. There, in case of a lengthy siege, he also stockpiled food and water, oxen for slaughter, and firewood. And to deprive the enemy of sustenance he denuded the area of food and shelter.

His masterstroke, however, was to use his herdsmen as a decoy on the emThonjaneni Heights, a few miles to the southeast of kwaGqokli Hill, in the hope that the Ndwandwe commander, Nomo-hlanjana, would send part of his army in pursuit. The herdsmen were to use smoke signals to indicate the position of the detached force.

For a time, Shaka's plan went like clockwork. The defenders at the river held the Ndwandwe back for more than a day, inflicting severe casualties, before withdrawing to the hill with the enemy hard on their heels. As he advanced, Nomohlonjana noticed the herdsmen and fell for Shaka's ruse by detaching part of his force to engage what he thought was a second Zulu *impi* (war band). With the bulk of his troops, around 7,000 warriors, he formed a semicircle round the base of kwaGqokli and opened the battle by advancing towards the first line of defenders, 1,500 strong. But, on Shaka's orders, the Zulus attacked first and, using their superior close-quarter fighting skills, hacked great gaps in the tightly packed Ndwandwe ranks.

When the Ndwandwe withdrew, Shaka took advantage of the lull to replace his frontline soldiers with men from his reserve, and at no time was his enemy aware exactly how many warriors he had at his disposal. Again the Ndwandwe attacked, this time round the whole base of the hill, and again were repulsed with heavy casualties, three Ndwandwe warriors dying for every Zulu. Nomohlonjana now tried a ruse of his own, instructing his men to feign a panicked retreat, but the sandalless Zulus were able to avoid the trap by outrunning the Ndwandwe reserve.

Assuming the Zulus were on the point of collapse, Nomohlonjana formed his remaining men into a huge column, 200 yards wide, and sent it up the hill. This gave

Shaka the opportunity to deploy his reserve in his favourite 'horns of the buffalo' formation, stopping the Ndwandwe column with his 'chest' and sending the two 'horns' to outflank it on either side. Nomohlanjana and four of his brothers were killed in the carnage, as were 4,000–5,000 of their men. It was a victory to rival Hannibal's at Cannae, though so serious were his casualties, and so severe the damage inflicted by the retreating Ndwande army to Zulu homesteads and crops, that Shaka had to move for a time nearer to the coast to build up his army and supplies. His victory was crucial to the survival of the fledgling Zulu state, though he knew it to be no more than round one in an ongoing struggle.

Shaka redoubled his efforts to increase the size of his army, and by 1819, through a combination of clever diplomacy and brutal conquest, he had brought all the tribes between the White Mfolozi and Tugela rivers under his control. This augmentation of force enabled him to rout the Ndwandwe again in 1819, forcing the tribe to move its power base north of the Phongolo into what is now southern Swaziland.

Shaka's military system

As Shaka's authority increased, so did the size of his army, with military conscription compulsory for all adult males. For three years, from the age of 14, boys lived in *amakhanda* (military kraals), where they herded cattle, tended crops and received military instruction. They were then formed into *amabutho*, or age-grade regiments, and spent another eight months together before returning to their homes where, for a quarter of the year, they served as reserves in the district *amakhanda*. Only for national festivals and in times of war would they remobilize as a regiment. Shaka even brought girls into the military system by grouping them in *amabutho* for the purpose of marriage. Not only did they have to wait for Shaka's permission to wed, they also had to choose their partners from those male *amabutho* who had been given leave to wear the *isicoco* (a fibre circlet sewn into the hair, coated with gum and then greased and polished), a privilege rarely granted before the age of 35. The award of the *isicoco* marked the attainment of adulthood, full acceptance into the village community and the right to marry and set up home. By withholding it until a relatively late age, Shaka was trying to keep young Zulu men more firmly under the authority of their tribal elders and, by extension, their king.

Within a few years Shaka's army had increased from its original nucleus of 500 to 20,000 men; his territory from 10 to 11,500 square miles. The many tribes he subdued even began to refer to themselves as Zulus, so that the original clan of 3,000 had soon swelled to a nation of a quarter of a million. Shaka was no longer fighting wars of survival but of conquest, and the Zulus, a pastoral people who measured their wealth in terms of cattle, grew rich on the huge herds they looted from their victims. By 1824 the Zulus had laid waste much of modern Natal and, in the process, had set off a stampede to the south that consumed clan after clan until it petered out on the borders of Britain's Cape Colony. This stampede was known as the *mfecane*, the 'crushing' (though in its widest sense the term applies to *all* the wars and migrations caused by rival emergent states north of the Tugela, and not just Zulu aggression).

The final showdown

One implacable foe had not gone away, however. Since retreating north of the Phongolo, the Ndwandwe had used the intervening years to re-gather their strength and build a new army. In the autumn of 1826, under the command of their young Chief Sikhunyana, they crossed the Phongolo into Zulu territory. Shaka responded by calling up his entire army, 20,000 warriors, and marching it north in a massive column, which, according to an early British settler called Henry Fynn, created huge clouds of dust. Fynn observed how each regiment was accompanied by *izimbongi* (praise singers) who hailed Shaka's heroic achievements. The warriors carried their own weapons, with their shields rolled up and strapped to their backs, and iron rations of maize grains and cooked cow's liver. Younger boys carried sleeping mats and drove the herds of cattle that provided the army with the bulk of its food.

After marching for ten days, the Zulu army rested on a sandstone ridge near to the battlefield of Kambula, where, fifty-three years later, the Zulus would be defeated by British troops armed with breech-loading rifles and cannon. From here Shaka sent out scouts and advance guards to gather intelligence and tempt the enemy into an attack. These spies revealed that Sikhunyana, in a mirror image of the Battle of kwaGqokli Hill, had concentrated the majority of his warriors just below the rocky summit of a peak in the izinDolowane Hills. Above them he had placed their cattle and, higher still, their women and children.

Given the confines of the battlefield, Shaka could not use his favourite tactic of envelopment. Instead his only option was a frontal attack that would, if all went well, pierce the Ndwandwe ranks and enable the Zulus to surround and destroy the broken remnants, a tactic known to Western generals as defeating in detail. As well as his peerless generalship, Shaka had one further advantage over the Ndwandwe: the firepower of Fynn and a small group of British settlers who had agreed to fight on his behalf.

Their opening volley of bullets into the tightly packed Ndwandwe ranks was the signal for the Zulu warriors to mount the first of a series of charges, which Shaka likened to waves striking the shore. As the third 'wave' swept into the Ndwandwe position, Shaka noticed from his vantage point on a nearby knoll that the enemy was beginning to waver; he took this as the cue to throw in his reserves. Like Alexander at Gaugamela, and Napoleon at Austerlitz, he had recognized the decisive moment in the battle and acted accordingly.

For a short time the Ndwandwe held their ground, but then a tiny gap appeared in their centre through which the Zulu reserves poured. Attacked from front and rear, the Ndwandwe broke and ran. Most were caught by their barefoot pursuers and killed, as were all the women and children. Among the handful of survivors was Chief Sikhunyana, who hid in a pit to avoid capture.

With this victory, Shaka finally removed the most dangerous and persistent threat to his power. In just ten years, thanks to his unequalled genius for war, he had created a huge empire that extended from Delagoa Bay in the north to the Mthamvuna River in the south, from the Indian Ocean to the Drakensberg Mountains. But he did not rule for much longer.

A tyrant's death

Shaka's people had grown tired of ceaseless war and their ruler's penchant for random executions (he once had an attendant brained for sneezing while he was eating). The final straw was his hysterical reaction to the death of his mother, Nandi, in October 1827. Thousands of mourners were bludgeoned to death, and for a year, on Shaka's orders, no women were to get pregnant, no crops to be planted and no milk drunk. After three months Shaka came to his senses and revoked the edicts; but the damage to his prestige had been done.

His assassins were his half-brothers Dingane and Mhlangana. On 24 September 1828, while the army was away campaigning and Shaka virtually unprotected, they launched their attack. As Shaka was stabbed by each brother in turn, he pleaded with them: 'What is the matter, children of my father?' They ignored his cries for mercy and finished him off in a flurry of thrusts from the weapon he had invented. He was 41 years old.

GARIBALDI

1807–82

LUCY RIALL

GIUSEPPE GARIBALDI was the greatest guerrilla leader of the nineteenth century, and possibly the century's most popular hero. His career spanned Europe and South America and, from these experiences, he adapted and pioneered a new style of warfare. A convinced revolutionary, he recognized the weakness of his forces relative to those of established regimes; and the tactics for which he became famous – commanding untrained men of varied capacities, using passion and courage as a weapon against an enemy superior in number and resources, relying on mobility and surprise to get ahead – were all designed to overcome this disadvantage.

Garibaldi's successes were still more important for the challenge they posed to perceptions of Italian decadence and cowardice. Before Garibaldi, all revolutionary uprisings against Italy's rulers ended in humiliating defeat, and had reinforced stereotypes of Italian military weakness associated with the peninsula's political decline. 'Italians don't know how to fight,' proclaimed General Oudinot, heading the army sent to Rome in 1849 to crush the short-lived revolutionary Roman Republic. Garibaldi's victory on that famous occasion tied his name for ever to a vision of Italian military resurgence – the *Risorgimento*.

Garibaldi's feats on the battlefield captivated the liberal public. Good-looking, brave and charming, he led an adventurous life that became the stuff of popular legend. In his self, he defied all military convention. His image was that of the radical soldier-hero, the embodiment of romantic rebellion, his long hair, exotic clothes and overt sexuality representing a drastic departure from the traditional, austere military type. Garibaldi's international fame also had a direct impact on his military successes. It guaranteed a steady supply of volunteers and money for his cause, while his fearsome reputation served to intimidate his adversaries, and often helped him gain the upper hand. Yet his extremism caused problems with the established authorities. Tensions with the regular military hierarchy tarnished the wars of Italian unification, and Garibaldi remained until his death a controversial figure, as disliked by conservative Europe as he was loved by radicals, outsiders and the poor.

Character and early career

Garibaldi's military career is inseparable from his belief in liberty and independence. As a young man in 1834, he deserted his post in the Piedmontese navy and was sentenced to death for his part in a nationalist conspiracy against the Piedmontese government. In 1835 he left for a new life as a merchant seaman in Brazil. There he became convinced of what he called a 'greater destiny', and abandoned commercial life to become a corsair for the Río Grande government, engaged in a war for independence from Brazil.

After four tough years of fighting at sea and on land, and as the war petered out into a bloody civil conflict, Garibaldi moved to Montevideo in Uruguay, where war had broken out between Uruguay and the Argentine confederation over control of the Río de la Plata region. He was to remain in Uruguay from 1841 until early 1848, first as a naval officer, then as the commander of the Uruguayan fleet, and finally as the head of the Italian Legion of Montevideo, organized to defend the city against the Argentine siege.

According to the liberal historian G. M. Trevelyan, Garibaldi's education at sea and on the plateaux of South America sheltered him 'from every influence which might have turned him into an ordinary man or an ordinary soldier'. His experiences there had a lasting impact on his political beliefs, and were especially crucial from a military

point of view. In Brazil, Garibaldi learnt the art of guerrilla warfare and how to ride a horse; in Uruguay, he
perfected these skills and discovered in himself the
outstanding talents of a naval and military leader. Although
doubts have always been cast on Garibaldi's achievements
(there were rumours of piracy and plunder, and he was
accused of insubordination), the skill with which he helped
put together a fighting force from the Italian community
in Montevideo seems harder to dispute. Here, as elsewhere
during his career, Garibaldi's personal qualities played a
vital role. With his officers, Garibaldi led from the front
and by example. They moved fast and light, and defeated
the enemy in surprise attacks; and when trapped or
outnumbered, as in the celebrated battle of San Antonio
del Salto in 1846, used the tactics of frontal assault to break
out and scatter their adversaries.

The Italian legionaries of Montevideo wore red shirts,
in an explicit reference to the colours of the French Revolution. In other aspects of their eclectic dress, and in their
manners and relationships, they copied the gaucho militias
of South America; Garibaldi, in the words of a British naval
officer who observed him at this time, resembled 'altogether
the beau ideal of a chief of irregular troops'. They attracted
publicity, and this publicity was used in the parallel propaganda war being waged against Argentina. The Legion itself,
and specifically its public commitment to the liberty of

Uruguay against the tyranny of Buenos Aires, embodied a spirit of combatant cosmopolitanism. Personal courage, flamboyant dress and international solidarity: all these were to prove lasting motifs for Garibaldi and his followers.

The Revolution of 1848–9

When Garibaldi returned to Italy in the spring of 1848 he was already a well-known figure. But his efforts to join the Piedmontese army, and to support Charles Albert of Piedmont-Sardinia in his self-proclaimed nationalist war against the Austrian Empire, were rejected by the king. Garibaldi's first Italian operation, conducting guerrilla action against the Austrian army in the Lake Maggiore area during August 1848, was also not a success.

All this changed at Rome in 1849. French military intervention at the end of April to restore the pope, who had fled the city following revolutionary disturbances there, should have spelt the immediate end to the isolated and largely undefended Roman Republic that had been proclaimed in February. But in one of the most spectacular episodes in his career, Garibaldi and his volunteer army met the French forces on the Janiculum Hill and led a massive bayonet charge on horseback that put the French to flight. He followed this up with two further victories, at the battles of Palestrina and Velletri.

The small Roman Republic was indeed doomed, especially after Garibaldi was tricked by the French, who broke a military truce and seized and held on to the vital strategic heights around Villa Corsini in early June. However, it is for these early, heroic victories in Rome that the Republic is most remembered.

At the time, and later, Garibaldi was criticized by other nationalist leaders both for disobeying orders and for suicidal attacks on unassailable positions (his attempt to retake Villa Corsini resulted in terrible casualties). That said, Garibaldi showed how to snatch moral victory out of certain defeat. Helped by able propagandists, the defence of Rome made front-page news in the international press, and made a villain of the pope and a hero of Garibaldi. Events thereafter – Garibaldi's departure from Rome in July, his march north across the mountains in an attempt to defend Venice from Austrian siege, and the death en route of Anita, his pregnant Brazilian wife – all turned him into a legend. Moreover, the spread and popularity of the volunteer movement, and their victories in the early summer, seemed to create a template for military success.

Exile and independence

After 1849 Garibaldi spent four years away, first in New York and then as a merchant seaman in the Pacific Ocean. Only in 1854 did he return to Europe. There, in a changing political climate, he seemed to abandon his republican convictions and to move closer to the moderate liberalism then being experimented with by the Savoy monarchy in Piedmont. When the 'National Society' was formed in 1857 to press for national unification in Italy under the leadership of Piedmont, Garibaldi was one of its first members.

Garibaldi's rapprochement with the new Piedmontese king, Victor Emmanuel II, and with Cavour, his prime minister, led to their alliance during the war of 1859. This war was the product of a secret agreement between France and Piedmont, and its purpose was to drive Austria out of northern Italy. Cavour made a number of promises in return for French military assistance, the most important of which was the cession of two provinces, Savoy and Nice, to France, and he also undertook to provoke Austria into declaring war on Piedmont. Garibaldi became a pawn in this plan of provocation: specifically, his name was used to encourage men to join volunteer militias, and his fame became part of the anti-Austrian agitation in the months leading up to the war.

The reality was that Garibaldi's role in the planned war with Austria was far from clear, and both the French and Piedmontese high command had severe misgivings about using him and the volunteers. In the end, however, they bowed to nationalist pressure, and Garibaldi was made a major-general in the army and allowed to organize three volunteer corps (the *Cacciatori delle Alpi*). Yet at the outbreak of war, he was given the oldest and least trained men and sent away from the main army into the mountains. Still Garibaldi won some notable victories over the Austrian forces there: first at Varese and then at San Fermo and Como.

The 1859 war ended with the compromise Peace of Villafranca, by which Austria held on to Venetia; this infuriated moderates and revolutionaries alike. Just as the French, by negotiating a separate peace with Austria, had reneged on the deal with Cavour, so had official Piedmontese obstruction hampered Garibaldi's progress during the 1859 war. Nevertheless, Garibaldi's skill as a guerrilla commander and in Alpine warfare was much in evidence in 1859, as was the population's enthusiastic support for both he himself and his cause. Garibaldi, commented one observer, 'did not seem to be a general as much as the leader of a new religion, followed by a fanatical rabble'. During the events of 1860 this popular fervour intensified still further.

'The Thousand'

In the spring of 1860, amid international condemnation, Piedmont ceded Savoy and Nice to France. For Garibaldi it represented a personal defeat. During the previous winter he had sought to continue the nationalist struggle against Austria by organizing a volunteer army 'made up of every man able to carry a firearm', along with a popular subscription to buy a million rifles. Blocked by Piedmontese officialdom, he had been forced to abandon these plans. The handover of Nice was even more of a blow. The town was Garibaldi's birthplace, and its cession cemented both his political frustration and sense of betrayal by Cavour: 'Thirty years of service for the cause of popular freedom,' he exclaimed, '[and] I will have won only the servitude of my poor land!'

In this mood, Garibaldi let himself be talked into leading a military expedition to Sicily, where the Bourbon government was said to be facing a serious insurrection. But the news from Sicily was vague, and when the expedition left Quarto, near Genoa, in early May, it comprised just over a thousand poorly armed volunteers (their rifles had been seized by the Piedmontese government). The men were crammed into two boats seized in Genoa, and they lacked a clear idea, or even maps, of their destination. What the volunteers did possess, however, was patriotic enthusiasm. Passion and bravery, disorganization and good fortune: these elements lay behind the story of 'the Thousand' and lent a miraculous quality to all that ensued.

The volunteers landed at Marsala in western Sicily, and quickly pressed into the interior. In the hill town of Salemi they joined forces with Sicilian revolutionaries, notably with some peasant irregulars (or *picciotti*). From here, against all odds, they overcame the enemy on a hillside at Calatafimi.

The Battle of Calatafimi (15 May 1860) was a tiny affair by modern standards, but it exemplifies Garibaldi's tactics, above all his capacity to surprise and improvise. The disadvantages he faced were evident from the outset. He was outnumbered (around 2,000 men against 1,200) and entirely outgunned. The Bourbon army had better and more rifles, and much more ammunition; they also occupied a defensive position on the top of a steep hill (the Pianto dei Romani) on which they placed two cannons.

Undaunted, Garibaldi relied on two elements to make his advance up the precipitous slope. The first was the intermittent, partly overgrown, terraces constructed on the hillside, which provided some cover from view. The second element was the fearless courage of his officers. It was Garibaldi himself who led the first rush up the hill, drawing his sword and shouting to his men to follow him. As one of the volunteers recounted: 'We thousand attacked, with the General in the lead: every last soldier was used without pause, without care, and without reservation because on that day rested the outcome of the whole expedition.'

Exposing himself recklessly to danger, Garibaldi fought up the hill while members of his staff sought to shield him from fire. Although the outcome of the battle was doubtful until the very last minute, the 'Thousand' kept up a relentless pressure on the enemy throughout the long, hot afternoon. At last, they stood on the final terrace before the summit. Garibaldi rallied his men for one more rush ('Italians, here we must die,' he reportedly told them), and, leaping over the bank in one final bayonet charge, they managed to scare the Bourbon soldiers into a full-blown retreat across the countryside.

Victory at Calatafimi changed everything. Its price was some thirty killed and over a hundred wounded, but it opened the road to Palermo and made the conquest of Sicily possible. The victorious leader, Garibaldi, acquired an aura of invincibility. The battle also began the process of demoralization that was to play a significant part in the defeat and collapse of the Bourbon kingdom in 1860.

In a masterstroke of guerrilla strategy, Garibaldi decided not to descend immediately into Palermo from the west but to remain hidden in the mountains, join up with more peasants, and enter the city from its most vulnerable point on the southeast side. The wounded were sent south on the Corleone road so that the Bourbons would believe that the *Garibaldini* were retreating, and send troops from Palermo to pursue them.

On the morning of 27 May Garibaldi and his men climbed silently down the mountain path from Gibilrossa to Palermo's Porta Termini, where only a temporary gate stood between them and the city. They took the troops guarding the city by surprise ('total surprise', one volunteer wrote in his diary), and under heavy fire charged into one of the main markets, the Piazza Fieravecchia, where they were greeted with enthusiasm. Garibaldi then went on to seize the municipal government building and the adjacent crossroads in the centre of town. There followed three days of street fighting during which Bourbon warships in the port opened fire on the city, while Garibaldi made a great show of his indifference, giving orders out in the open while the shells crashed around him. On 30 May the Bourbon government requested a truce, which was negotiated by a British naval commander in Palermo; the truce was extended until 6 June, when the government capitulated entirely and agreed to withdraw all 20,000 troops from the city.

Sicily was Garibaldi's moment, on which much of his status as a great commander rests. To this day, there remains something astonishing about what he achieved. In less than a month, a handful of poorly armed civilians had challenged and overthrown a regular army, relying on little more than daring, local knowledge and luck. Although the weakened state of Bourbon bureaucracy played a role in its army's defeat, much of the credit must go to Garibaldi. Apart from his ability to continually wrong-foot the enemy, perhaps the most important element in explaining his success was his use of the volunteers. As Calatafimi showed, their courage and self-motivation could make the difference in close-combat situations using the bayonet. 'It was not long shots that imposed on the well-armed Neapolitans [Bourbons]', Garibaldi told his men in 1860, 'but a determined rush in advance.'

These same tactics worked at the Battle of Milazzo in July, and in his army's rapid sweep through Calabria and the southern mainland towards Naples in August. When Garibaldi arrived in Salerno, south of Naples, in early September he was moving so fast that he had left most of his army behind. His progress so disheartened the enemy that, according to one observer, 'Garibaldi ... [had] gradually assumed the nature and the form of Fate.' On 7 September Garibaldi took a train from Salerno to Naples and entered the capital to a vociferous public welcome. The Bourbon king, Francis II, had abandoned the city days before and had retreated to the fortress of Capua some miles to the north.

Unification

After Naples, Garibaldi won one more battle, on 1 October on the River Volturno against a Bourbon counter-attack with 50,000 men (Garibaldi's army was now some 20,000 strong). The battle lasted two days, and Garibaldi proved a master at maintaining offensive–defensive tactics along the whole line of attack. The point is worth stressing because, in the same period, he also allowed himself to be politically outmanoeuvred by the Piedmontese. During the summer

Cavour had become alarmed at Garibaldi's progress, and came under international pressure to protect Rome and the pope from his threatened invasion. Accordingly, Cavour sent an army through the Papal States towards Naples and, at the end of October, Garibaldi met King Victor Emmanuel II and quietly handed power over to him.

The story of Italian unification was beset by rivalries within the nationalist movement, and 1860 was no exception. By giving the Bourbon kingdom to the king of Piedmont, Garibaldi abandoned the hope, long-cherished by republicans, that Italy would be united by the people. Until his death in 1882 he continued to campaign tirelessly for radical reform in the new liberal state, but the political defeat suffered in Naples put a halt to his heroic progress and overshadowed the rest of his career.

Garibaldi was involved in four military campaigns between 1860 and 1882, and they reflect his awkward position in a united Italy. In 1866 he fought with the king against Austria, and saw Venetia absorbed into the kingdom of Italy. Twice during the 1860s – in 1862 and 1867 – he led attempts to march on Rome and seize the city from the pope, but the first time he was stopped by Italian troops at Aspromonte (and badly wounded in the foot), and on the second occasion he was defeated by the French at Mentana. The French forces were equipped with the chassepot rifle, which allowed for fast reloading, and Garibaldi's tactics of rushing forward with the bayonet were no match for this weapon. Despite defeat at Mentana, in 1870 Garibaldi left for France to help defend the newly formed Third Republic against Prussian invasion. He was now old and ill, and the campaign was ineffective. However, Garibaldi's actions in France affirmed the principle of international solidarity; they were a reminder of his glory days in Brazil and Uruguay fighting for the freedom of oppressed peoples.

Revolutionary precursor

By the end of his life Garibaldi had become an uncomfortable presence, his skills supplanted by innovations in military technology. Still he represents much more than a parenthesis between the land battles of the Napoleonic period and the trench warfare of 1914–18. He was a precursor of the revolutionary militias of the twentieth century, and was the first to bring guerrilla tactics from America to Europe. He was a leading tactician of the volunteer movement, a crucial organization in the mid nineteenth-century world. He was an exceptionally versatile commander, equally at home on land and at sea, and able to command field armies as well as guerrilla bands. Garibaldi may make us nostalgic for a time when courage could make the difference in battle; yet his military victories were also modern, linked to the uses of publicity, fame and the press, and these tactics were not lost on the generations that followed.

ROBERT E. LEE

1807–70

JOHN A. BARNES

ROBERT E. LEE was the most successful Confederate general in the American Civil War. His leadership is widely credited with preventing Union forces from overcoming the Confederate government in Richmond, Virginia, for nearly three years. Given the encrustation of political and historical agendas that attached to his name in the decades after the war and his own death, however, an objective assessment of his military reputation has proved difficult. Only in recent years has more scholarship in this area been undertaken, work that has revealed Lee as a bold tactician, but a deeply flawed strategist.

The family into which Robert Edward Lee was born on 19 January 1807 was one of the most distinguished in America. Lee's father, Revolutionary War hero Henry 'Light Horse

Harry' Lee, served as a governor of Virginia and a US congressman, but he nevertheless disgraced the family name by his profligate spending and was twice imprisoned for debt. Young Robert and his siblings grew up in homes borrowed from wealthy relatives.

Lee's desire to erase this disgrace has been cited by biographers, notably Emory Thomas, as the source of his fabled rectitude, his drive to succeed and his devotion to what he saw as his duty. When he graduated second in his class from the US Military Academy at West Point in 1829, he was one of only a handful of cadets in the history of that institution to complete the course without incurring a single demerit.

Early career and Mexican War experience

Commissioned into the elite Army Corps of Engineers, Lee spent the first decade and a half of his military career working on various engineering projects in Virginia, New York, Maryland, Georgia and Missouri. In 1831 he married Mary Anne Randolph Custis, the daughter of George Washington's adopted son, which brought him the Custis mansion in Arlington, overlooking Washington, DC.

Like his future antagonist Ulysses S. Grant, Lee's major pre-Civil War experience was the Mexican War. Attached to the staff of Major General Winfield Scott, Lee demonstrated his personal bravery on several occasions, distinguishing himself at the battles of Cerro Gordo, Contreras and Churubusco, and the final, war-winning assault on Chapultepec.

The war gained Lee valuable combat experience, though some historians (notably Edward H. Bonekemper III) think that Lee might well have drawn erroneous conclusions from that war about the value of audacious tactics and the efficacy of frontal assaults. While frequently successful against poorly trained and led Mexican infantry equipped with smoothbore muskets, such tactics would be far more problematic fifteen years later against Union soldiers firing rifled muskets.

The Civil War: early frustrations
Lee returned to garrison life following the Mexican War, serving for several years as superintendent (commanding officer) of the US Military Academy at West Point. In 1856 he accepted appointment as lieutenant colonel and executive officer of the 2nd US Cavalry Regiment in Texas.

A dramatic side-event of these years was Lee's capture of the anti-slavery zealot John Brown in October 1859, after Brown seized the federal arsenal at Harper's Ferry, Virginia, in an abortive effort to provoke a slave uprising in the South. The efficiency of Lee's operation further enhanced his reputation in Washington circles.

On the recommendation of Winfield Scott, Lee was offered overall command of US forces after the commencement of the Civil War in April 1861. Lee declined, however, since his native state of Virginia had chosen to secede and Lee resigned his commission. He was almost immediately commissioned a major general in the Virginia militia, and later a full general in the new Confederate States Army. He was also named military adviser to President Jefferson Davis.

The immediate problem facing the new Confederate government was the northwestern counties of Virginia, where there were few slaves and the bulk of the population opposed secession. Union troops swiftly occupied most of this area (the future state of West Virginia).

Davis dispatched Lee on 22 July 1861 with vague orders to 'inspect' and 'consult' on the campaign. Once on the scene, Lee declined to bring order out of the chaos, sticking instead to the letter of his instructions to act merely as an observer. Later in the summer and autumn, he took a more active role, becoming de facto commanding officer, but this did little to salvage the situation. Although his forces actually outnumbered those of his Union opponents, the campaign ended in a complete rout for the Confederates.

For the next eight months Lee would operate under the cloud of this disaster. On 6 November he was dispatched to South Carolina to supervise the construction of defences in that region, a posting that earned him the nickname 'the King of Spades' from his soldiers as they dug in. For Lee, it was a backwater posting. He remained in the southeast until early March 1862, when he was recalled to Richmond to resume his post as Davis's chief military adviser.

The Seven Days Battle and the emergence of Lee

On 31 May 1862 General Joseph E. Johnston, who was commanding Confederate forces defending Richmond against the approach of Union Major General George McClellan's huge force on the Virginia Peninsula, was wounded at the Battle of Seven Pines. Davis named Lee as Johnston's successor, changing the character of the war entirely.

Lee succeeded in pushing the Union forces back from the gates of Richmond in the conclusion of the Battle of Seven Pines. Later in June he embarked on what became known as the Seven Days Battle, employing what came to be seen as the hallmark of his style: seizing the initiative with highly complex plans that involved aggressive attacks on Union forces; however, while these plans often resulted in tactical victory, it was only at the expense of high casualties to his own forces.

It was during this campaign that Lee began his famed partnership with an intense western Virginian named

Thomas Jonathan Jackson (see pp. 341–57). The nickname of 'Stonewall' that Jackson earned at the First Battle of Manassas (also known as the First Battle of Bull Run) might indicate a preference for defensive tactics, but this was in no way true. Jackson turned out to be virtually the only one of Robert E. Lee's immediate subordinates who thrived under Lee's habit of issuing discretionary orders.

Commander of the Army of Northern Virginia

Having removed the threat to Richmond by mid July 1862, Lee wasn't about to rest on his laurels. With Union forces reorganizing in northern Virginia, Lee struck in that direction. With the audacious 'Stonewall' Jackson at his side, Lee routed Union forces under John Pope at the Second Battle of Manassas (also known as the Second Battle of Bull Run). Within two months Lee had moved the seat of battle from the gates of the Confederate capital of Richmond to the gates of the Union capital of Washington. At the same time, his popularity with the Southern people soared. Talk of 'the King of Spades' was gone.

At the same time, however, these victories were costing Lee in treasure he could not afford: manpower. Of the 95,000 men he had inherited on 1 June 1862, 30,000 had become casualties less than two months later. Union losses were also high, but less so in proportional terms, as the Union had a far larger population base on which to draw.

Lee was demonstrating that he was all too willing to order the death of that which he loved: his army.

At least in part because of these losses, Lee promptly planned another offensive, this time north of the Potomac River into Maryland. The latter was a slave-holding state, but one that had been kept in the Union by the Lincoln administration through a combination of force and subterfuge. Lee believed that if his victorious army entered the state, pro-Confederate Marylanders would flock to fill its depleted ranks.

It was not to be. On 3 September Lee's army crossed the Potomac into the western part of the state, led by a band playing the pro-Confederate anthem, 'Maryland, My Maryland'. Unfortunately for Lee, this portion of the state was pro-Union and unlikely to be susceptible to secessionist appeals. The new recruits on which Lee premised the campaign stayed away in droves.

On the Union side, although it was as slow-moving as usual, McClellan's Army of the Potomac was not idle. While moving to intercept Lee, a group of Union soldiers from an Indiana regiment discovered, under a tree and wrapped around three cigars, a copy of Lee's orders. These revealed that Lee had divided his forces in the face of the enemy, as he often did, to create the impression he had a much larger army than was actually the case. How the famous 'Lost Order' came to be lost remains a mystery –

although one of Lee's shortcomings as a commander was that his staff was far too small for the tasks assigned to it, and in retrospect it is amazing that more crucial orders did not go astray.

Such an intelligence bonanza should have resulted in a crushing victory for any general but George McClellan. Instead, the result was the bloody but inconclusive Battle of Antietam on 17 September 1862. Outnumbered more than two to one and with its back to the Potomac River, Lee's army came to the brink of defeat several times. Each time, however, through a combination of luck, daring and Union ineptitude, Lee staved it off.

Tactically, Antietam ranks as one of Lee's great battles. Strategically, however, the campaign was a disaster for Lee and the Confederacy. Not only had the hoped-for recruits failed to materialize, but Lee had suffered a terrible 11,700 casualties, nearly a quarter of his men. Worse, Lee's retreat in the wake of the battle across the Potomac back into Virginia looked ignominious. A few days later, Abraham Lincoln felt sufficiently confident to issue his preliminary Emancipation Proclamation, declaring that unless the Confederate states abandoned the war and returned to the Union by 31 December, all the South's slaves would be 'henceforth and forever free'. Given the battle's outcome and the issuance of the Proclamation, the prospect of British and French intervention – always the Confederacy's most realistic hope for independence – dimmed considerably.

Lincoln sacked McClellan a few months after Antietam, replacing him with Ambrose Burnside, who had won some minor victories early in the war. Burnside proved no saviour. In a grim preview of the Western Front in the First World War, on 13 December 1862 he sent wave after wave of Union infantrymen against Lee's solidly entrenched army at Fredericksburg, Virginia. The result was Lee's most lopsided victory, incurring only 4,700 casualties to nearly 11,000 for the Union.

Lee wrote frequently of his desire to inflict a 'Cannae' on the Union army, referring to Hannibal's victory of 216 BC in which his forces killed an estimated 50,000 Romans. Lee probably missed his best chance at Fredericksburg by failing to follow up his tactical success on 13 December with an attack late that day or early the next. Fredericksburg illustrates the key flaw in Lee's generalship: although his tactical gambles won him successes, he proved unable to cash in these successes for strategic victory.

The road to Gettysburg

As 1863 dawned, the Union Army of the Potomac received yet another commander, Major General Joseph Hooker, who replaced the hapless Burnside. Hooker made a good start with a decent plan that caught Lee napping on

27 April 1863, when the 130,000-strong Union force crossed the Rappahannock River to face Lee's army, which was only half as strong. The result was the Battle of Chancellorsville, Lee's greatest military success.

Hooker had devised a bold plan, using four corps to slip past Lee's left flank and into his rear, interposing themselves between Lee and his capital of Richmond. The remaining corps would occupy Lee by feinting through Fredericksburg on his right. Meanwhile, some 7,500 cavalry under Major-General George Stoneman would raid deep into the Confederate rear, cutting Lee's lines of communication and supply.

But having seized the initiative, Hooker failed to hold it. Instead, he abruptly halted, hunkered down on the south side of the river, and dared Lee to attack his superior force. Lee and Jackson took the gamble, with Lee agreeing to divide his already greatly outnumbered army further and to allow Jackson to take the bulk of it on a roundabout march around Hooker's unsecured right flank.

For the plan to work, everything had to go perfectly from the Confederate point of view. Incredibly, everything did. 'Stonewall' Jackson achieved total surprise in his flank attack late of the afternoon of 2 May, routing the Union XI Corps. The blow was not fatal, however. Hooker's huge force could have absorbed it and bounced back, but the commander was psychologically shattered. He withdrew across the Potomac River.

Lee's tactical victory at Chancellorsville, so unlikely in almost every respect, seems to have bred an arrogance of its own in both Lee and his soldiers. The latter came to believe in their general as a god-like miracle-worker, while the former seemed to believe he could ask anything of his men and they would loyally deliver. It was to prove a fatal combination at Gettysburg two months later.

The most consequential result of Chancellorsville was the death of 'Stonewall' Jackson. 'He has lost his left arm, but I have lost my right,' lamented Lee upon hearing that Jackson had been accidentally wounded by his own men at the climax of the battle. This led to complications, and Jackson died of pneumonia a week later. Thus was Lee deprived of his most reliably aggressive commander.

Despite this crushing loss, Lee planned his most ambitious campaign: a second invasion of the North, this time into Pennsylvania. The precise reasons for this adventure Lee never adequately articulated. He was apparently hoping that a major victory won on Northern soil would persuade the North to sue for peace or, failing that, convince the European powers to enter the war on the Confederacy's side. As the Germans were to discover at Verdun in 1916, a vague hope of breaking your enemy psychologically is a thin reed on which to rest a major campaign.

Lee never intended to fight at Gettysburg. As usual, he had divided his army, and only hastily decided to concentrate it in the small Pennsylvania town after he learnt, to his surprise, that the Army of the Potomac was closing rapidly on his position. This unwelcome news was a result of Lee having lost contact with his cavalry commander, Major General J. E. B. Stuart. The latter, following vague and contradictory orders from Lee, had ridden off on an independent operation, leaving Lee 'blind'.

The entire campaign was plagued by such errors, most of them traceable to Lee himself. Thanks once more to vague orders, on the first day of the battle, 1 July, an opportunity was missed to capture a commanding hill. On the second day Lee insisted on attacking the Union forces in their strong position on Cemetery Ridge, against the advice of such trusted subordinates as Lieutenant General James Longstreet, who favoured waiting for the Union forces to attack, as they had at Fredericksburg. Lee compounded his error on the third and final day when he launched the near-suicidal 'Pickett's Charge', in which some 12,500 Confederate troops advanced across a mile of open ground swept by artillery and musket fire from defenders ensconced on high ground behind a stone wall.

Gettysburg exposed all of Lee's major weaknesses as a commander: an excess of aggression, overly complex battle-plans, a tendency to issue vague orders vulnerable to interpretation, and a curious refusal to take determined charge of the battlefield. As Lee's army began the inevitable retreat to Virginia on 4 July in driving rain, it was with staggering casualties: 22,600 out of 75,000 men engaged in the battle (see also pp. 364–6).

On the same day, Major General Ulysses S. Grant captured Vicksburg, Mississippi, cutting the Confederacy in two (see pp. 383–5). Lee had refused to send any of his troops west to Vicksburg, insisting they would be better employed in Pennsylvania. Now Vicksburg was lost, and the Pennsylvanian campaign had ended in failure. Lee's lack of strategic vision was starkly revealed.

Lee vs Grant

Such losses dictated the cessation of any further major Confederate offensives. Not unlike Napoleon's Grande Armée in 1813–14, the Army of Northern Virginia remained tactically dangerous, but its strategic circumstances were dire. As the spring campaigning season approached in 1864, Lee's only real hope was to inflict such punishment on the Army of the Potomac that a war-weary Northern public would vote out the Lincoln administration in the November elections.

It was Lincoln who first realized that the manpower of the Army of Northern Virginia was fatally depleted, and his appointment of Grant as commanding general of all

Union forces in March 1864 reflected this. Grant's grand strategy was to attack simultaneously all along the front, putting maximum pressure on both Lee and the Western theatre in Tennessee and Georgia, preventing one part of the front from reinforcing another. Eventually, the thinning grey line would crack.

It wasn't that simple, of course, and Lee's resourcefulness and legendary luck – not to mention some incompetence on the part of Grant's subordinate generals – combined to make it a very close-run thing. Ultimately, however, Grant's theory proved correct. The Confederate line did indeed crack, but in Georgia, not Virginia. William T. Sherman's spectacular capture of Atlanta in September 1864 saved Lincoln's re-election two months later. Lee's short-sighted focus on Virginia and his neglect of the Western theatre of operations proved his own – and his cause's – undoing.

Assessment

Lee is the only general in the English-speaking world to become the object of a personality cult. Embittered white American Southerners – the only English-speakers ever to experience defeat in a total war – elevated him to near god-like status in an attempt to make sense of their own suffering. Lee, and, by implication, all Southerners, were undone exclusively by the North's superior resources and numbers of men.

ROBERT E. LEE

Decades of such thinking prevented a realistic appraisal of Lee's qualities as an army commander, at least by American historians. By contrast, British historians, notably J. F. C. Fuller and Basil Liddell Hart, penned far more critical portraits. Fuller described Lee as 'in several respects ... one of the most incapable Generals-in-Chief in history'.

Looking at the totality of Lee's record, that conclusion seems hard to escape. Not only did Lee never devise a strategy for winning the war – and history is replete with examples of weaker powers defeating stronger ones – his audacious, costly attacks and stubborn insistence on having his own way served to undermine whatever strategy the Confederacy possessed.

What then, of Lee the tactician? It must be pointed out that, with the sole exception of Grant, Lee's direct Union opponents were mediocre commanders at best. The likes of John Pope and Ambrose Burnside are hardly yardsticks against which greatness is measured. Nor can the 'Jackson effect' be discounted. Lee won every single one of his victories with 'Stonewall' Jackson at his side. Once Jackson was gone – the one general who thrived under Lee's 'hands-off' style of leadership – the thunder and lightning went out of the Army of Northern Virginia. It never again won another major victory.

A test of a great commander is his legacy to the future. Ulysses S. Grant bequeathed not only a united country poised on the cusp of world-power status, but a strategy and approach to war-fighting that remain the basic doctrine of the US Army to this day. 'Stonewall' Jackson's 1862 'Valley Campaign' is still studied as an example of how a smaller, weaker army can have an impact out of all proportion to its actual size.

Lee's strategy and tactics, by contrast, have less to offer today's commanders. His iconic status, therefore, owes more to the political needs of the post-war South than to the actual value of his military record.

'STONEWALL' JACKSON

1824–63

RICHARD J. SOMMERS

THE LEGENDARY 'STONEWALL' JACKSON was the second greatest Confederate general in the American Civil War. He proved equally effective as battle brigadier, small-army strategist and big-army executive officer. His death in the middle of the war leaves unanswered the question as to how the conflict might have developed had he lived.

Thomas Jonathan Jackson was born in Clarksburg in what is now West Virginia on 21 January 1824. He graduated from West Point, seventeenth of fifty-nine, in 1846. His classmates included twenty-four future Civil War generals, among them the Union commander George B. McClellan and the Southerner George E. Pickett.

Early career

The Mexican War was already raging when Jackson graduated from West Point. Brevetted second lieutenant and posted to Company K/1st US Artillery, he served with that company, acting as infantry, at Vera Cruz and Cerro Gordo. Promoted second lieutenant on 3 March 1847, he soon transferred to Light Battery G/1st US Artillery under Captain (later Confederate Major-General) John B. Magruder. With that famous fighting formation, Jackson earned promotion to first lieutenant, plus brevets as captain and major for his 'gallant and meritorious conduct' at Contreras, Churubusco and Chapultepec.

Back in Company K, Jackson left Mexico for New York harbour in 1848. In 1850 he was detailed to Company E in Florida during the Seminole troubles. There he clashed with company commander Captain (later Union Major-General) William H. French, whose drunken, libertine behaviour offended the dour, devout Presbyterian Jackson. Jackson left Florida in May 1851 and resigned his commission on 29 February 1852.

That resignation proved anti-climactic. Since August 1851 Jackson had been professor of natural philosophy and artillery tactics at the Virginia Military Institute (VMI) in Lexington. Both happiness and sadness awaited him there. He married Elinor Junkin in 1853, but the following year she died in childbirth. He married again in 1857; his second wife, Anna Morrison, was the sister-in-law of future Confederate Lieutenant General Harvey Hill. Hill was an engaging, if argumentative, professor, but Jackson proved an uninspiring pedagogue, whose eccentricities were derided by the cadets. Indeed, had he not become famous, even these oddities would probably have remained unrecorded.

The coming conflict

The growing sectional strife between North and South was to transform Jackson's prospects. John Brown captured the federal arsenal at Harper's Ferry on 16–17 October 1859, hoping to spark a slave insurrection. Instead, counter-attacking US regulars and state militia suppressed his abortive rebellion. Convicted of treason against Virginia, Brown was hanged on 2 December; at the execution, Jackson commanded the VMI artillery to prevent any attempts to release the condemned man.

Brown's uprising was over, but a bigger conflict was about to start. After the Civil War erupted on 12 April 1861, Jackson, as a VMI professor and Virginia militia officer, became an officer of the commonwealth's army and of the Confederacy. He initially, on 20–22 April, led the VMI cadets to Richmond to train volunteers. He himself remained only until 28 April. Now a major in the Virginia army, he took charge of militia at Harper's Ferry. In his first – but not last – show of aggressiveness, he crossed the Potomac to occupy the commanding Maryland Heights, but was soon withdrawn lest Maryland take umbrage.

Less than a fortnight later, Brigadier General Joseph E. Johnston superseded Jackson as commander at Harper's Ferry. As senior subordinate, Jackson commanded the 1st Brigade of Johnston's army: the 2nd, 4th, 5th, 27th, and 33rd Virginia Infantry Regiments, soon to be immortalized as 'the Stonewall Brigade'. A Confederate brigadier general himself as of 17 June, Jackson repelled a Union incursion across the Potomac at Falling Waters on 2 July.

A much bigger victory came on 21 July at the First Battle of Manassas (also known as the First Battle of Bull Run), where Johnston's army had been transferred. As the Northerners overran the Confederate left, one of Jackson's fellow generals spotted Jackson's soldiers atop Henry House Hill. 'There is Jackson standing like a stone wall,' he shouted; 'let us determine to die here, and we will conquer.' Despite a severe wound in his left hand, Jackson stood firm and repulsed the Union forces, leading to a great Confederate victory. Henceforth, the general and his brigade were nicknamed 'Stonewall'.

Independent command

This victory earned Jackson promotion on 7 October to major-general (backdated to 7 August), and command of one of Johnston's four divisions. Even greater responsibility came on 5 November, when he took charge of the Valley District – the Shenandoah Valley west to the Allegheny Mountains. Although still subordinate to Johnston, Jackson was now detached from the main army with his own semi-independent command.

The new command involved a large territory and considerable responsibility – but few troops, even after the Stonewall Brigade joined him; his other forces consisted of inexperienced militia brigades and undisciplined cavalry companies. The arrival of William Loring's veteran division in December brought more men and more headaches. Loring, formerly a US army colonel, resented being subordinated to pre-war 'Lieutenant' Jackson. Isolated in icy Romney, Loring protested to Secretary of War Judah Benjamin, who recalled his division to the Shenandoah Valley. Outraged, Jackson resigned, and was persuaded to stay in service only with great difficulty. Instead, it was Loring and two brigades who departed. The remaining two joined Jackson's 'Army of the Valley', now a division of four brigades – three infantry and one cavalry.

The move to Romney plus earlier strikes toward the Potomac aimed to cut coal supplies via the Baltimore and Ohio Railroad and the Chesapeake and Ohio Canal. Jackson also sought to mask his weakness with activity, and to keep the Union forces so busy defending they could not attack. He even began planning to carry the war into the North.

These operations thus foreshadowed his great Valley Campaign of 1862.

The Shenandoah Valley Campaign of 1862

March 1862 witnessed massive movements by Northern forces in Virginia: George McClellan's main army against Manassas, Nathaniel P. Banks's three divisions up the Shenandoah Valley, and John C. Frémont's three brigades eastward from what is now West Virginia toward the Shenandoah Valley. The Confederate forces in those sectors – respectively under Joseph E. Johnston, Jackson and Edward Johnson – retreated before this onslaught.

Instead of pursuing, McClellan sent one division to Frémont and moved his main army by water to Fort Monroe to attack Richmond from the east. One of Banks's divisions joined that transfer toward Richmond; another began marching east from the Shenandoah Valley into the Piedmont. Johnston correspondingly moved his army from the Rappahannock River to the Peninsula. He left only Richard S. Ewell's division in the Piedmont and a brigade at Fredericksburg.

Jackson, too, abandoned Winchester. Rather than yield the entire Shenandoah Valley, however, on 23 March his small division pounced on a supposedly isolated detachment at Kernstown – which proved to be a strong division under James Shields that beat Jackson badly. Tactically, First

Kernstown was a handsome Federal victory. Strategically, it was a striking success. That Jackson felt strong enough to attack so alarmed President Lincoln and Secretary of War Edwin Stanton that they left Banks's two remaining divisions in the Shenandoah Valley. Even more significantly, they retained McClellan's largest corps in the Piedmont as an independent command under Irvin McDowell.

Banks moved southward far up the Shenandoah Valley before withdrawing to Strasburg. He then sent Shields east to McDowell at Fredericksburg. McDowell's strengthened force was to move southward against Richmond, which McClellan threatened from the east.

Jackson, who had withdrawn all the way to Swift Run Gap, did not remain idle but challenged the Yankees for the strategic initiative. He brought Ewell west to hold the gap, then moved his own Stonewall Division westward to join Johnson. At the battle of McDowell on 8 May they beat Frémont's vanguard, which retreated northward. Jackson then moved down the Shenandoah Valley and the parallel Luray Valley with ten brigades – his own, Johnson's and Ewell's. They captured a regiment at Front Royal on 23 May, then routed Banks's three brigades at First Winchester two days later. As the Federals fled across the upper Potomac, Jackson threatened Harper's Ferry.

The government in Washington exaggerated this thrust into a threat against the capital itself. New York militia mobilized, raw volunteer regiments rushed to Harper's Ferry, and Frémont's six brigades were ordered to enter the Shenandoah Valley near Strasburg to cut off Jackson. Even worse, McDowell's drive on Richmond was cancelled. He was directed to take two divisions westward to Front Royal to intercept Jackson.

Theoretically, uniting Frémont and McDowell in Jackson's rear might have proved the latter's undoing. But as it happened, coordinating two distant columns in rainy, mountainous country proved impossible. Jackson's hard-marching 'foot cavalry' escaped the trap, smacked Frémont's van at Strasburg on 1 June and withdrew up the Shenandoah Valley. Frémont followed. McDowell's leading division under Shields moved south in a parallel route up the Luray Valley.

On 6 June Jackson lost his inspiring if undisciplined cavalry commander, General Turner Ashby, in bloodying Frémont's pursuit at Harrisonburg. Two days later Ewell defeated Frémont's entire army at Cross Keys, and on 9 June Jackson thrashed Shields's two leading brigades at Port Republic. Frémont and Shields retreated down their respective valleys. At this point the victorious Jackson even considered invading Pennsylvania, but he was transferred east to save Richmond and to try to destroy McClellan.

The eight battles of the Valley Campaign, including seven Confederate victories, are fascinating in themselves.

The campaign's inherent importance, however, lies in its strategic impact. With sometimes only four brigades and never more than ten, Jackson challenged seemingly over-whelming Federal forces of thirty brigades intent on over-running the Shenandoah Valley and central Virginia, then joining McClellan at Richmond. Rather than let them concentrate, Jackson, with swift, bold strokes reminiscent of Frederick the Great's a century earlier, beat some of the Union forces and diverted the rest, leaving the planners in Washington distracted and distraught, and disrupting their entire campaign plan. Jackson succeeded in delaying eight brigades from joining McClellan, and prevented the other twenty-two altogether. He thus changed the course of the campaign and thereby the war. In late March 1862, Union victory in Virginia had seemed certain. Three months later, thanks to Jackson, Washington's plans lay in ruins, and the Confederacy appeared ascendant.

Surprises strategic and psychological

The Valley Campaign of March–June 1862 was Jackson's greatest success. But before June ended, he suffered his greatest failure: the Seven Days Battle. At first the Confed-erate strategists considered sending Jackson's victorious veterans to invade Pennsylvania, but they decided instead to bring them east to relieve beleaguered Richmond. Jackson's force, now increased to nine infantry brigades grouped into three divisions, moving by rail and road, was to surprise and envelop the right-rear of three Union divisions isolated north of the Chickahominy River. Three other Confederate divisions would simultaneously attack their front. General Robert E. Lee, Johnston's successor as commander of the Army of Northern Virginia, hoped thereby to crush the Union V Corps and raise the siege of Richmond.

With his brigades in transit, on 23 June Jackson rode ahead to confer with Lee, the first meeting of the two greatest Confederate commanders. Since Jackson's force had to travel farthest, he was allowed to set the attack date. He confidently picked 25 June; at James Longstreet's suggestion, 26 June was chosen instead. Even that later date proved over-optimistic. The primitive logistical infrastructure of the Confederacy, plus poor staff work and Jackson's own neglect, made him miss that mark. Unthreatened from their right-rear, the Federals repulsed Lee's frontal assaults at Mechanicsville. Now alert to the danger, V Corps withdrew overnight to Gaines' Mill, where, on 27 June, it once more parried Lee's thrusts. Again Jackson was slow in striking, finally engaging in mid afternoon. Several hours later, two of his brigades pierced the Union centre to gain the one clear-cut Confederate tactical victory of the Seven Days Battle.

Though driven from the field, the Federals escaped

south of the Chickahominy. Both sides spent the following day manoeuvring. When fighting resumed on 29 June, Jackson took no part in it. The crisis came on 30 June. While three Confederate divisions attacked retreating Union forces south of White Oak Swamp, Jackson's four divisions were to fight their way across the swamp into the Union rear. Other than desultory skirmishing and shelling, however, Jackson did nothing. With their rear unthreatened, the Federals repelled the other attacks. They then escaped to Malvern Hill, where, on 1 July, they repulsed repeated onslaughts, including six from Jackson's brigades. The Federals then safely withdrew to the James River. Richmond had been saved, but the Union army had not been crippled or destroyed, largely due to Jackson's failures.

Jackson's uncharacteristic performance in the Seven Days Battle is mystifying. Blaming either his supposed reluctance to fight on Sundays (sometimes offered as an explanation of his inaction on 29 June) or his alleged unwillingness to be subordinated is unfair. He fought on Sundays when necessary, and he later became a model subordinate. A better explanation is the Valley Campaign itself. Its rapid marches and sterling successes had made him overconfident, while its fatiguing operations had left him and his men physically exhausted. Psychological exhaustion further sapped his energy to press the enemy.

Spearhead of success

Relative rest restored Jackson's resolve and his soldiers' strength. By August, they were facing John Pope's new army in central Virginia. One of Pope's corps attacked Jackson at Cedar Mountain on 9 August, and actually made early progress. Confederate counter-attacks, however, secured the field.

Both Lee and Pope sparred along the Rapidan and upper Rappahannock rivers. Then in a bold surprise turning movement, Lee sent Jackson's three divisions north through Loudoun Valley, then east across Bull Run Mountains into Pope's rear. On 26 August Jackson captured the main Union forward supply base at Manassas Junction and crushed a brigade at Bull Run Bridge.

Tactical success, strategic surprise and supply windfall were Jackson's means of implementing Lee's seizure of the strategic initiative. Yet Jackson in Pope's rear was a vulnerable target until Lee's main body rejoined him. Bagging Jackson was not easy, however. On 27 August he held back his pursuers at First Bristoe Station, and the next day at Groveton fought a stand-up battle to a standstill. The Groveton fighting alerted Pope to Jackson's location, and over the next two days Jackson and his men came under massive assaults; but Jackson firmly held his ground along a railroad embankment. Longstreet's arrival led to a great counter-attack on 30 August, which made the Second Battle of Manassas Lee's first great victory. Jackson's effort to exploit that success at Chantilly on 1 September produced only limited gains, however.

Pope's ensuing retreat into the defences around Washington virtually cleared Virginia of Union forces. Lee then carried the war across the Potomac in the hope of liberating Maryland and crippling the Northern war effort, long one of Jackson's goals. Jackson led the advance, which began on 4 September. Two days later his new horse injured him, but he resumed command within days. He then led his three divisions westward to isolate Harper's Ferry, while three other divisions helped surround the town itself. His and their successful attacks on 14 September doomed the Union position. The capitulation of its 12,400 defenders the following day was the largest US surrender until Bataan in the Philippines in 1942.

Such a triumph proved risky, however. Lee had boldly scattered his army from Harper's Ferry almost to Pennsylvania. When his dispersal order fell into Federal hands, Union commander George McClellan had a great opportunity to beat the Confederates in detail. McClellan secured South Mountain, but failed to exploit his advantage. Jackson's capture of Harper's Ferry emboldened Lee to remain north of the Potomac. Jackson joined him at Sharpsburg on 16 September, and the following day, at Antietam, held the Confederate left. The first Federal onslaught inflicted terrible losses on Jackson, but reinforcements restored his lines. Antietam proved the bloodiest day of the Civil War. Lee finally withdrew into Virginia, on 18/19 September.

Promotion and promising prospects

Lee's battered army spent October in the Shenandoah Valley, resting and refitting. While there, his two senior subordinates, Longstreet and Jackson, were promoted to the newly created rank of lieutenant general (Jackson ranking from 10 October). On 6 November their 'wings' were officially designated the I and II Corps of the Army of Northern Virginia. Jackson's II Corps contained the three divisions that had served under him since August, plus Harvey Hill's division.

This respite ended in late October as McClellan's final campaign drew both armies east of the Blue Ridge. McClellan's successor, Ambrose E. Burnside, advanced further southeast to Falmouth. Lee countered by moving Longstreet to Fredericksburg and shifting Jackson further downstream towards Port Royal. Burnside crossed the Rappahannock River at Fredericksburg on 11 December. Two days later, he frontally assaulted Lee's position. On the Confederate left, Longstreet repulsed successive Union attacks, but on the right Jackson, who had returned from Port Royal, was having a harder time defending his position. A Union division under George G. Meade actually penetrated a gap in the Light Division, which was holding Jackson's front, but Jackson's counter-attacks restored his line. Not content with such defensive success, Jackson wanted to drive the defeated and demoralized Union troops into the Rappahannock, but he was thwarted by the early December dusk and by Federal artillery fire from the left bank. On the night of 14/15 December the Union forces withdrew across the river.

By the end of January the opposing armies had gone into winter quarters. The fighting resumed in late April, when the new Union commander, Joseph Hooker, sent eight divisions upstream to envelop Lee's left-rear. By then, three of Longstreet's divisions had gone south, and Lee had only six infantry divisions to meet this threat. Jackson left one division to confront eight Union divisions at Fredericksburg, and formed the remaining five divisions facing west to meet the turning movement. Jackson's bold show of strength and combative counter-jabs on 1 May punctured Hooker's pretensions to power, and the formerly aggressive Union general withdrew into the Wilderness to defensive positions around Chancellorsville plantation.

With audacity born of confidence in his troops and in his executive officer, Lee again divided his forces. He kept one division at Fredericksburg and two facing Hooker's thirteen divisions at Chancellorsville. On 2 May Jackson boldly marched the remaining three divisions westward, across the entire front of the Yankee army, from its far left to its far right. The Wilderness concealed him, and the closed minds of the Union commanders, who also suffered from overconfidence and lack of initiative, failed to comprehend that Jackson would undertake such a move. His own great ability enabled him to carry it out. In the late afternoon of 2 May Jackson routed the Union right flank west of Chancellorsville, crushing XI Corps. The resulting victory proved to be Lee and Jackson's greatest battlefield success.

For Jackson, it also proved to be his last. As he reconnoitred in the darkness that evening for ways to exploit his initial success, his own men fired on him in error, seriously wounding his right hand and left arm, which was subsequently amputated just below the shoulder. He appeared to recover, but died of complications eight days later. He is buried in Lexington.

Assessment

From First Manassas to Chancellorsville, 'Stonewall' Jackson was the great popular hero of the Confederacy. Such adulation left him untouched. His stern Calvinism led him to attribute his successes to God's will. Moreover, he understood that, to be meaningful, battlefield victories must translate into strategic success. His Valley Campaign of 1862 best represents such strategic success. Other instances are Second Manassas, which not only drove the Federals from the field but from Virginia, and Harper's Ferry, which netted numerous prisoners. Chancellorsville, unquestionably a masterful tactical triumph, might have become a strategic victory had Jackson lived. Even the follow-up at Fredericksburg and the Romney campaign represent unfulfilled quests for strategic victory. Such major strategic gains more than offset the disappointing Seven Days and precarious Antietam. They mark Jackson as the best executive officer of the American Civil War.

GEORGE MEADE

1815–72

RICHARD J. SOMMERS

GEORGE MEADE was a competent professional soldier who earned promotion after promotion during the American Civil War, until, during the greatest crisis of that war, he was unexpectedly given command of an entire army. Rising to his new responsibilities, he won a great victory at Gettysburg, repelling a Confederate invasion of the North, and thus affecting the entire outcome of the war.

George Gordon Meade was born on 31 December 1815 in Cadiz, Spain, where his American parents were on business, but was raised in Philadelphia. Graduating from West Point in 1835, nineteenth of fifty-six, he went on to serve sixteen months as a second lieutenant in the 3rd US Artillery Regiment, campaigning in the Second Seminole War and escorting 400 Seminoles on the 'Trail of Tears' to Indian

Territory (present-day Oklahoma). He resigned on 26 October 1836 and practised civil engineering.

In May 1842, seventeen months after marrying Margaretta Sergeant in Philadelphia, Meade re-entered service as a second lieutenant in the Topographical Engineers. For nineteen years thereafter he made maps and designed, built and maintained lighthouses from Florida to New Jersey and Michigan. During the Mexican War he undertook topographical surveys from Palo Alto to Vera Cruz, and then he honourably returned to Washington in March 1847, before the drive to Mexico City was launched. Promoted to captain in 1856, he was engaged in lake survey work in Detroit when the Civil War broke out.

The battling brigadier

Many officers in the Corps of Engineers and the Topographical Engineers, largely upper graduates at West Point, immediately received high command on the outbreak of hostilities in April 1861. Perhaps because Meade had middling standing at the Military Academy and became a 'Topog' only indirectly, he initially languished in Detroit, despite desiring active service. Probably thanks to his wife's politically influential family, however, he was commissioned brigadier general of volunteers on 31 August.

On 16 September Meade assumed command of the 2nd Brigade of the Pennsylvania Reserve Division, which was among only a few Federal divisions entirely from one state. He and his first two fellow generals of brigade rose to great eminence. John F. Reynolds was a wing commander when killed at Gettysburg. Both Meade and Edward Ord commanded armies at Appomattox. Like most of George B. McClellan's army, the Pennsylvania Reserves spent seven months training, first north of the Potomac and from October onwards in Virginia. The following March they participated in the meaningless move to Manassas. As part of Irvin McDowell's I Corps, they remained in northern Virginia when McClellan's main body transferred to Fort Monroe to attack Richmond from the east.

McDowell occupied Fredericksburg and intended continuing south against Richmond. He was, however, ordered westward in a vain effort to trap 'Stonewall' Jackson. During that chase the Pennsylvania Reserve Division, commanded by George A. McCall, remained around Fredericksburg until 9 June, when it sailed to join McClellan. By 18 June the Reserves held McClellan's far right, north of the Chickahominy River just northeast of Richmond.

There they lay exposed to Robert E. Lee's great strategic counter-attack, the Seven Days Battle, which reversed the course of the war in the east. However, numerous Confederate errors cost Lee a victory of annihilation. Those shortcomings cannot eclipse the valour of the Reserves and the skill of their generals in resisting

Confederate attacks throughout that prolonged battle. On 26 June, the Pennsylvanians repeatedly repulsed Confederate onslaughts at Mechanicsville. Meade, originally in reserve, fed his forces forward to bolster the front. Overnight the Federals withdrew to Gaines' Mill, where a bigger battle erupted the next day. McCall initially remained in reserve (Meade on the left, Reynolds on the right, 3rd Brigade further back). As the Union position progressively deteriorated, the Pennsylvania regiments reinforced the front or resisted breakthroughs piecemeal. When the whole Union position collapsed, Meade used his topographical skills to lead survivors safely south of the Chickahominy.

The weary V Corps, including McCall, was spared fighting for two days as McClellan's army shifted southward towards the James River. The crisis of the campaign came on 30 June, as Lee intercepted that lateral march at Glendale. Charles City Crossroads proved key. Meade, reconnoitring southwestward from there, alerted McCall to the danger. The 2nd Brigade held McCall's right. In the heaviest fighting of the Seven Days Battle, the Pennsylvanians blunted the Confederates' blow. Although yielding some ground, McCall secured the crossroads and assured the five divisions behind him safe passage to the James River. At the height of the battle Meade was severely wounded in the right arm and possibly the right kidney. He tried to ride away but grew faint from bleeding and had to be carried off. He was among the 2nd Brigade's 1,400 casualties in the Seven Days Battle, which accounted for almost half of McCall's 3,100 casualties. McCall and Reynolds had been captured; another brigadier was killed. Only one general remained with the division when it finally reached the James.

On 17 August Meade resumed command; by then his brigade (now redesignated the '1st') was back near Fredericksburg. In the ensuing Second Battle of Manassas (Second Bull Run) on 30 August Meade helped secure Henry House Hill against James Longstreet's great counterattack, thus preventing defeat from becoming disaster. Meade lost 185 men in the battle.

Division and corps command

Prior to late June 1862 Meade had not led even a platoon in combat, but over the ensuing two months his prudence, skill and inspiration commanding a brigade in battle earned him promotion. It came on 12 September, when he succeeded Reynolds as commander of the Pennsylvania Reserve Division.

Two days later Meade delivered the decisive charge that drove the Confederates from South Mountain. Two days after that, he and John B. Hood tangled in the East Woods at Antietam. Then, on 17 September, Meade's devastating charge through Miller's cornfield nearly wrecked

Jackson's wing. Meade again penetrated Jackson's centre at Fredericksburg on 13 December, the one bright spot in that dismal Union defeat. At both Antietam and Fredericksburg, Meade, left unsupported, was eventually driven out, but he demonstrated continued competence as a battle leader at this higher level of command. His casualties on 14 and 16–17 September and on 13 December were 393, 573 and 1,853 respectively.

His service earned him higher rank. As of 29 November he became a major-general of volunteers, and on 26 December he took command of V Corps. At Chancellorsville in the spring of 1863 (pp. 334–5) his corps spearheaded the drive into the Confederate left-rear. On 1 May, however, Jackson's stiffening resistance caused the Union army commander, Joseph Hooker, to go on the defensive. He thereby forfeited the initiative to Lee and Jackson, who won their greatest victory. Guarding the Union left, Meade saw little action in the decisive fighting of 2–3 May, suffering only 700 casualties in the entire battle.

In June Lee seized the strategic initiative and moved down the Shenandoah Valley into Pennsylvania. As Hooker repositioned his forces in reaction to Lee's strike, Meade's corps supported heavy cavalry fighting east of the Blue Ridge Mountains. Meade then crossed the Potomac and bivouacked near Frederick, Maryland, on 27 June.

Battles great and small

That night a War Department staff officer roused Meade from sleep. The general, who was among many senior subordinates openly critical of Hooker, feared he was being arrested. Instead he received command of the Army of the Potomac. In less than a week he led that army to victory at Gettysburg.

Throughout the month leading up to the battle the army had manoeuvred defensively, shielding Washington and Baltimore. Lee, invading Pennsylvania, controlled the strategic initiative. Meade immediately changed that. Prudently but boldly, he advanced into Pennsylvania on 29–30 June, to challenge Lee. Meade thereby won the strategic duel. No longer could Lee advance unimpeded. He had to re-concentrate and respond to Meade. Thereafter each side sought victory on the battlefield, where the superior numbers and equipment of the North would count – if well led.

Meade provided that good leadership. He massed his largest force under his best subordinate, Reynolds, in the most threatened sector, the westerly left wing. The battle opened on Wednesday 1 July, when Confederate troops encountered that wing at Gettysburg, and attacked and defeated it. Despite this setback, Meade accepted Reynolds's and Hancock's recommendations that Gettysburg was the place to fight, and moved his remaining forces there.

Meade perceptively understood that Lee's offensive strategy mandated offensive tactics. To meet those attacks, Meade made excellent use of terrain. His 'fishhook' formation gave him interior lines, which allowed ready reinforcement of threatened sectors. Lee, in contrast, suffered from exterior lines.

Such reinforcements first saved the Union left, which Longstreet overran on Thursday afternoon. They similarly secured Meade's centre and right through Thursday night and Friday morning. Meade resolved to keep fighting on 3 July. That afternoon Hancock repulsed Lee's last great onslaught, Pickett's Charge.

During the night of 4/5 July Lee withdrew. Meade had won the battle. Now he tried reaping its fruits. Only two divisions chased the Confederates, while his main army rushed to Maryland, thence westward to intercept their retreat. Meade found them unable to cross the flooded Potomac, but fortified on defensible ground; he judged his own battered army too weak to attack. On the night of 13/14 July Lee escaped across the river.

Meade immediately continued southward across the Potomac east of the Blue Ridge. Again he did not chase the Confederates from behind but sought to confine them west of the mountains. His slow vanguard, however, was repulsed at Wapping Heights on 23 July, and the Confederates crossed the mountains further south. The Gettysburg campaign ended on 1 August, as both exhausted armies rested near Warrenton.

How fared Meade in his first five weeks of army command? Strategically, he immediately seized control of the campaign and forced Lee to react to him. Tactically, he took excellent advantage of terrain and skilfully deployed and redeployed troops to contain or repel attacks. Unquestionably, the Confederates made many mistakes. Equally clearly, Meade took advantage of them. One measure of a good general is how well he fights a flawed foe.

Nor should Meade be blamed for not counter-attacking at Gettysburg on 3–4 July, or for not assaulting on the Potomac on 13 July. So costly and close-run a victory as Gettysburg, with its terrible losses of soldiers and leaders (23,000 Northerners, 28,000 Southerners), left Meade too crippled to attack tactically. His decision not to attack is thus justifiable, and critics (including President Lincoln) who have said otherwise are being unfair. Indeed, Meade deserves credit for his aggressive strategic pursuit, from Gettysburg to Warrenton, with such a battered army. Contrast him with McClellan, stalled in Maryland for six weeks after the Battle of Antietam.

Gettysburg was the largest battle ever fought in the Americas. It did not end the war, nor could it have. The war, however, did change there. Meade deserves great credit

for winning so tactically important and strategically significant a victory. His victory ended the Southern invasion of
the North, and the Confederates withdrew to central Virginia.

After resting, refitting and sending troops north to
suppress draft riots, Meade resumed his advance on 13
September. He crossed the Rappahannock, easily overran
Culpeper County and reached the Rapidan River. He had
already detached one division to South Carolina; the
requirement now to send four more to Tennessee stalled
his advance. Lee, despite having sent off three divisions
himself, took the initiative and tried to cut off the Union
forces in Culpeper. Meade skilfully withdrew across the
Rappahannock and Bull Run on to the fortified Centreville
Heights, beating back the Confederates at Second Bristoe
on 14 October.

Lee then withdrew behind the Rappahannock, but on
7 November Meade's victories at Rappahannock Station
and Kelly's Ford again brought Culpeper County under
Federal control. Late that month he crossed the Rapidan
to turn Lee's right. Fighting flared at Payne's Farm on 27
November, but Meade thought assaulting fortifications along
Mine Run too risky. The Unionists withdrew into Culpeper
a few days later, and went into winter quarters. Critics
branded this operation 'the Mine Run Fiasco'. Actually,
Meade deserves credit for his moral courage in refusing to
squander his men in senseless slaughter.

Winning the war

Few fights flickered along that front during the winter of 1863/4. Spring saw the arrival of new General-in-Chief Ulysses S. Grant, who (unlike his predecessor, the desk-bound Henry W. Halleck) established headquarters 'in the field' in Virginia, operating directly against Lee. Meade magnanimously offered to step aside, so Grant could take immediate command or install some preferred replacement. However, Grant left Meade in charge, while himself assuming the role, to use a modern term, of 'army group' commander, overseeing both Meade's Army of the Potomac and the independent IX Corps and later the Army of the James.

Grant wisely sought to work with and through the generals under his command, not around or without them. Over the ensuing twelve months, moreover, many of them earned his respect. Grant already knew of Meade by repu-tation; Gettysburg, after all, occurred at the same time as Grant's greatest victory, Vicksburg. Meade now confirmed that reputation. On 23 January 1865 Grant affirmed that 'Gen. Meade is one of our truest men and ablest officers … I defy any one to name a commander who could do more than he has done with the same chances.' Grant thereby assured Senate confirmation of Meade as major-general of regulars, as of 18 August 1864. (Meade had, after Gettysburg, already been promoted to brigadier general of regulars.)

Grant's professional respect for Meade is unmistakable. Yet they were not friends (Grant was closer to Ord, William T. Sherman and, increasingly, Philip H. Sheridan), nor was their relationship harmonious. Proud, patrician, sensitive and well-connected, Meade, the hero of Gettysburg, chafed and seethed, imagining slights where Grant intended none. Too good a soldier to erupt against his superior, Meade lashed out at subordinates, including such old friends as Gouverneur K. Warren, Horatio G. Wright and even Winfield Scott Hancock. Meade particularly resented the growing prominence and influence of Sheridan, the coarse cavalry commander, one of the few outsiders whom Grant installed in the Army of the Potomac. The long, hot, dry summer of unfulfilled operations worsened frustration and tension among all parties. Already called 'Old Snapping Turtle', the acerbic Meade confirmed his nickname that summer.

Beyond personalities, the new institutional arrangements increased Meade's frustration. Previously he had made the fundamental decisions on starting, conducting and ending campaigns. Those decisions now rested with Grant, who functioned not only as grand strategist for the Union war effort but also as strategist for the eastern theatre and 'army group' strategist. Though nominally still army commander, Meade was, in effect, reduced to operations officer, responsible simply for troops and tactics to implement Grant's strategy. Grant respected Meade, and frequently deferred to his recommendations on operations. Yet they remained just recommendations. The final say was now with Grant.

Despite such institutional and personal problems, these two consummate professionals worked together to win the war in the east. Grant, through Meade, fought a series of bloody field battles in May and June 1864 – Wilderness, Spotsylvania, North Anna, Cold Harbor – which forced the Confederates from the Rapidan to Richmond. From the middle of June Grant waged the prolonged siege of Petersburg on both sides of the James River. Both Petersburg and Richmond fell on 3 April 1865. Six days later, Lee surrendered at Appomattox.

Throughout those eleven months, Meade remained directly under Grant. When a new field army was created in August 1864 to conquer the Shenandoah Valley, Sheridan, not Meade, received that quasi-independent command. The latter general was considered for that post in October, but only because Sheridan, the junior officer, might be needed in Missouri. However, Sheridan remained in the Valley, and Meade remained at Petersburg. Even at Appomattox, Sheridan and Ord, who had blocked Lee's escape, were present for his surrender; but Meade, who had battled Lee for twenty-two months and was in hot pursuit of the Southerners on 9 April, was not invited.

Grant did not mean to slight his subordinate, but Meade took offence, nonetheless.

Post-war career

The Army of the Potomac conducted its grand review in Washington on 23 May 1865. Five weeks later it ceased to exist. Meade immediately took command of the Military Division of the Atlantic, a position he held until 1868 and again from 1869 to 1872. Within that division he also headed the Department of the East, from 1866 to 1868. In 1868–9 he commanded the Third Reconstruction District, later the Department of the South. During his sojourn in the South he sought reconciliation in Georgia, Florida and Alabama (later in the Carolinas, too), and was spared most of the odium associated with Reconstruction. Nor did he fight Native Americans. His one post-war military operation involved intercepting a Fenian invasion of Canada in 1866.

Active service fighting Native Americans went to Grant's favourites, Sherman and Sheridan. When Grant became president on 4 March 1869, Sherman succeeded him as general-in-chief. That promotion vacated the one lieutenant-generalcy. The three contenders for that coveted third star were George H. Thomas, long Grant's enemy; Meade, Grant's proven subordinate; and Sheridan, Grant's favourite. Unsurprisingly, it was Sheridan who was promoted. Being again overlooked broke Meade's heart. He died on 6 November 1872, aged only 56, and is buried in Philadelphia.

Meade excelled commanding a brigade or a division in battle. His understanding of terrain, tactics and troops enabled him to maximize effectiveness offensively and defensively. Chancellorsville suggests he would have done well as a corps commander, too.

Yet army command is where Meade must be evaluated. That record is mixed. Genius he lacked. Other hallmarks of great captains – boldness, strategic insight, tenacity – Meade possessed only to a limited degree. Two years of army command show him a sound, competent, capable leader, well above average for the Union army but hardly in the front rank, either in the American Civil War or in other eras. If left in charge in the east without Grant, Meade was capable enough not to lose the war but not good enough to win it.

What entitles Meade to his place in this book is not his entire career but his greatest victory. Less than one week into army command, he defeated the best Confederate army under the best Confederate general (who really was a military genius). He thereby saved the North from invasion and reversed the course of the campaign. More than that, Gettysburg – together with major Union victories in the west in early July 1863 – changed the entire course of the American Civil War. Only rarely thereafter did the Confederates regain the strategic initiative. Never again did they mount a major invasion of the North (managing only two sizeable raids into Maryland and Missouri in 1864). His victory at Gettysburg rightly ranks Meade among the great commanders of history.

ULYSSES S. GRANT

1822–85

JOHN A. BARNES

ULYSSES S. GRANT was the most successful military commander in American history, and was primarily responsible for the Union victory in the American Civil War. Undefeated on the battlefield, he forced the surrender of three enemy armies, including the most important, Robert E. Lee's Army of Northern Virginia. Every Union victory of any significance in the war, with the sole exception of Gettysburg, was won either by Grant personally, or under his overall direction. His legacy as a strategist influences the US and other armies to this day.

Grant's rise is also one of the most meteoric in military and political history. A clerk in his father's leather-goods store in the tiny town of Galena, Illinois, at the outbreak of the war in April 1861, he would become, within three years, the first American to hold the permanent rank of lieutenant general since George Washington. In less than eight, he would take office as president of the United States.

A soldier made, not born

The men who become professional soldiers and who grow into great military commanders seem to choose this career path very early in life, often as a result of having military ancestry. Robert E. Lee and George S. Patton, for example, were both descended from war heroes and settled on military careers while quite young. Ulysses S. Grant does not fit this pattern.

Hiram Ulysses Grant (the name Ulysses Simpson Grant was a result of an army clerical error at West Point) was born on 27 April 1822 to a prosperous local businessman in Point Pleasant, Ohio. If Grant had any thoughts of a military career as a young man, he kept them well to himself; his appointment to the West Point class of 1843 was arranged by his father without his knowledge. The young man baulked at first, according to his own account, giving in only when his father insisted.

Again, according to his own account, Grant did not enjoy his four years at the military academy. Nevertheless, he did quite well there, finishing twenty-first in a class of thirty-nine graduates. (Thirty-six cadets who entered with Grant in 1839 failed to graduate at all.) In addition to doing well in mathematics (which was also Napoleon's best subject), he was excellent at drawing (which improves the eye for topography) and served as president of the cadet literary society, thus displaying an interesting (and rare) blend of the precise and the artistic. He was also a superb horseman, setting a jumping record that stood at the academy for decades following his graduation.

Experience in the Mexican War

The United States declared war on Mexico on 13 May 1846; at the time Grant was a young lieutenant with the 4th US Infantry stationed near St Louis, Missouri. He was still ambivalent about his choice of a military career, admitting later that, as he faced his first action, 'I felt sorry I had enlisted.'

Grant had been appointed his regiment's quartermaster, a highly responsible position that meant he was in charge of providing everything the soldiers might need (except food, which was the responsibility of the commissary). In theory, this staff position should have kept him out of action, but Grant soon discovered that exposure to enemy fire did not 'un-man' him, and he sought out opportunities to engage the Mexicans. On one occasion he put his exceptional skills as a horseman to work by clambering atop a horse and riding pell-mell through a hail of enemy fire to bring back a re-supply of ammunition. The critical importance of this particular commodity was not lost on him, and in his later career he would ensure that adequate ammunition was always available.

Grant's other major experience in the war was in serving under both of its major commanders, Winfield Scott and Zachary Taylor. While both were excellent generals, Scott was a military showman, wearing, it was said, every inch of gold braid the regulations permitted, while Taylor tended towards extreme simplicity of dress and manner. Grant emulated Taylor, who was elected president of the United States in 1848. Grant also saw what could be achieved when commanders were sufficiently bold and daring.

Civilian life

Assigned to garrison duty in California after the war, Grant was quickly bored. He also missed his wife Julia and new family (including a son he had never seen), who had remained behind in St Louis. This was the period when he probably acquired his reputation for heavy drinking, although contemporaneous evidence for it is lacking. Seeing no other way to reunite his family, Grant resigned from the army in 1854, just after receiving his promotion to the rank of captain.

Returning to St Louis, Grant took to farming the land that his father-in-law had given to him and his wife as a wedding present. With his restless mind and wanderlust, however, a man with less aptitude for the settled life of a farmer than Grant would have been hard to imagine. While he did well enough for the first few years, the economic depression that struck in 1857 hit him hard. Thus began his period of working as a debt collector, firewood salesman, and, when he had no other options, as a clerk in his father's leather-goods business.

Return to military service

The fall of Fort Sumter to Confederate forces on 14 April 1861 ignited the Civil War. Attending a public meeting in Galena, Grant resolved to return to the service. Getting back into the army, however, proved far more difficult than leaving it.

A surplus of serving and former officers, as well as a preference for commissioning officers who could raise regiments on their own, kept Grant from winning the colonelcy to which he believed his training and experience entitled him. (This was not a case of inflated ego; George McClellan, who had also left the army as a captain three years after Grant, was commissioned a major-general in 1861.)

It took two months and some good luck, but in June 1861 Grant won a colonel's commission and command of the 21st Illinois Volunteer Regiment. At almost the same time, he got another piece of good news. Through the efforts in Washington of Elihu B. Washburn, Grant's congressman and a friend of Lincoln's who had taken positive notice of the leather-store clerk back in Galena, he was commissioned a brigadier general.

Even in these very early days, Grant displayed the major characteristic of his generalship: aggressively seeking out the enemy and endeavouring to bring him to battle. Approaching a small Confederate force encamped near the Salt River in Missouri, Grant apprehensively deployed the 21st Illinois for what he assumed would be its first engagement. But as he approached the site of the enemy camp, Grant found it hastily abandoned. The Confederate commander, Grant realized, 'had been as afraid of me as I had been of him'. It was a lesson Grant did not forget.

Early victories

The Mississippi River bisects the North American continent, with major tributaries such as the Missouri and Ohio cutting far to the east and west. Grant early realized the vital necessity to the Union war effort of controlling this waterway, and set about securing it while politicians in Washington and lesser generals obsessed over capturing the Confederate capital of Richmond, Virginia.

Belmont, Missouri, is a small town overlooking the Mississippi, directly across from the town of Columbus, Kentucky. Both towns were occupied by Confederate forces in early November 1861, and were being used to blockade the river to Union traffic. On 7 November Grant decided to see if he could scare the Confederates out of Belmont.

Assembling what would today be called a combined-operations task force, Grant loaded 12,000 men, along with supporting cavalry and artillery, aboard naval vessels at Cairo, Illinois, and sailed downstream to Belmont, landing 3 miles north of the Confederate encampment. Completely surprised, the Confederates scattered.

But the effect was only momentary, as the Confederates soon regrouped and counter-attacked, seeking to cut the Union troops off from their transport. Thanks to the artillery and cavalry Grant had brought along, these efforts failed, and the Union troops returned safely to Cairo.

Belmont wasn't much more than a big raid, but it was victory enough for a Northern public already growing wearily familiar with bad news from the front. The battle was also significant in that it featured what would later become Grant's trademarks of speed and surprise, and it was the first major use of what would later be called amphibious warfare.

Grant's successful cooperation with the navy – daring and innovative for the time – continued with his next major operation, against the Confederate strongholds of Fort Henry on the Tennessee River and Fort Donelson on the Cumberland River.

The movement against the two forts – made much against the will of Grant's superior, Major General Henry Halleck – illustrates Grant's innovative approach to waging war. While other Union generals were thinking in European terms of capturing cities – notably the Confederate capital of Richmond – or taking territory and holding it, Grant was thinking in terms of North American geography.

The Mississippi, Tennessee and Cumberland rivers all bit deep into the Confederacy. Unlike railroads, the rivers couldn't be severed by Confederate cavalry raiders. Using them as highways to move far inside the South, Union forces could cut the Confederate forces off from their sources of food and war materials. The cities and territories those armies were defending would then fall as ripe fruit from a tree.

The fall of the two forts, on 6 February and 16 February 1862 respectively, was the first significant Union victory of the war. Their capture made Grant a national hero, earning him the nickname, based on his initials, of 'Unconditional Surrender' Grant.

Shiloh: victory into defeat

Grant was a hero, but that fact also excited jealousy and envy among his fellow officers, particularly the scheming Henry Halleck. Incredibly, in the weeks following the fall of the two forts, Halleck plotted to have Grant removed.

The only result of all this backstage manoeuvring was to yield the initiative to the Confederates.

In early April 1862 Grant's Army of the Tennessee was encamped near a country church called Shiloh, awaiting reinforcement from Brigadier General Don Carlos Buell's Army of the Ohio prior to moving into northern Mississippi. Confederate General Albert Sidney Johnston, who used the six-week pause after the fall of forts Henry and Donelson to assemble an army of 50,000 men in northern Mississippi, decided to strike Grant before Buell could join him.

The Battle of Shiloh, which began on the morning of 6 April 1862, was not merely the bloodiest battle of the war to that point, but its 24,000 total casualties exceeded those of all previous American wars combined. Grant had chosen his ground carefully, however, and the Confederates never came close to overrunning his position. Buell's troops joined him on the night of 6/7 April and Grant counter-attacked the next day, driving the Confederates from the field. The Union also achieved the grim bonus of the death of Johnston.

But the size of the butcher's bill stunned the Northern public. There was some wildly irresponsible reporting of the engagement, and the people who had lauded Grant only a few weeks earlier now turned viciously against him. Faced with demands for Grant's dismissal from influential members of Congress, President Lincoln is supposed to have replied, 'I cannot spare this man; he fights.' In his memoirs, Grant states that Shiloh was the battle that convinced him definitively that the war would be a long and costly one. Operating under this cloud, Grant nevertheless undertook his next objective: reducing the Confederate fortress of Vicksburg, on the Mississippi river.

The Vicksburg Campaign: The First Blitzkrieg

The essence of what came to be known in the Second World War as 'blitzkrieg' or 'lightning war' was the winning of a great strategic prize at high speed and at relatively low cost in men and matériel. The first modern practitioner of this form of 'shock and awe' warfare was Ulysses S. Grant in his campaign to take Vicksburg, Mississippi, between May and July 1863.

Dubbed the 'Gibraltar of the West' by Confederate President Jefferson Davis, the town of Vicksburg stands on a high bluff overlooking a hairpin bend in the Mississippi river, making it a natural fortress. In Confederate hands, it blocked the flow of Union commerce on the river, cutting off the vast interior heartland of the Union from access to the port of New Orleans (Union-held since April 1862). 'Vicksburg is the key,' Abraham Lincoln told his advisers. 'The war cannot be brought to a close until the key is in our pocket.'

Grant began manoeuvring against Vicksburg in the autumn of 1862, trying a variety of plans to invest and take the city, all without success. His movements, however, succeeded in thoroughly confusing Confederate Lieutenant General John C. Pemberton, the commander of Vicksburg. In April 1863 an increasingly demoralized Pemberton sent a telegram to his superiors: 'Enemy is constantly in motion in all directions.'

Grant now set in motion what he later said was the only plan in which he really had confidence. He would come at the city through the 'back door' – its lightly guarded southern approaches. Marching his army south along the western bank of the river opposite Vicksburg, Grant transported it across the river via steamboats and transports that had run the gauntlet of the city's guns in a nerve-wracking operation on the night of 16 April 1863. (Army–navy cooperation is a much-overlooked hallmark of Grant's campaigns, just as air–ground cooperation marked the German blitzkrieg campaigns of 1939–41.)

The stage was set for the main action of the campaign. Between the time Grant's army landed on the eastern bank of the river below Vicksburg on 30 April and the start of the siege of the town on 18 May 1863, it would march over 200 miles, take and burn the Mississippi state capital of Jackson, and fight and win five battles, before locking Pemberton's army inside Vicksburg, where it languished without hope of relief until its surrender on 4 July. All the while, Grant's army lived off the land, without a supply line. Grant thus pocketed Lincoln's 'key' at a cost of fewer than 10,000 men killed, wounded, captured and missing.

Wrapping up the west

Following Vicksburg, it had been Grant's intent to strike against the port of Mobile, Alabama, and then north to the southern railhead of Atlanta, Georgia. Combined with simultaneous thrusts from Tennessee and Mississippi, the Confederate armies in the field would be deprived of the men and supplies they needed to operate. Their choice would then be surrender or starvation, as at Vicksburg. Other considerations intervened, however. French intervention in Mexico in 1862 tied down Union forces in Louisiana, and Union forces in Tennessee were decisively beaten at the Battle of Chickamauga in September 1863 and forced back on Chattanooga, where the Confederates besieged them.

The need to lift the siege became paramount, and Lincoln placed Grant in command of all Union forces west of the Appalachian mountain chain. When Grant arrived at Chattanooga he found plans in place for breaking the siege, but Union General William Rosecrans apparently lacked the will to implement them. Grant did not. Between 23 and 25 November 1863, Grant's forces defeated those of Confederate General Braxton Bragg, driving them back in the direction of Atlanta.

Lincoln had seen enough. In March 1864 he took the obvious (in retrospect) course of naming Grant commander-in-chief of all Union forces, with responsibility for finding a way to win the war.

Grant vs Lee

Grant was still in favour of the Mobile operation and several simultaneous thrusts into the heart of the Confederacy, but by the spring of 1864 there was no longer time. Lincoln was facing a difficult re-election campaign that November; a direct confrontation with Confederate General Robert E. Lee on his home ground of northern Virginia was no longer avoidable.

Grant understood the strategic problem of confronting a foe who enjoyed the advantage of interior lines of commu-nication. Until then the Confederacy was able to cope with widely separated Union thrusts by shuttling troops from one threatened sector to another – much as the Germans tried to do in both world wars. Grant prevented this in the same way that Eisenhower and Zhukov prevented it eighty years later: he launched simultaneous offensives in both the Virginian and western theatres. The latter would be commanded by William T. Sherman, while Grant would personally superintend the former.

Grant's aim was simple: he would grab hold of Lee's Army of Northern Virginia and refuse to let it go, denying Lee the initiative. From the opening of the Overland campaign on 4 May 1864 until the final surrender at Appomattox on 9 April 1865, the two armies would never be out of contact (except for a few days in mid June 1864).

Grant has been accused of wantonly squandering the lives of his men during this campaign. While his losses were indeed high (around 50,000 in May and June 1864), recent scholarship has shown that, proportionately, Lee's losses were even higher. The casualty list might also have been shorter had Grant been able to get better service out of the Army of the Potomac's officer corps, which was never able to entirely shake off its lethargic habits, nor its terror of Robert E. Lee.

Lee's only real hope during this period was to inflict such punishment on the Union armies that the Northern public would revolt and turn out the Lincoln administration. Had the Confederacy's western armies been able somehow to defeat Sherman, this strategy might have succeeded. But since the Confederates were outnumbered two to one, and even more inferior in terms of supplies, there was little hope of that. Lincoln's re-election in November 1864 and the thrashing of the Confederacy's western armies at the Battle of Nashville on 15 December

1864 essentially ended the war. All that remained was for Lee to recognize that fact, which he did at Appomattox.

Post-war career

The Appomattox campaign was Grant's last. Following Lee's surrender, he spent three years as general-in-chief of the US army, based in Washington, DC. Concerned that the election of a Democratic candidate in the 1868 election would rob the nation of 'the fruits of victory', he reluctantly agreed to run for president as the Republican candidate, and was elected. He spent much of his time in the White House trying to protect the rights of newly freed blacks in the South, a policy that became increasingly unpopular as time went on, and which was abandoned when he left office in 1877.

Grant died of throat cancer at Mount McGregor, New York, on 23 July 1885. His memoirs, published after his death, sold more than 300,000 copies.

Assessment

Grant deserves to be ranked among the great captains of history. He skilfully handled huge armies that were separated by thousands of miles. Unlike Napoleon or Frederick the Great, who each tasted the bitterness of defeat more than once, Grant never lost a battle, whether facing mediocre opponents or highly talented ones.

Defying the Peter Principle, Grant never rose to a level of military incompetence. Whether a junior officer in Mexico or the highest-ranked since George Washington, he moved into each new role – which called for different skills and abilities – with seeming ease. In all these respects, he very closely parallels Wellington.

Grant also competently employed radical new military technologies with which no previous commander had had to cope: the telegraph, the rifled musket, the railroad and the steamship. He used all of these to their fullest advantage at the time, something none of his opponents managed, and only Sherman came close to matching.

Grant's legacy is still felt in today's US army, which combines a devotion to logistic mastery with speed, surprise and unmatched firepower. The 1991 Gulf War campaign was modelled closely on Grant's Vicksburg campaign.

In the light of these facts, the reality of Grant's genius emerges. His success set a very high standard for his successors.

WILLIAM T. SHERMAN

1820–91

RICHARD J. SOMMERS

SHERMAN WAS THE SECOND BEST Union commander of the American Civil War. His keen intellect perceived the interrelationship between the fighting front and the home front, and by crippling the will of Southern civilians to continue waging war, he undercut Confederate military power and thereby contributed decisively to the Union victory.

William Tecumseh Sherman was born in Lancaster, Ohio, on 8 February 1820. Orphaned nine years later, he was raised by US Senator Thomas Ewing, an influential Whig, and married the senator's daughter Ellen in 1850. Ewing secured Sherman a place at West Point, where he graduated sixth of forty-two in the class of 1840.

Early career

Commissioned as a second lieutenant in the 3rd US Artillery
Regiment in 1840 and promoted first lieutenant in 1841,
Sherman helped garrison Charleston, South Carolina,
where he came to appreciate antebellum Southern society.
In the Mexican War he accompanied his regiment on its
fourteen-week trip around Cape Horn to California, but by
the time he got there it was already under US control, and
the war was virtually over. Unlike many senior Civil War
commanders, Sherman saw no combat in the Mexican War,
and all that remained was garrisoning California. He
performed staff duty at San Francisco headquarters and
was promoted to captain (Commissary of Subsistence) on
27 September 1850.

The Gold Rush of 1849 lured many soldiers to desert,
but Sherman faithfully remained on duty for four more
years. On 6 September 1853 he resigned and went into
banking in San Francisco. The panic of 1857 doomed the
bank, and for the next two years he practised law in Leav-
enworth, Kansas Territory, with two of his brothers-in-law,
Hugh and Thomas Ewing (both future Union generals).
From 1859 to 1861 he served as first superintendent of the
new Louisiana Military Academy in Pineville (forerunner
of Louisiana State University).

Early years of the Civil War

Abraham Lincoln's election as president caused seven Southern states to secede, including Louisiana on 26 January 1861. Even before officially leaving the Union, Louisiana occupied some Federal installations, and the state's military school and its superintendent were expected to support these actions. Unlike some Northerners living in the South who fought for the Confederacy, Sherman never wavered. Despite his deep and genuine admiration, respect, even affection for the South and its people, he remained loyal to the Union. He promptly resigned and moved to St Louis, Missouri, where, ironically, he was almost killed on 10 May during street riots in that torn city following the Camp Jackson affair.

Sherman was still a civilian at this point, but within days he would be back in uniform, beginning four years of tumultuous military service – years full of anxiety and uncertainty, confidence and insight, tactical defeat and strategic success. Sherman would emerge from those four years as one of the foremost Northern generals, and one of the great commanders of military history.

On 14 May 1861 Sherman was appointed colonel of the 13th US Infantry, one of eleven new regiments in the regular US army. Almost all other colonels of new regiments had distinguished records fighting Mexicans and Indians. Sherman, by contrast, had never been under fire until, as a civilian, he had been caught up in the St Louis riots. His selection is unmistakably attributable to political and family connections: his father-in-law was now an elder statesman in the new Republican Party, while his brother John was a US senator, and it was their political influence that landed him the coveted appointment. This is not to say Sherman was a 'political general'. Indeed, he disdained politics and explicitly refused to exploit military service for political advantage. Yet his selection underscores the reality that in mid nineteenth-century America, even quintessential career regulars like Sherman benefited from patronage (his future friend Ulysses S. Grant comparably had a political sponsor). For Sherman, both political and family connections served him well.

Tactical defeat, strategic doubt

Such connections secured Sherman further promotion on 3 August 1861, as brigadier general of volunteers, back-dated to 17 May, and he served briefly on General-in-Chief Winfield Scott's staff. On 30 June he took command of the 3rd Brigade, 1st Division, Army of Northeast Virginia, and three weeks later he took part in heavy fighting and in the ensuing Union defeat and rout at the First Battle of Manassas (First Bull Run). Then in August he had to suppress a near mutiny among some of his troops, who mistakenly thought their service had expired.

Despite this inauspicious beginning, Sherman was appointed in late August by his Old Army friend Robert Anderson (the hero of Fort Sumter) as his senior subordinate in the new Department of the Cumberland (Kentucky and Tennessee). Both North and South strove to secure the strategic state of Kentucky, and in the end it was junior Federal officers who turned the tide for the Union. Anderson himself deserves little credit: overburdened by weighty responsibilities, he could not act vigorously. On 8 October he was gently shelved, and Sherman succeeded him.

Sherman, although younger and more energetic than Anderson, fared no better. His keen insight recognized the magnitude of the Civil War and of the force needed to win it: not content with the 20,000 soldiers on hand, he called for an army of 200,000. In retrospect, he appears far-sighted, but at the time he seemed unrealistic and alarmist. Unquestionably, he exaggerated Confederate strength and capabilities, and their supposed threat vexed him to distraction. The Federal government feared he would suffer a nervous breakdown, and on 9 November it engineered the department out from under him by transferring its areas of responsibility to other departments. Left without a command, Sherman went home to Ohio and then St Louis.

Bloody redemption

St Louis, fortunately, was headquarters of another Old Army friend, General Henry W. Halleck. Halleck, recognizing Sherman's abilities, gave him time to rest and then on 14 February 1862 restored him to command by putting him in charge of the District of Cairo. Sherman's new responsibility involved forwarding troops to support Grant's decisive breakthrough of the main Confederate line across Kentucky and Tennessee. On 1 March Sherman formed some reinforcements into what would gain immortality as the 5th Division, Army of West Tennessee (the future Army of the Tennessee). A week later he led that division up the Tennessee River to northern Mississippi, where flooding prevented him from landing to cut a key railroad. He then dropped downriver and went ashore on the left bank at Pittsburg Landing, Tennessee, near a country church called Shiloh.

Four of Grant's five other divisions soon joined him there. The Federals drilled, massed and prepared to move against the Southern stronghold of Corinth, Mississippi. But they did not fortify their own position, and they did not guard against the contingency that the Confederates might strike first. Yet on 6 April, the Confederates did attack. Ever afterwards, Grant and Sherman denied they were caught off guard. Tactically Shiloh was not a surprise, but strategically it was. For eleven weeks everything in the western theatre had gone the Union's way. Southern resistance seemed near collapse. Union planners – Sherman, Grant, Halleck – did not consider that the Confederates might counter-attack. Yet when they did, Sherman's tactical skills blunted the blow and extracted a heavy price, before he was obliged to yield his advance ground. He thus bought time for reinforcements to bolster the defence, then to counter-attack on 7 April. Shiloh was the bloodiest battle in American history up to then. This potential disaster turned into strategic success forged a friendship between Grant and Sherman that lasted the rest of their lives.

Vicksburg and Chattanooga

Promoted major-general of volunteers, Sherman participated throughout May 1862 in the First Corinth campaign. His greatest service in that summer of stagnation was keeping the despondent Grant from resigning. Sherman's responsibilities progressively increased, and on 21 July he was given command of Memphis. From there in November he led three divisions into northern Mississippi during Grant's first drive against Vicksburg. Concern that the political Union general John A. McClernand might take that stronghold led Grant to rush Sherman's four divisions down the Mississippi to capture that city first. Sherman, however, was repulsed at the end of December at Chickasaw Bayou. McClernand then arrived, assumed command (with

Sherman subordinated to corps command) and, on 11 January 1863, captured Arkansas Post.

Grant shifted most divisions to the Mississippi and absorbed McClernand's force. Within that expanded army, Sherman's command (the 5th, 8th and 11th Divisions) became XV Corps. In March he led that corps to rescue the US navy trapped up Steele's Bayou, then in May helped to capture Jackson (the Mississippi state capital), and shared in Grant's repulses at Vicksburg (see pp. 383–5). As the siege continued, Sherman took charge of the rear line facing east against Joseph E. Johnston's relieving army. Once Vicksburg surrendered on 4 July, Sherman led IX, XIII and XV Corps against Johnston and reoccupied Jackson on 21 July.

Victory at Vicksburg earned Grant promotion to command the new Military Division of the Mississippi, encompassing the entire western theatre, and on 24 October Sherman (now brigadier general of regulars) succeeded him in command of the Army of the Tennessee. Sherman was fortunate to be available then, because only a couple of weeks earlier he had narrowly evaded capture, perhaps death, near Colliersville, Tennessee, while isolated from his forces.

Sherman went on to lead four divisions to help relieve Chattanooga. Grant gave him the main attack, turning the Confederate right, but on 25 November his charges were repeatedly repulsed. However, his West Point classmate

George H. Thomas, now commanding the Army of the Cumberland, stormed Missionary Ridge to win a great victory. Sherman then led IV, XI and XV Corps to relieve Knoxville in early December. He returned to Vicksburg in January 1864, and the following month led XVI and XVII Corps eastward to capture Meridian, Mississippi. The Meridian campaign entailed little fighting, but it confirmed the lesson Grant had demonstrated the previous May: Federal forces could cut loose from supply lines, penetrate deeply into the Confederacy and live off the land. Before 1864 ended, Sherman would apply this lesson with devastating effect.

The Great March

In mid November 1864 Sherman massed fourteen divisions (thirteen infantry and one cavalry) in Atlanta, divided into Oliver O. Howard's right wing (the Army of the Tennessee) and Henry W. Slocum's left wing (the Army of Georgia). These 60,000 veterans struck devastatingly deep into the Confederacy.

Sherman cut loose from his supply line to Chattanooga, burned Atlanta, and on 15 November began his 'March to the Sea', living off the land. He could have headed south for the Gulf of Mexico or east for Charleston. Instead, he advanced southeast toward Savannah. Uncertain of his destination, Southern commanders dispersed their forces. He compounded their confusion by demonstrating with his right against Macon and with his left against Augusta. Then he penetrated the unguarded centre and captured Milledgeville, at that time Georgia's state capital, unopposed on 22 November. He continued southeastward and on 13 December stormed Fort McAllister, thereby making contact with the US navy. Savannah fell on 21 December, but its garrison escaped.

These elegant manoeuvres demonstrate Sherman's deftness as a strategist. Yet they also reflect the reality that he faced minimal opposition. He could not have operated so boldly or broadly if Hood's army had still confronted him. But Hood had gone to Tennessee – and annihilation at Nashville on 15–16 December. The strategic success of Sherman's march might have been minimized, even nullified, save for George H. Thomas's great battlefield victory there.

Both generals accomplished their missions. Sherman's success lay in demonstrating Federal ability to penetrate the South, unimpeded. The Confederacy could not protect its citizens. It was not through wanton plunder but through systematic strategic devastation of the home front that Sherman 'made Georgia howl'. He thereby crippled civilian commitment to the war and undercut the Confederate soldiers' morale.

A worse fate awaited South Carolina, the 'Cradle of Secession', beginning in February 1865. Sherman again feinted leftwards toward Augusta and rightwards toward Charleston, then swooped through the unguarded centre and took South Carolina's state capital, Columbia, which was burned on the night of 17/18 February. Sherman convincingly claimed he did not order its destruction, but destroyed it was. Its fall, moreover, doomed Charleston, which was abandoned on the same dates.

Sherman followed Charleston's fleeing garrison into North Carolina and took the arsenal city of Fayetteville on 11 March. The Charleston garrison gave Slocum a good fight at Averasboro on 15–16 March. Then at Bentonville on 19 March Johnston (restored to command) delivered a heavy counter-attack with local divisions and Nashville survivors. Slocum withstood this blow, and two days later Sherman almost severed Johnston's escape route, but the Southerner was too experienced in retreating to be intercepted.

Sherman reached Goldsboro on 23–24 March, where John M. Schofield's Army of the Ohio awaited him. He rested for seventeen days, met Lincoln and Grant in Virginia, then resumed advancing on 10 April. For reasons of both strategy and policy (to allow eastern armies to win the eastern war), Sherman no longer headed north toward Virginia. He turned west, occupied Raleigh on 11 April, and received Johnston's surrender at Durham.

From Atlanta to Durham via Savannah, Columbia, Goldsboro and Raleigh, Sherman marched virtually a thousand miles. He devastated the interior of the South, destroyed its already limited logistical infrastructure, demoralized its populace and depleted the determination of its defenders to sustain the struggle. Strategically, he caved the western front almost into the rear of the eastern front; psychologically, he destroyed the enemy's will to wage war. He became the decisive element in Grant's grand strategy of devouring the rest of the Confederacy while Grant pinned Lee in Virginia. Together, these two great commanders, who had become fast friends at Shiloh, won the American Civil War.

Advance to Atlanta

Saving Chattanooga earned Grant promotion to general-in-chief in March 1864. He chose to operate in Virginia against the greatest Confederate commander, Robert E. Lee. On 26 March Sherman succeeded him in command of the western theatre, centred on Chattanooga. Near there he massed 100,000 men in twenty-two divisions, grouped into seven corps and three armies. (Three more divisions, comprising an additional 13,000 men, arrived in June and July.)

Pursuant to Grant's grand strategy to advance simultaneously on major fronts, on 7 May Sherman moved against Johnston's army in northwestern Georgia. They battled at Rocky Face Ridge on 8–11 May. Sherman sent his former Army of the Tennessee, now under James B. McPherson, through Snake Creek Gap into Johnston's left-rear at Resaca. McPherson failed to press his advantage, however, and withdrew into the gap. Alerted to the danger, Johnston retreated to Resaca, where Sherman fought him on 13–15 May. The Confederates fell back across the Oostenaula River and then across the Etowah. Light fighting flared at Cassville and Kingston, and then in late May and June heavy combat erupted around Dallas, Gilgal Church and Kolb's Farm. Sherman's massive frontal assault on Kennesaw Mountain on 27 June proved a bloody failure. Despite such repeated tactical setbacks, Sherman enjoyed strategic success, pressing ever more deeply into Georgia to the Chattahoochee River.

Beyond the Chattahoochee lay Atlanta – and a more combative Confederate commander, John B. Hood. Sherman crossed the river unopposed, but was then attacked by Hood in late July at Peach Tree Creek, Decatur Road and Ezra Church. The Federals withstood such blows and throughout August tightened their siege of Atlanta. Late that month most of Sherman's army swung south-west, cutting the final two railroads into Atlanta. The Confederates failed to stop him at Jonesborough (31 August – 1 September), and that night Hood abandoned Atlanta. Northern troops occupied the city the next day – a strategic success that brightened a dreary summer and helped to re-elect President Lincoln.

Bitter aftermath

Johnston surrendered twice, on both 18 and 26 April, because Sherman's first terms were so generous they were called the 'Sherman–Johnston Treaty.' Sherman thought them consistent with Lincoln's intent to hasten reconciliation. By then, however, Lincoln was dead. Anger over his assassination caused Washington scornfully to repudiate Sherman's offer and to compel him to insist on the same terms Grant accorded Lee. Such abuse of a victorious commander at the height of success embittered Sherman and estranged him from Halleck. At the grand review of his troops in Washington on 24 May, Sherman publicly refused to shake hands with Secretary of War Edwin M. Stanton, whom he blamed for such mistreatment.

The three grand reviews were triumphal marches symbolizing the Union victory. On 27 June the great volunteer armies that won the Civil War were discontinued, and the US army began shifting to a peacetime footing. By then Sherman had been a major-general of regulars for some ten months, and when Grant was promoted to full general on 25 July 1866 Sherman succeeded him as lieutenant general of the army. Then when Grant became president, on 4 March 1869, Sherman received a fourth star and became general-in-chief. First as commander of the Military Division of the Missouri, 1865–9, and then as commanding general of the army, Sherman remained discontented with political interference in the military – somewhat ironically, since he had re-entered service in 1861 through his political connections. To help immunize the army from such influences and heighten its capabilities, he enhanced its school system – the military dimension of the increased professionalization of American society in the Gilded Age. He adamantly refused to run for president himself.

Sherman stepped down as general-in-chief on 1 November 1883, and retired three months later. He died on 14 February 1891 and is buried in St Louis.

Assessment

Sherman was a strategist, not a tactician. Although he fought well defensively at Shiloh, most of his tactical attacks failed, from Chickasaw Bayou to Missionary Ridge, from Kennesaw Mountain to Bentonville.

The realm of strategy was where he excelled. His brilliant mind recognized key strategic objectives and how to attain them. Even more crucially, he understood that in a republic at war, civilian support for the war effort is essential. To cripple that support is to cripple the enemy, no matter how brave and well led are the enemy armies. Through his

'March to the Sea' and his Carolinas campaign, he won the war on the home front – and thereby won the war. In so doing, he did not revive the horrors of the Thirty Years War, which the genteel dynastic wars of eighteenth-century Europe had striven to avoid. Nevertheless, by re-introducing the home front into the equation of war, he foreshadowed the total wars of the twentieth century.

Thus, not only in the American Civil War but also in the continuity of command from Gustavus Adolphus and Tilly through Marshal Saxe and Frederick the Great to Yamashita and Zhukov, William T. Sherman holds an important place among the great commanders of history.

FURTHER READING

MAURICE OF NASSAU

Marco van der Hoeven (ed.), *The Exercise of Arms: Warfare in the Netherlands, 1568–1648* (Brill, Leiden, 1998).

B. H. Nickle, *The Military Reforms of Prince Maurice of Orange* (Ann Arbor, MI, 1981).

Jan den Tex, *Oldenbarneveldt* (2 vols, Cambridge University Press, Cambridge, 1973).

GUSTAVUS ADOLPHUS

Michael Roberts, *Gustavus Adophus: A History of Sweden 1611–1632* (2 vols, Longman, London, 1953–8).

Geoffrey Parker (ed.), *The Thirty Years War* (second edition, Routledge, London, 1997).

COUNT TILLY

Michael Kaiser, *Politik und Kriegführung: Maximilian von Bayern, Tilly und die Katholische Liga im Dreißigjährigen Kriege* (Aschendorff, Münster, 1999).

C. V. Wedgwood, *The Thirty Years War* (London, 1938).

Georg Gilardone, *Tilly, der Heilige in Harnisch* (Kosel und Pustet, Munich, 1932).

Onno Klopp, *Tilly im Dreißigjährigen Kriege* (2 vols, Stuttgart, 1861).

OLIVER CROMWELL

Micheál Ó Siochrú, *God's Executioner: Oliver Cromwell and the Conquest of Ireland* (Faber, London, 2008).

Barry Coward, *Oliver Cromwell* (Longman, Harlow, 2000).

Tom Reilly, *Cromwell: An Honourable Enemy* (Brandon, Dingle, 1999).

Christopher Hill, *God's Englishman* (Penguin, London, 1990).

VICOMTE DE TURENNE

Jean Bérenger, *Turenne* (Fayard, Paris, 1987).

Max Weygand, *Turenne* (George G. Harrap & Co., London, 1930).

DUKE OF MARLBOROUGH

Winston S. Churchill, *Marlborough: His Life and Times* (George G. Harrap & Co., London, 1947).

David Chandler, *Marlborough as Military Commander* (The History Press, Stroud, 2003).

PRINCE EUGÈNE OF SAVOY

Nicholas Henderson, *Prince Eugen of Savoy* (Weidenfeld & Nicolson, London, 1964).

Derek McKay, *Prince Eugène of Savoy* (Thames & Hudson, London, 1977).

CHARLES XII

Ragnhild Hatton, *Charles XII of Sweden* (Weidenfeld & Nicolson, London, 1968).

Robert I. Frost, *The Northern Wars, 1558–1721* (Longman, Harlow, Essex, 2000).

Peter Englund, *The Battle of Poltava: The Birth of the Russian Empire* (Gollancz, London, 1992).

MAURICE, COMTE DE SAXE

Comte Maurice de Saxe, *My Reveries upon the Art of War*, in T. R. Phillips (ed.), *The Roots of Strategy* (Stackpole Books, Harrisburg, PA, 1985), pp. 189–257.

J. E. M. White, *Marshal of France: The Life and Times of Maurice, Comte de Saxe, 1696–1750* (Hamish Hamilton, London, 1962).

FREDERICK THE GREAT

Giles MacDonogh, *Frederick the Great: A Life in Deed and Letters* (Weidenfeld & Nicolson, London, 1999).

David Fraser, *Frederick the Great* (Allen Lane, London, 2000).

Christopher Duffy, *Frederick the Great – A Military Life* (Emperor's Press, London, 1995).

Dennis E. Showalter, *The Wars of Frederick the Great* (Longman, London, 1996).

ROBERT CLIVE

Michael Edwardes, *The Battle of Plassey* (Batsford, London, 1963).

Mark Bence-Jones, *Clive of India* (Constable, London, 1974).

Robert Harvey, *Clive: The Life and Death of a British Emperor* (Hodder & Stoughton, London, 1998).

Thomas Babington Macaulay, *Essay on Clive* (London, 1840).

JAMES WOLFE

Stephen Brumwell, *Paths of Glory: The Life and Death of General James Wolfe* (Continuum, London, 2006).

C. P. Stacey, Quebec: *The Siege and the Battle* (Macmillan, Toronto, 1959).

NATHANAEL GREENE

Terry Golway, *Washington's General: Nathanael Greene and the Triumph of the American Revolution* (Holt, New York, 2005).

John Ferling, *Almost a Miracle: The American Victory in the War of Independence* (Oxford University Press, New York, 2007).

NAPOLEON BONAPARTE

David Chandler, *The Campaigns of Napoleon* (Weidenfeld & Nicolson, London, 1966).

Philip Dwyer, *Napoleon: The Path to Power, 1769–1799* (Bloomsbury, London, 2007).

Charles Esdaile, *The Wars of Napoleon* (Longman, London, 1995).

Charles Esdaile, *Napoleon's Wars: An International History, 1803–1815* (Allen Lane, London, 2007).

DUKE OF WELLINGTON

Elizabeth Longford, *Wellington: The Years of the Sword* (Weidenfeld & Nicolson, London, 1969).

Richard Holmes, *Wellington* (HarperCollins, London, 2002).

Gordon Corrigan, *Wellington: A Military Life* (Hambledon Continuum, London, 2001).

Alessandro Barbero, *The Battle: A New History of the Battle of Waterloo* (Atlantic Books, London, 2005).

LOUIS-NICOLAS DAVOUT

John G. Gallagher, *The Iron Marshal: A biography of Louis N. Davout* (1976; reissued by Greenhill Books, London, 2000).

Daniel Reichel, *Davout et l'art de la guerre: recherches sur la formation, l'action pendant la Révolution et les commandements du maréchal Davout, duc d'Auerstaedt, prince d'Eckmühl, 1770–1823* (Centre d'Histoire et de Prospective Militaires, Neuchâtel, 1975).

Joseph, Comte Vigier, *Davout: maréchal d'empire, duc d'Auerstädt, prince d'Eckmühl, 1770–1823* (2 vols, Paul Ollendorff, Paris, 1898).

MIKHAIL KUTUZOV

Roger Parkinson, *The Fox of the North* (Purnell, London, 1976).

Christopher Duffy, *Borodino* (Sphere, London, 1972).

L. G. Beskrovny, *The Patriotic War and Kutuzov's Counter-Offensive* (Moscow, 1951).

A. Brett James, *1812, Eyewitness Accounts of Napoleon's Defeat in Russia* (Macmillan, London, 1966).

Adam Zamoyski, *1812: Napoleon's Fatal March on Moscow* (HarperCollins, London, 2004).

Alan Palmer, *Napoleon in Russia* (Deutsch, London, 1967; revised edition, London, 1999).

Alan Palmer, *Russia in War and Peace* (Weidenfeld & Nicolson, London, 1972).

Alan Palmer, *Alexander I: Tsar of War and Peace* (Weidenfeld & Nicolson, London, 1974).

CARL VON CLAUSEWITZ

Michael Howard and Peter Paret (eds), *Carl von Clausewitz: On War* (Princeton University Press, Princeton, NJ, 1989).

Raymond Aron, *Clausewitz*, translated by Christine Booker and Norman Stone (Routledge, London, 1983).

Christopher Clark, *Iron Kingdom: The Rise and Downfall of Prussia 1600–1947* (Allen Lane, London, 2006).

SIMÓN BOLÍVAR

John Lynch, *Simón Bolívar: A Life* (Yale University Press, New Haven and London, 2006).

David Bushnell, *Simón Bolívar: Liberation and Disappointment* (Prentice Hall, New York, 2004).

David Bushnell (ed.), *El Libertador: Writings of Simón Bolívar* (Oxford University Press, Oxford, 2003).

Daniel Florencio O'Leary, *Bolívar and the War of Independence*, translated and edited by R. F. McNerney, Jr (University of Texas Press, Austin, TX, 1970).

R. A. Humphreys (ed.), *The 'Detached Recollections' of General D. F. O'Leary* (Athlone Press, London, 1969).

SHAKA ZULU

Ian Knight, *The Anatomy of the Zulu Army: From Shaka to Cetshwayo 1818–1879* (Greenhill Books, London, 1995).

John Laband, *The Rise and Fall of the Zulu Nation* (Arms and Armour, 1997).

Donald Morris, *The Washing of the Spears* (Simon and Schuster, New York, 1966).

Alan Mountain, *The Rise and Fall of the Zulu Empire* (kwaNtaba, 1999).

GIUSEPPE GARIBALDI

L. Riall, *Garibaldi, Invention of a Hero* (Yale University Press, London & New Haven, 2007).

D. Mack Smith, *Garibaldi: A Great Life in Brief* (Hutchinson, London, 1957).

G. M. Trevelyan, *Garibaldi* (3 vols, Longman, London, 1907–11).

ROBERT E. LEE

Edward H. Bonekemper III, *How Robert E. Lee Lost the Civil War* (Sergeant Kirkland's Press, San Diego, CA, 1998).

J. F. C. Fuller, *Grant and Lee: A Study in Personality and Generalship* (Indiana University Press, Bloomington, IN, 1982).

Gary W. Gallagher (ed.), *Lee the Soldier* (University of Nebraska Press, Lincoln, NE, 1996).

Alan T. Nolan, *Lee Considered: Gen. Robert E. Lee and Civil War History* (University of North Carolina Press, Chapel Hill, NC, 1996).

Emory M. Thomas, *Robert E. Lee: A Biography* (W. W. Norton & Co., New York, 1997).

'STONEWALL' JACKSON

George F. R. Henderson, *Stonewall Jackson and the American Civil War* (Longmans, Green and Co., London and New York, 1898).

James A. Kegel, *North with Lee and Jackson* (Stackpole Books, Mechanicsburg, PA, 1996).

James I. Robertson, *'Stonewall' Jackson: The Man, the Soldier, the Legend* (Macmillan, New York, NY, 1997).

Frank E. Vandiver, *Mighty Stonewall* (McGraw-Hill Book Company, New York, NY, 1957).

GEORGE MEADE

Freeman Cleaves, *Meade of Gettysburg* (University of Oklahoma Press, Norman, OK, 1960).

Edwin B. Coddington, *The Gettysburg Campaign: A Study in Command* (Charles Scribner's Sons, New York, 1968).

David W. Lowe (ed.), *Meade's Army: the Private Notebooks of Lt. Col. Theodore Lyman* (Kent State University Press, Kent, OH, 2007).

George Meade, *The Life and Letters of George Gordon Meade* (Charles Scribner's Sons, New York, 1913).

ULYSSES S. GRANT

Edward H. Bonekemper III, *A Victor Not a Butcher: Ulysses S. Grant's Overlooked Military Genius* (Regnery Books, Washington, DC, 2004).

Josiah Bunting, *Ulysses S. Grant* (The American Presidents Series, Times Books, New York, 2004).

Ulysses S. Grant, *Memoirs and Selected Letters, 1839–1865* (Library of America, New York, 1990).

Michael Korda, *Ulysses S. Grant: The Unlikely Hero* (Eminent Lives series, HarperCollins, New York, 2004).

Brooks Simpson, *Ulysses S. Grant: Triumph Over Adversity, 1822–1865* (Houghton Mifflin, Boston, 2000).

WILLIAM T. SHERMAN

Lloyd Lewis, *Sherman: Fighting Prophet* (Harcourt, Brace and Company, New York, 1932).

John F. Marszalek, *Sherman: A Soldier's Passion for Order* (The Free Press, New York, 1993).

William T. Sherman, *Memoirs of General William T. Sherman by Himself* (D. Appleton and Company, New York, 1885).

Brooks D. Simpson and Jean Berlin (eds), *Sherman's Civil War: Selected Correspondence of William T. Sherman, 1860–1865* (University of North Carolina Press, Chapel Hill, NC, 1999).

INDEX

Aboukir 242
Aboukir Bay, Battle of
   216–17
see also Nile, Battle of the
Abrantès, duchesse d' 252
Adrianople 118
Aelian 31
Africa, sub-Saharan 296–7
Aix-la-Chapelle, Peace of
   148, 166, 184
Alabama 371, 385
Albert 141
Albrecht, archduke of
   Austria 28
Aldringen, Johann von 60
Alexander the Great 296,
   308
Alexander I, tsar of Russia
   218–19, 221–2, 247,
   248, 255, 257–60,
   263–4, 267
Algiers 91
Allahabad 177
Alost 81
Alsace 50, 79, 139, 140
   defence of 76, 83–8
Alt-Breisach 78, 139
Altmark 35
Altranstädt, Treaty of 126
Alushta 256
Alva, Duke of 22
amabutho 305
amakhanda (military kraal)
   304–5
American Civil War 1,
   325, 328–41, 343–75,
   378–90, 392–405
   end of 1, 368, 388, 403
   Great March and Carolinas
      campaign 398–401,
      405
   home front in 390, 399,
      405

outbreak of 328, 343, 359,
   374, 378, 392
Overland campaign 387
Valley campaign 340,
   346–9, 351, 356
American War of Independ-
   ence 195–210
Amherst, Jeffrey 185, 186,
   189
Amiens, Peace of 217–18
Anderson, Robert 394
Andes mountains 281,
   289–90
André, John 205
Andrews, Joseph 293
Angers Military Academy
   227
Angostura 289
Anna of Saxony 17
Anne, queen of Great
   Britain 95, 103
Antietam, Battle of 332,
   353–4, 357, 362–3
Antwerp 48, 140, 142, 147
Appomattox 360
   surrender 370, 387, 388
Arcola, Battle of 215
Arcot, siege of 167–70
Ardennes 102
Argenson, René-Louis de
   Voyer, marquis d' 139
Argentina 313
Arkansas Post, capture of
   397
Arleux 102
Arlington 326
Arminians 29–30
Arni, Battle of 169
Arnim, Hans Georg von
   35, 58
Arnold, Benedict 205
Asfeld, Claude François
   Bidal, marquis d' 137

Ashby, Turner 348
Aspern-Essling, Battle of 3,
   223
Aspromonte 323
Assaye, Battle of 228
Atatürk 13
Ath 81, 141
Atlanta 338, 385, 386,
   398, 401–2
Auerstädt, Battle of 164,
   221, 244–6, 270
Augsburg, War of the
   League of 109
Augusta 399, 400
Augustus II (the Strong),
   elector of Saxony 121,
   122–6, 132
Augustus, prince of Prussia
   269
Austerlitz, Battle of 218–20,
   244, 258, 308
Austria 54, 96, 113,
   117–19, 241–2, 278
see also Austrian Succession,
   War of the; Seven Years
   War
and Italian unification 314,
   315, 316–17, 323
and Napoleonic Wars 215,
   217–19, 223, 224, 247,
   257–9
and Silesian Wars 152–5
Thirty Years War 39
and War of the Spanish
   Succession 110
Austrian Netherlands 140,
   142
Austrian Succession, War of
   the 135, 137–48, 182
Auxerre 241
Averasboro 400
Axel 144
Ayacucho, Battle of 292

413